It's all About Showing Up

I0559167

THE POWER IS IN THE ASKING

Vol. 3

Lady Amb. Dr. (h.c.) Robbie Motter
& Amb. Reverend Dr. (h.c.) Christine Park D.D.

HAVANA BOOK GROUP LLC.
HAVANABOOKGROUP.COM

HAVANA BOOK GROUP LLC
2173 SALK AVE, SUITE 250
CARLSBAD, CA. 92008

COPYRIGHT 2021 All rights reserved.
ISBN: 9798989191864

Preface

The Power of Presence:
Why Showing Up and Asking Changes Everything

Book Overview

In a world bustling with opportunities yet saturated with self-doubt, we often hesitate to step forward, fearing rejection or feeling unworthy. However, when we embrace the power of showing up and asking, we unlock a transformative journey toward personal and professional growth. These chapters in this book will delve into the significance of being present, the courage it takes to voice our needs, and practical tips to help you embrace this empowering philosophy. We want to also share some additional insight with you.

The Importance of Showing Up

Imagine a room filled with potential connections and opportunities. Each one of us has faced the intimidating prospect of walking into such a space. The first step—showing up—can feel monumental. Yet, it is in these very moments that we discover the courage within ourselves to embrace what lies ahead.

Building Confidence Through Presence

Show up. These two simple words hold immense power. They serve as a reminder that your voice matters, and your presence can change the dynamics in any space. When you choose to show up, you affirm your worth and the unique contributions you bring. Each event you attend—be it a conference, networking session, or casual gathering—presents an opportunity to expand your horizons. Remember, even the most accomplished women and men were once beginners who dared to step forward.

Cultivating Authentic Connections

The beauty of showing up extends beyond personal aspirations; it's about fostering connections. Relationships are built through shared experiences, and showing up allows for authentic interaction. You become part of a community, and that sense of belonging can fuel both personal and professional growth. Connect with others, who inspire you; they might just be waiting for someone to reach out, too.

The Art of Asking

Once you've shown up, the next vital step is asking. Unfortunately, many of us have been conditioned to shy away from asking for what we need. Whether it's seeking assistance, requesting a raise, or expressing an interest in a project, the fear of judgment can silence our voice. However, understanding that asking is a form of self-advocacy can shift our perspective.

The Strength in Vulnerability

Asking for help or guidance can be daunting, yet it reveals a strength in vulnerability. When you ask, you are acknowledging your needs and desires. This act not only enriches your own life but empowers others to step forward in their own journeys. People lifting People is an essential mantra, and it begins when we allow ourselves to be vulnerable.

Transforming Rejections into Lessons

Fear of rejection is a common barrier that prevents people from asking. However, every "no" can be reframed as a lesson. Each rejection is an opportunity to gain insights into what works and what doesn't, providing essential feedback for future endeavors. Embrace these moments; they are steppingstones on the path to success.

Practical Tips for Showing Up and Asking

Here are some actionable strategies to help you cultivate the habit of showing up and asking:

1. Set Intentions

Before attending an event or meeting, set clear intentions. What do you hope to gain? Who do you want to connect with? When you approach each situation with purpose, you are more likely to engage and ask questions that will lead to meaningful interactions.

2. Practice Mindfulness

Being mentally present enhances your ability to connect with others. Practicing mindfulness through meditation or breathing exercises can help center your thoughts and increase your confidence in social settings.

3. Start Small

If the idea of asking feels overwhelming, start small. Begin by asking a colleague for advice on a project or inquiring about someone's career journey. Each small step can build your confidence and help you get accustomed to voicing your needs.

4. Create a Support Network

Surround yourself with a community of supportive people. Whether through formal mentorship programs or informal friendships, having a network provides encouragement and accountability as you practice showing up and asking.

5. Celebrate Your Wins

Acknowledge and celebrate your efforts, whether successful or not. Every time you show up or ask, recognize it as a victory. Journaling these experiences can help you see the growth that comes from taking risks.

Real-Life Stories of Impact

The stories in this book will give you real impact in addition below are a few stories we are sharing to give you additional ideas.

Story 1: The Reluctant Speaker

Ella, a young professional, often felt overshadowed in meetings. One day, she decided to show up early to a presentation and volunteered to introduce a guest speaker. Despite her nerves, she used the opportunity to ask questions afterward. This small act of showing up led to her being recognized for her insights and eventually being offered a leadership role in her team.

Story 2: The Power of Community

A group of women in a small town came together to form a networking group, driven by the belief that their combined voices could create change. Each meeting encouraged every member to share their challenges and ask for help. Over time, this collective effort not only fostered personal growth but also led to the creation of a local business incubator supporting women entrepreneurs.

Conclusion

The journey toward personal and professional growth begins with the courageous act of showing up and the empowering choice to ask. Each effort, no matter how small, plants a seed of change that can blossom into extraordinary opportunities.

We all possess the innate strength to support one another through our vulnerability and courage. By embracing the power of presence and the art of asking, we not only elevate ourselves but also inspire a global community of women and men to rise together. Remember, the world is waiting for your unique voice—show up, ask, and let your journey unfold.

We send you continued success, love and happiness. We are Lady Ambassador Dr. Robbie Motter, GSFE Founder/CEO. Ambassador Reverend Dr. Christine Park, Ambassador Dr. Angela Covany CEO/Founder of Havana Book Group Publishers LLC and Ambassador Dr. Marcy Decato, Graphic Artist. We send you love and wish you great journeys in SHOWING UP and ASKING and hope you enjoy this Anthology with our wonderful contributing authors that we loved compiling together for you.

It's all
About
Showing
Up

FOREWORD

There's something truly powerful about sharing stories of showing up, even when it's hard. These narratives of courage and resilience can inspire us to face our own challenges with renewed determination.

This book is a collection of these experiences, shared authentically, that can become a beacon of hope for anyone feeling lost or uncertain. It reminds us that we're not alone in our struggles, and that even small acts of bravery can have a ripple effect.

This book has the potential to be a source of immense comfort and motivation for readers from all walks of life.

Through this book, we all show up from a diverse creed, race, religion, sexual preference, age, ethnic identity, color, and gender to create a better world and take a step.

This book highlights stories by various leaders about how showing up is more than just being physically present, it can also mean being present in mind, body, and spirit. It can involve putting in effort, even when you don't feel like it.

Being present can make all the difference.

Showing up demonstrates commitment and a willingness to engage. It allows you to learn, contribute, and be a part of something meaningful. Even when things are challenging, your presence can inspire and motivate others. Remember, sometimes simply showing up is a victory in itself.

Through this book you will learn how your presence can inspire others and create positive momentum. Showing up is a testament to your resilience and dedication.

Showing up can expose you to new ideas, perspectives, and industry trends that you may not have encountered otherwise.

Showing up consistently can help strengthen relationships and build trust. It can also help create opportunities that might not have been obvious at first.

By showing up, you can learn new ideas and advice. Learning new ideas and advice is a fantastic way to grow as a person. It broadens your horizons and helps you see the world from different angles.

Through showing up, one can discover innovative solutions and approaches that you may never have considered before.

The book will also highlight the importance of showing up as a team.

Together, we can be the force that shifts the tide, one ripple of change at a time. Let's make our mark on the world, leaving it a little better than we found it.

Face-to-face interactions are essential to building trust and establishing rapport with others and can lead to new opportunities and collaborations.

Embrace the opportunity to expand your knowledge and understanding, as it can be truly enriching.

Remember, showing up is often the most important step you can take. It can increase your chances of finding opportunities you're looking for.

It takes courage to envision a better world, but even more to step forward and make it a reality.

In this book, some of the leaders have highlighted how every act of kindness, innovation, and perseverance contributes to a brighter future by showing up.

In conclusion

Remember to keep an open mind and never stop seeking new information and perspectives.

Never underestimate the power of showing up and the power of your actions, however small they may seem.

Being present, both physically and mentally, demonstrates respect and dedication. Showing up consistently builds trust and strengthens relationships. Your presence can inspire others and create a positive impact. Even when inconvenient, ultimately, showing up matters, as it lays the foundation for success and fulfillment.

By showing up, you might find yourself in the right place at the right time.

Showing up can lead to greater joy and stronger bonds when you appreciate yourself, your achievements, and your impact on others.

Professor Caroline Makaka, PhD

It's all
About
Showing
Up

TESTIMONIALS

"High praise for Robbie Motter's brilliant "Showing Up Series"- Read all to catch the golden nuggets of inspiration and motivation that will inspire you to boldly jump into life as you show up and ask for what you truly want and need to become the person who has always been inside you- WAITING to come out!"

Barbara Berg, LCSW
Author of "Ring Shui- Move Your Rings, Change Your Life!"

"I love the stories submitted for this third volume of Show Up and Ask! They're both interesting and inspirational. Robbie Motter can draw from her vast network of friends and fans as well as 300+ international members of the Global Society for Female Entrepreneurs she founded and runs. This ocean of outstanding women is incredibly diverse by age, race, religion, politics, geography, and any other measure, yet they all have in common at least one story of changing their lives by showing up and asking!"

Carol Liege, Founder and CEO
The Legacy Factory LLC
Carol@TheLegacyFactory.com
+1 612-227-0752

"All the books on "It's All About Showing up" belong on everyone's bookshelf and we all need to share these books with each other too. They are filled with short inspiring stories about how just by showing up, your life, business, even your bank accounts can change in that moment. Pick up these books today and start reading and be inspired!"

AMB Dr. (h.c.) Nanciann Horvath
Professional speaker/author/nurse/mental health advocate/ Business Owner/ GSFE member
IMPROV FOR HEALTH
https://www.ImprovForHealth.com
ImprovForHealth@gmail.com

"The GSFE compilation of stories about the power of "Showing Up" is a game changer!

I have read the chapters in the past volumes of books. I was honored to have been asked to submit my story in Vol ll. As a collection, they carry individual themes of "Showing Up."

The stories have compelling messages with sage advice to keep going. They are culturally diverse, with a continentally rich perspective. The books are chronologically represented, and time tested. This makes the book a good read for young people as well as those of us who have lived and learned from every season. We bring the wisdom of our lessons; and the encouragement for taking risks. They all have an account of coming through it all with a sound mind and stronger for it. We must keep showing up.

These anthologies are coffee table books as well as a reference book for your personal libraries. I can't wait to read your review of the books once you have read and enjoyed them."

Dr. (h.c.) Stone Love Fauré
Certified Pilates Instructor
International Speaker & Retreat Leader
Stonelovesays@gmail.com

"It's All About Showing Up: The Power Is in the Asking" Volumes 1, 2, and 3 by Lady Dr. Robbie Motter are inspiring books that encourage readers to seize control of their lives through active participation and presence. Dr. Motter stresses the significance of showing up and articulating one's needs, which can lead to unexpected opportunities and connections. The volumes feature personal stories, practical advice, and motivational insights that motivate individuals to overcome challenges and pursue their goals. Volume 3 expands upon the themes of the first two installments, offering even more exciting and informative content. With a mix of expertise and personal experiences, Dr. Motter and the Co-authors foster resilience and effective networking among readers. Overall, these volumes are essential for anyone looking to enhance their personal and professional lives, making them a powerful resource for those ready to unlock their potential and embrace the importance of asking for what they want."

Amb. Rev. Dr. (h.c.) Christine Park, DD
International Best-selling Author, Inspirational and Motivational Speaker, Business and Personal Coach

"Where women come together and "show up" amazing things happen for ourselves, our communities, and the world."

Dame Shellie Hunt
Founder: The Women of Global Change
Shellie hunt@thewomenofglobalchange.com

"It's All About Showing Up: The Power Is in Asking is a transformative guide that emphasizes the importance of seizing opportunities by simply showing up and asking for what you want. Through real-life stories, practical advice, and motivational insights, this book reveals how the courage to ask can unlock doors, create connections, and lead to success in both personal and professional endeavors.

As someone who highly recommends It's All About Showing Up, I can attest to its life-changing impact. This book empowers readers to step out of their comfort zones and embrace the possibilities that come with boldness and initiative. Whether you're looking to advance your career, build stronger relationships, or achieve personal growth, this is the roadmap to making it happen. The power is in your hands—if you just ask."

Dr. Dawn Anderson, DHL
The Media Monetization Strategist
Leverage the power of media to change the world
MediaMonetizationStrategist.com
CelebrityBoss.com

"As the person who formats these books, and a co-author on the first volume, I have learned to appreciate the writing, the stories, and the heart of the women who share in these books. "It's All About Showing Up – The Power is in The Asking" is a concept that opens up a diversity of thoughts and conversations and every one of the authors in the 3 volumes share valuable information worth reading.

Thank you to Robbie Motter for pushing me to write, and for valuing my style, even though, English is my second language, she feels I have a place in her books.

Thank you to Angela Covany from Havana Book Group Publishers, for hiring my services and always appreciating my creativity.

Being a part of this anthology has been an incredibly rewarding experience. It's a privilege to stand alongside such talented writers, each contributing their unique voice and perspective to a collection that speaks to diverse themes. The collaborative nature of this project has deepened my appreciation for storytelling and the impact we can have when we come together. I'm honored to have my work included and excited for readers to embark on this journey with us."

Marcy Decato
Co-Owner
Creative Solutions Marketing & Printing, Inc.

marcy@creativesolutionsmktg.com
951-707-6338
www.creativesolutionsmktg.com

It's all
About
Showing
Up

Chapter Overview

Faith, Fear, and the Strength to Show Up
By Alex Ann Rathjen

The journey of my life has been shaped significantly by the simple yet profound act of showing up. It's a lesson I've learned time and again. Showing up is more than just being present; it's about stepping into opportunities, even when they seem overwhelming, inconvenient, or downright impossible.

I've learned that showing up is often the hardest part, especially when we're not certain of the outcome. Yet, it's in these moments, when we push past fear, exhaustion, or doubt, that miracles happen. The act of showing up opens doors, creates connections, and leads to opportunities we never could have anticipated. It's what has shaped my path, from being an athlete competing with the best in the world to stepping into rooms where I didn't feel like I belonged, to taking on challenges I wasn't sure I was ready for.

In each of these pivotal moments, the decision to show up laid the foundation for growth. While the rewards weren't always immediate or obvious, they came—sometimes in unexpected ways that revealed themselves only much later. Showing up has benefited me in every stage of my life, often in ways I never saw coming. There is power in showing up, in trusting the process, and believing that every small effort builds toward something greater.

It started on the volleyball courts when I was young, taking on the pressures of competition, the demands of discipline, and the relentless pursuit of excellence. From the moment I joined my first recreational volleyball team, I felt a spark. I was hooked by the thrill of the game, the sense of connection with my teammates, and the challenge of bettering myself. At first, it was fun—a way to spend my evenings—but as my skills grew, so did my desire to push myself further. What started as a recreational activity soon transformed into something more demanding.

In club volleyball, the expectations were higher, the competition tougher. My life quickly became consumed with practice schedules, weekend tournaments, and constant drills to improve my form, speed, and precision. I loved the sport, but it wasn't always easy to show up. It wasn't long until my skills earned me a spot on the varsity team as a freshman. I was now waking up at 5 a.m. for weight training, practicing for three hours with the varsity team, and then heading straight to club practice for another two hours—my body ached, and there were many mornings when I simply didn't feel like lacing up my shoes. The demands of the sport, combined with maintaining good grades in school, often felt overwhelming.

Yet, I showed up. Each day, I got myself out of bed, reminding myself of the bigger picture: my passion for volleyball and my desire to compete at the highest level. There were times when I doubted myself, feeling exhausted and mentally drained. I was constantly competing with girls who were at the top of their game, playing alongside some of the best. My coaches were some of the toughest and most respected in the game, pushing me to break through my physical and mental limits. I vividly remember the intensity of hell week and coming home on the last day and crying for hours.

Despite the challenges, I continued to show up. Each practice, each game, each weight-lifting session, I gave everything I had. For four years, I played

varsity volleyball, growing stronger not only as an athlete but as a person. I even played beach volleyball, learning a whole new dimension of the sport, adjusting to the sand, and to the unique demands of the outdoor game. Volleyball taught me resilience, teamwork, and how to push through discomfort. I became a two-time Junior Olympian, accomplishing my goal of competing against the best players in the world.

The sacrifices were immense—early mornings, late nights, sore muscles, and the constant pressure to perform at a high level—but I learned that showing up was more than just being physically present. It was about showing up with purpose, with the determination to improve, and with the belief that every small effort compounded into something greater.

I was reminded of this fundamental lesson one sunny, summer day when I was fresh out of high school. My dad, a man of unwavering perseverance, invited me to join him knocking on doors. It was my first day of canvassing with the goal of setting appointments for a solar company.

At the time, I was shy and nervous, more comfortable in my own world than venturing into the unknown. The thought of knocking on doors and talking to strangers made my heart race. I vividly recall the sinking feeling in my stomach as we drove to our first location. My dad, sensing my apprehension, turned to me and said, "This is my contribution to your education." I was hesitant but his words deeply resonated, and I agreed to step out of my comfort zone.

As we approached the first house, I felt like I was standing on the edge of a diving board, staring into a vast pool of uncertainty. I could feel my palms sweating and my heart pounding. "Just take a deep breath and remember, I'm right here with you," my dad reassured me. He stood beside me, offering silent strength, and I knocked on the door, unsure of what to expect. The first few doors were the hardest. I could barely get a word out. My dad patiently encouraged me. I remember feeling so small, my childhood instinct kicking in as I wanted to put my head between my legs and hide. With each knock, I pushed myself a little further with resilience and determination to overcome my fears and to learn this valuable skill of canvassing. My dad taught me that 95% of success is showing up.

After a few attempts, I began to find my voice. Each interaction, whether a friendly face or a harsh refusal, built my confidence. I was learning the invaluable skill of communication—how to connect with people, listen to their concerns, and articulate my thoughts. Day after day, I continued to show up, and gradually, I began to develop a sense of ease that was once foreign to me.

It wasn't long before I transitioned from canvassing to petitioning. Armed with the communication skills I had learned through those door-to-door experiences, I began gathering signatures to qualify initiatives. I spoke to thousands of people, and what was once nerve-wracking became second nature. I was confident and found joy in the connections I made with people.

Reflecting on those early days, I recognize the profound impact showing up had on my life. It was the beginning of a journey that would lead me to greater opportunities, including my decision to apply for recognition of prior learning for the opportunity to earn an MBA. With a heart full of hope and a mind eager for knowledge, I submitted my application, sharing my life experiences and the skills I had acquired. Three days before my thirtieth birthday, I received the news that my request had been granted. It felt like the culmination of all those moments I had chosen to show up. The hard work and dedication have paid off, and I am on my way to earning a degree that will open even more doors. As I am currently navigating through the MBA program, I continue to embrace the importance of showing up. There are times when I don't know the outcome of my efforts, but I am determined

to learn.

It was summertime and my close friends invited me to a camping trip in Sedona, Arizona. I was short on money, but I made a promise that I would show up. I used what resources I had and pawned all the jewelry and gold I owned. I knew it would be a trip to remember. When I arrived, they were happy to see me and as time went on, they became curious of my deep connection and personal relationship with God. I reflected on the time I lost my son when he was eight days old and how my relationship with God was strengthened. I experienced a peace that surpassed all understanding, a love that conquered all and a grace that was sufficient. I trusted God and made peace with him through faith. My relationship with God was deepened, leading me to a place of healing and resilience. It was on this trip I had a dream to write a book on my testimony that would help others searching for peace.

Through my petitioning network, I met a woman named Diana Londyn, who quickly became an incredible friend. We shared similar interests of creating a better world. She invited me to a dinner hosted by the Global Society for Female Entrepreneurs. Initially, the drive felt daunting. The distance, combined with my already busy schedule, made me question whether it was worth the effort. I had just gotten done petitioning and decided I was too tired and not properly dressed so I turned around to go home.

As I drove, I felt a stirring in my heart. I heard God's voice urging me to turn back around and go to the dinner, telling me that he had a gift waiting for me there. It was a voice I had learned to trust, especially after experiencing profound peace and strength during one of the most challenging times of my life when I lost my son. I had learned that sometimes the greatest blessings come from moments we initially resist. Despite my reluctance, I

turned back around and headed to the dinner, knowing that I had to show up.

When I arrived, I felt out of place, underdressed while the other women were dressed to impress. The room was filled with talented, accomplished women. They looked at me with curiosity, and I felt a wave of self-doubt wash over me. I reminded myself of my journey, and with confidence, courage, and a warm smile, I introduced myself. Not knowing who she was at the time, I sat next to a woman named Robbie Motter, the founder of the Global Society for Female Entrepreneurs. I recalled a mentor's advice: "Be interested, not interesting," words I first heard from Tom Chenault, one of the top network marketers in the world. I began asking questions, eager to learn about these remarkable women. To my surprise, they had not met in person since COVID-19 had disrupted their lives. I just so happened to be there on that night. It was as if I was meant to be there, like a thread woven into the fabric of their collective narrative.

That evening, I was informed about an exciting opportunity to write in a book titled Voices of Peace, featuring 100 co-authors sharing their stories of resilience and the quest for peace in a chaotic world. The moment I was invited to join, I felt an overwhelming sense of gratitude. It was a reminder of how pivotal the decision to show up had been. Tears of gratitude and astonishment filled my eyes on the drive home from dinner as I received the gift God promised me. My dream was coming true. Voices of Peace is now an international best-selling book, and I had the privilege of sharing my testimony.

After a few months, I received an invitation to attend a book signing with my co-authors at a beautiful winery in California. I was ecstatic yet apprehensive. I had nothing to wear and felt insecure about my appearance. I had an earlier commitment that day, and time was slipping away. As I

searched for an outfit, nothing seemed to fit right, and I began to convince myself that I should skip the event. I was already an hour late and an hour away from the event without any idea of what to wear.

I heard Gods voice speak to me once again, reminding me of the weight of regret. I had learned that showing up was better than hiding away. So, despite feeling less than perfect, I decided to make the drive. As I arrived at the winery, the gentle strumming of guitar strings greeted me, weaving through the air like a warm embrace. The ambiance was peaceful, with the co-authors celebrating our book's success. It felt surreal to be part of a collaborative effort that required all our voices to shine through. I spoke with fellow authors, as we signed books, I shared my story about the dinner I almost missed. I spoke of how I almost let fear and uncertainty dictate my decisions, but ultimately, I chose to trust God and show up. That evening was a testament to the miracles that can happen when we take that leap of faith.

The next morning, I received a call from Robbie Motter. She offered me the chance to be part of another book, this one centered on the theme of showing up, the book you are reading today. I was filled with gratitude, recognizing the divine timing of it all. It was another opportunity to share my story and inspire others to embrace the power of showing up.

If I had not shown up as an athlete, I might never have developed resilience. If I hadn't knocked on that first door, I might not have discovered the confidence to petition. Without the necessary experience, I wouldn't have dared to apply for a recognition of prior learning, which opened the door to pursuing an MBA. If I hadn't made that last-minute decision to attend the dinner, I would have missed the incredible opportunity to co-author a best-selling book on peace, and if I hadn't shown up to the book signing, you wouldn't be reading this chapter today.

I want to emphasize the significance of showing up—not just in the big moments but in the small ones as well. Life is full of choices, and sometimes, the hardest decision is simply to be present. Every time we choose to show up, we open ourselves to the possibility of growth, connection, and unexpected blessings.

As I reflect on my life, I give all the glory to God. He has guided me through the valleys and mountain tops. Even as I journeyed through the unknown, each step only served to strengthen my faith. I encourage you to embrace the power of showing up. Whether you're facing fear, uncertainty, or self-doubt, remember that your presence matters, and that God has a plan for your life. You never know what doors may open when you take that courageous step forward. Trust the process, lean into your faith, and show up—because the world is waiting for your unique contribution.

Alex Ann Rathjen is an entrepreneur and U.S. and international best-selling author of Voices of Peace: A Global Perspective. Currently pursuing her MBA at Oneday in London, UK, she is the founder of Bugsno, a startup focused on creating sustainable, natural alternatives to traditional bug repellents and insecticides. Her work reflects a passion for innovation, environmental sustainability, and supporting global health initiatives. Alex has contributed to qualifying over 300 initiatives as a traveling petitioner, advocating for social impact. She is the founder of Sweaters and Souls, a nonprofit organization dedicated to providing warmth and essential resources to those in need while sharing the message of the gospel. Originally from Riverside, California, Alex enjoys cooking, exploring new places, and hiking.

(951) 963-1994
alexannrathjen@gmail.com

It's all
About
Showing
Up

"Show Up" For Yourself in Life
By Ambassador Dr. (h.c.) Angela Covany

This book, in subsequent volumes, has been a testament to times in life when "Showing Up" has changed the trajectory of life courses and the "Ask" stories that have also shown how the "Power in the Asking" has changed life paths. As we all have in us many stories throughout life that these powerful mantras have happened for us to reflect on, I realized the biggest "Show Up" story I have is learning how to Show Up for myself in life and do what is best for me. Beginning the Self-Love Journey that I started 5 years ago has been the most challenging and rewarding endeavor that I have ever embarked upon. After leaving a 20+ year marriage and raising 5 children, a new chapter of my new life began. I realized a lot of people say they love themselves but continue to prioritize others before themselves, and don't practice self-love practices for many reasons. When you put others' needs above your own as a wife, mother, caregiver, or full-time employee how can you? Often, we ourselves get lost in the routine of life. How can you give from an empty cup? Below is a list of things I have learned on my journey.

It's okay to say No!

It's healthy. I'm a natural helper. If I can, I will. This was a big lesson for me. You do not need to over-extend yourself.

It's okay to take mental health days off.

Even if you need the money from your job or a day off from school it won't set you back too far academically. I raised my children to take time when time is needed. Don't push yourself or your children to achieve perfection at the cost of peace of mind.

It's okay to be unapologetic for being your authentic self.

Speak the truth and own it. No one can but you. No one is perfect nor should they think they need to be.

It's okay to choose what makes you happy.

This is the only life you get. You don't have to feel guilty to choose you and your carefully thought-out choices.

Self-love isn't selfish, it is required.

You deserve healthy relationships.

You deserve to live and work in non-toxic environments. Only keep real friends and partners that recognize your strengths and nurture your growth without judgement. It's okay to love others from a distance and keep them in prayer. The world will judge everything about you. What you did, what you said, what you didn't do, what you should've done, family included. Friends are the family you choose and feel valued by. Family is the one thing that will never change. That is one thing I heard that made me think a lot. Value the family you have even if you don't know how at any given moment.

After my divorce, we call ourselves my favorite ex-husband and favorite ex-wife even though we have both only been married one time. We are better friends than ever because the core value of family first has never changed.

You deserve to be appreciated.

You deserve to pursue your own dreams.

Even if that road gets lonely, as it often will, because your vision is yours alone. No one will truly understand your vision, your life calling or purpose but you in the way it was given to you. They will probably not choose to support, recognize, or value it as most people choose to stay in their own lane. Be okay with that and stay true to you.

Be proud of your accomplishments big and small, even if no one else is.

Look back frequently and see how far you have come and let go. Don't get lost in thought of how far you think you should be, you are always right on time in life.

You don't need validation from others to feel or be complete.

This is another milestone that I reached on my journey from codependency to independence. So many times, I have heard no one is going to save you and I have felt that on a core level over the last five years, but I have realized the truth in that. It is crucial you realize you are worthy of all good things, and you must be your own savior. I personally believe that I am never alone, and that GOD has guided me and helped to meet great teachers, mentors, and friends in my life that have helped me with this lesson.

Choose you and desire to continue to push yourself through the hard times knowing you deserve what is right on the other side of what you can't see.

"Don't let the fear of what could go wrong deprive you of what can go right."

As my beautiful sister Joan Wakeland taught me.

Gratitude breeds more gratitude.

Be grateful for what was, what is, and what will be. Gratitude is a game changer. It can elevate you to choose optimism over negative mental chatter.

Remember that you have control of your future.

The past is the past and if there is something you want to do, do it NOW. Tomorrow isn't promised to anyone. I believe wholeheartedly. Depression is wishing the past was different. Anxiety is being unsure of the future and peace of mind is appreciating and trusting in God, how it will unfold.

Procrastination deprives you of the rewards of doing.

You are worth investing in.

Believe and know you are.

"Show Up" and become the best version of yourself every day, even when it's difficult.

Your best is the greatest gift you can give to others because when you feel proud of yourself, your integrity and discipline speak. Your cup will be overfilled. People will not always remember your name, your face, or accomplishments. On a deeper level they will remember how you made them feel. They will remember their admiration for your tenacity, character, your ability to shine and thrive. You will inspire others through the adversities they watch you face and overcome.

Choose you first!

Even if that means some people will fall out of your life. Those who are meant to stay for you will.

Ambassador Dr. (h.c.) Angela Covany

Angela Covany is the CEO/Founder of HAVANA BOOK GROUP PUBLISHERS LLC., a publishing company located in the

United States. She serves on the Advisory Board of GSFE. She was a former Director of the Global Society for Female Entrepreneurs (G.S.F.E) for the Temecula, California chapter and previously Co-director for Menifee, Ca. She has also been the Director for Ventura and Santa Barbara, California chapters of National Association of Female Executives (N.A.F.E). Both companies serve to empower women personally and professionally to reach their fullest potential. Angela is a #1 Best-selling Author, Artist, and Illustrator. Some of her published works include Silver Lining Abstracts, a contributing Author in "Entrepreneurial Women of Faith Anthology", "It's All About Showing Up: The Power is in the Asking", "Holiday Express", "100 Most Successful Women from around the World", and her self-compiled Anthology entitled, "LOVE YOUR HATERS: How to harness the power

of self-love and embrace the peace found in forgiveness," and "Expert World leaders: Reaching beyond Boundaries Volume 2". Angela has a passion to help others connect through written and spoken words.

Her publishing company allows others to have a platform to help uplift, educate, and build living legacies. She feels a great sense of alignment in combining passion with purpose. Angela has been recognized with 3 separate awards by 3 seated presidents from 2016-2022 for her

dedication to her community. One of these awards was the Lifetime Achievement Award from President Barack Obama. Angela has been awarded by many city and state municipalities, recognizing the effort

she has made to help others personally and professionally. Angela has recently been the recipient of the Most Inspirational People in the World from (SIMA Global Awards 2022) She Inspires Me Award. She has received the international award "Beautiful Survivors Reaching Beyond Boundaries" from (LOANI) Ladies of All Nations International. She has most recently been honored with an Honorary Doctorate Degree in Humanitarianism from (GIA) Global International Alliance for her desire to continue to be a service driven leader and has been awarded recently with an Ambassadorship.

Contact Information:

WWW.HAVANABOOKGROUP.COM
WWW.HOWTOLOVEYOURHATERS.COM
HAVANABOOKGROUP@MAIL.COM

It's all
About
Showing
Up

Take Your Power Back

By Ambassador Dr. (h.c.) AnGéle Cade

The Power of Asking:
How a Single Question Transformed My Business

In the world of small business ownership, asking is a skill that many underestimate or overlook. As the founder and owner of Executive On the Go, I've spent years sitting across from clients, prospects, and even partners, all while grappling with the fear of "asking," whether it's asking for money, a sale, or simply knowing and asserting my own worth. It's an experience that most entrepreneurs can relate to, the uncertainty, the vulnerability, and the sinking feeling that perhaps you're asking for too much. Yet, I've learned that asking is a form of power. And in today's business world, power, when used wisely, can be the gateway to a life we deserve and a life worth asking for.

Power is often misconstrued as dominance or control. But in my experience, true power is the ability to confidently ask for what you need, what you want, and what you're worth and be able to do it without fear of rejection or inadequacy. Power doesn't have to be loud or aggressive; it can be quiet and self-assured. It's knowing that you are enough, and that the value you bring to the table deserves recognition. When I reflect on the role of power in business, I realize that it's not just about the ability to make deals or close sales; it's about understanding that the act of asking itself can be the most powerful tool we have as entrepreneurs.

Early in my career, I feared the ask. I feared it so much that I often didn't ask for what I needed at all. I would walk into client meetings with anxiety swirling in my stomach, hoping that they would see my value without me having to say it. I assumed they would offer me what I was worth if I just did a good job. But the harsh reality is, no one is going to hand you what you deserve on a silver platter. You have to ask for it.

I remember vividly the moment that encapsulated my struggle with asking. I was sitting across from a prospect, a potential client who could have been a game-changer for my business. My husband and I had poured hours of effort into preparing the perfect pitch. We believed in our work, and we believed in the value we brought to our clients. But when the moment came to talk about pricing, my confidence wavered. As the negotiation began, the prospect questioned our pricing. Instead of standing firm on the worth of our services, I hesitated.

In that instant, I discounted our price. I discounted it not because it made sense for the business, but because I feared the rejection that might come if I asked for what we were truly worth. I discounted down with defeat in my heart, and even though the client accepted the new price, I left that meeting feeling smaller. It was a win on paper, but a loss in every other sense.

The moment haunted me. I realized that in the process of trying to secure the sale, I had undervalued myself and my business. The fear of asking for the right price, the fear of hearing "no," had cost me more than just a few dollars. It had cost me my confidence and my sense of self-worth. In that

moment, I knew something had to change.

It wasn't long after that my husband and I stumbled upon a book by a business expert who had helped countless entrepreneurs overcome their own challenges. One piece of advice from her book stood out to us like a beacon of light in the fog of our self-doubt. She suggested a simple but powerful shift in the way we approached our pricing conversations. After presenting your price, she advised, ask, **"How would you like to pay for that? **

At first glance, it seemed almost too simple to make a real difference. But we decided to give it a try. The next time we sat across from a prospect, I presented our pricing confidently and then, with a steady voice, I asked, "How would you like to pay for that?" The effect was immediate and profound.

Instead of waiting for the prospect to react to the price or opening the door to negotiation, we had subtly shifted the conversation from "Is this price, okay?" to "This is the price, now let's talk logistics." It was a subtle but powerful difference. By asking how they would like to pay, we implicitly communicated that the price was non-negotiable, but we were willing to work with them on the terms of payment. The prospect, instead of pushing back on the price, responded with options for payment. The deal was closed.

That question changed our business. In fact, over the next few months, we saw a 35% increase in our sales. Who would have thought that a single question could hold so much power? But the power wasn't just in the words; it was in the confidence that came with asking. By reframing the way, we asked for what we deserved, we unlocked a new level of success that we hadn't even realized was possible.

I'm not alone in my fear of asking. So many business owners, especially small business owners, struggle with the same challenge. We worry that if we ask for too much, we'll scare clients away. We worry that if we assert our value, we'll be seen as arrogant or difficult to work with. And so, we undersell ourselves. We offer discounts before they're even requested. We downplay our achievements and capabilities in an effort to seem more likable or agreeable.

But here's the thing: asking is not a selfish act. It is not arrogant to ask for what you are worth. It is not greedy to charge a fair price for the value you provide. In fact, the act of asking is an acknowledgment of your own value. It's a way of saying, "I know what I bring to the table, and I believe it is worth this much." The fear of asking is, at its core, the fear of rejection. But rejection is not the end of the world. What's far worse is the slow erosion of your confidence and self-worth that comes from constantly under-asking and under-selling.

The power of asking is deeply intertwined with knowing your worth. In business, as in life, people will treat you according to the value you place on yourself. If you ask for less, they will give you less. If you act as though your services are worth discounting, they will assume the same. But if you stand firm in your value, if you ask for what you deserve, you'll find that people respect that.

For many years, I struggled to understand my own worth. I thought that being likable or accommodating was the key to success in business. But I've learned that likability and accommodation should never come at the expense of your own value. It's okay to be firm. It's okay to set boundaries. And it's okay, NO, it's necessary to ask for what you deserve.

Power is in the Asking

Asking is powerful because it opens doors. It invites conversation, negotiation, and, most importantly, possibility. The act of asking whether it's for money, for a sale, or for help it signals that you are willing to engage, to move forward, and to grow. It's a declaration of intent: I know what I want, and I'm not afraid to ask for it.

Throughout my journey, I have been fortunate to learn from my mentor, Robbie Motter, who embodies and champions the power of asking in every aspect of life. Robbie has shown me that asking is more than a business tool—it's a life philosophy. Whether advocating for herself or helping others, she consistently demonstrates how asking can turn visions into reality. Robbie's influence on me, and on so many others, has been profound. She taught me that asking isn't just about seeking opportunities for yourself but also about helping others access their own potential. Her leadership and ability to open doors through the simple act of asking have created ripples of impact across our communities.

In business, as in life, asking is a way to signal your intentions and to activate the possibilities around you. It's about initiating conversations and building connections. It's about taking the bold step to request what you need—whether it's resources, guidance, support, or opportunities. This is something Robbie taught me: when you ask, you give others the chance to be part of your journey, to contribute, and to help you grow.

For small business owners, the power of asking extends far beyond the confines of client meetings. It's about asking for the resources you need to grow your business, asking for advice from mentors like Robbie, asking for help from peers, and asking for feedback from customers. The more you ask, the more you learn, and the more you grow. This growth doesn't just benefit you—it benefits your entire network and creates a culture of collaboration and shared success.

In my journey as a small business owner, I've come to realize that the only thing standing between where I was and where I wanted to be was my own fear of asking. For years, I hesitated, unsure if my requests were reasonable or if they would be met with rejection. But once I learned to embrace the power of asking, everything changed. My business—and my life—began to transform. We started closing more deals, we stopped discounting our worth, and we built stronger, more trusting relationships with our clients.

The power of asking opened new doors I didn't even know existed. We began partnering with more businesses, expanding our reach, and stepping into opportunities that had previously seemed out of reach. Most importantly, asking helped us build confidence in ourselves and our value, enabling us to live the life we had always envisioned—a life worth asking for.

The power of asking is not limited to business transactions; it's a philosophy that can elevate every area of life. Robbie Motter continues to remind me of this. Her unwavering belief in the importance of asking has allowed her to open doors not just for herself but for so many others. She embodies the truth that when we ask, we don't just seek something for ourselves—we create pathways for others to follow, opening up possibilities for collaboration, growth, and shared success.

In every aspect of life, remember: the power of asking is the gateway to achieving your dreams. Don't be afraid to ask for what you need, to request what you're worth, and to engage with the world around you. The more you ask, the more you open the door to the future you deserve. A Life Worth Asking For.

The power of asking isn't just about business; it's about living a life that reflects your true worth. When you ask for what you need, you open yourself up to opportunities, relationships, and experiences that you might otherwise miss. You begin to live a life that is aligned with your values, your goals, and your purpose.

As I look back on my journey, I realize that the fear of asking is something that will always be there in some form. But the difference now is that I know how to overcome it. I've learned that asking is not a weakness; it's a strength. It's the key to unlocking the life you deserve, the success you seek, and the power within you.

So, the next time you find yourself sitting across from a prospect, a partner, or even a friend, remember the power of asking. Ask for what you're worth. Ask for what you deserve. And when the time comes to close the deal, don't forget to ask, "How would you like to pay for that?" You might just be surprised at the doors that question opens.

As I look forward to the future, I think not just about my journey, but about the legacy I want to leave behind for my son, Aundon, and for the generations that will follow—my future grandchildren, and beyond. The power of asking has transformed my life and my business, but more importantly, it has shaped the way I view the world, the opportunities around me, and my own ability to create a life of purpose. My hope is that this legacy of asking will become a guiding principle for my family, inspiring them to live boldly, pursue their dreams, and never be afraid to ask for what they deserve.

For my son, Aundon, I want him to know that his voice matters. In every room he enters, every opportunity he encounters, and every challenge he faces, I want him to feel confident in his ability to ask. Whether it's asking for help, guidance, resources, or simply standing firm in his worth, I want him to understand that the act of asking is his key to unlocking endless possibilities. He should never fear rejection or feel diminished by the word "no," because every ask is an opportunity to learn, grow, and push closer to his goals.

The same holds true for my future grandchildren and their children. I want them to live with the courage to ask, knowing that the world is full of opportunities waiting to be discovered. I want them to see asking not as a sign of weakness or uncertainty, but as a powerful tool to shape their futures. When they encounter obstacles or moments of doubt, I hope they will remember that they come from a legacy of boldness, a family that believes in the power of asking.

I envision a future where my family stands tall, knowing their worth, confident in their purpose, and unafraid to take risks. A future where they ask without hesitation, trusting that each question brings them closer to their dreams. As they navigate life's challenges, I want them to remember that the power to ask is within them—and with that power, they can achieve anything.

Living in the power of asking is not just about success; it's about living fully, with intention and courage. It's about embracing every opportunity, forging meaningful connections, and creating a life that is aligned with your highest purpose. This is the legacy I want to leave—a legacy that extends beyond wealth or accomplishments and speaks to the heart of what it means to live a life of purpose, integrity, and fearlessness.

To my son, Aundon, and to my future grandchildren: Always live in the power of asking. Never be afraid to use your voice, to seek out opportunities, and to claim the life you deserve. The world is yours for the asking.

Ambassador Dr. (h.c.) AnGéle Cade

ANGELE M. CADE is a consulting expert, who has dedicated the last twenty years to helping entrepreneurs develop effective corporate structures. With a pointed emphasis on current and future business goals, AnGèle truly walks alongside her clients to make sure they are set up with security and success. AnGèle is the CEO and Co-Founder of Executive On the Go, Inc., a thriving consulting firm for today's entrepreneurs. After nearly two decades spent developing, supporting, and counseling thousands of local, national and international businesses, AnGèle is recognized as the "Go To" expert for structural professional business needs. When AnGèle is not consulting, she can be found speaking, teaching, and training on the best practices to set goals, create priorities and attain support for their vision. She is passionate about sharing down to earth, real world business experience to help solve problems and empower those around her.

AnGèle is also a happily married, devoted wife to Brandon and a loving, proud mother of Aundon, to whom she dedicates her legacy work.

The Treasure Map of Life: Navigating Opportunities by Showing Up

By Dr. Angelica Benavides

Before diving further into the power of showing up, allow me to introduce myself. I am Dr. Angelica Benavides, often known as Dr. B., The Ultimate Legacy Builder. My passion lies in helping others, especially women, share their stories and leave a lasting legacy. I believe deeply in the power of storytelling as a way to inspire, motivate, and uplift others. My mission is to empower women to reclaim their superpower of confidence, enabling them to step fully into their greatness.

As an international publisher, I help people not only write and share their stories but also become comfortable using AI technologies to assist in the writing process. Whether it's creating books, content, or courses, AI has become a powerful tool in my mission to help others step into their creative potential. I embrace both tradition and innovation, allowing people to tell their stories in ways they never imagined possible.

In addition, I am the founder of the Alive and Beautiful Foundation, where I help women, men, and children affected by cancer to rebuild their lives and rediscover their inner strength. Through festivals, fashion shows, and mentorship programs, I celebrate their resilience and guide them on their path to success. It is my life's mission to ensure that every individual understands they can leave a lasting impact, not only for themselves but for future generations.

Success Isn't Just About Talent or Skill—it's about showing up

Through my journey, I've come to realize that success isn't just about talent or skill—it's about showing up, embracing the opportunities presented, and being willing to say "yes" when the right moment arises.

Life often feels like an intricate treasure map, full of winding paths, hidden opportunities, and unexpected connections that guide us to where we are meant to be. The key to unlocking these treasures is simple: you have to show up. Over time, I have come to realize that the power of saying "yes" and showing up when opportunities align with who you are and what you do can transform your life in ways you never imagined. Whether it's attending an event, joining a project, or accepting an unexpected meeting, the magic lies in being present and open to possibilities.

By showing up, I have made invaluable connections and forged deep friendships that have shaped my journey. For instance, I met Ambassador (h.c) Dr. Randi D. Ward, who is not only a great friend but also my editor. Through her, I was introduced to Prof. Caroline Makaka, a global leader with Leaders of All Nations International (LOANI), who has also become an amazing friend and has played a pivotal role in transforming my life. Prof. Caroline, in turn, introduced me to Lady Ambassador (h.c) Dr. Robbie Motter, an incredible force for empowering women worldwide.

Every place where I've chosen to show up has rewarded me with a "golden nugget"—a meaningful friendship or an opportunity that has allowed me to grow personally and professionally on a global scale. Showing up has truly been my key to unlocking the treasures of life.

The Treasure Map of Life: Unlocking Opportunities

Imagine life as a vast, complex treasure map. Each step forward, each "yes" you say, each event you attend, opens a new path, unveils a new connection, and brings you closer to hidden treasures you may not have even known existed. We often find ourselves at a crossroads, wondering if a particular opportunity is worth our time or energy, but it's in these moments of indecision that the treasure map beckons us forward.

Last year, I found myself standing at one such crossroads. I was invited to attend an event in the Philippines. At the time, I already had another commitment—a project I was passionate about—but at the last minute, it was canceled. I was left wondering: Should I take this unexpected opportunity to go to the Philippines, or should I stay where I was? Despite my reservations, I said "yes". And that one decision changed everything.

In the Philippines, I had the privilege of meeting Lady Robbie Motter, someone I had heard of but had never met in person. She welcomed me into her organization, the Global Society for Female Entrepreneurs (GSFE), which shares a mission similar to mine—empowering women to grow both personally and professionally. My connection with Lady Robbie has introduced me to other remarkable women, expanding my network, broadening my vision, and opening new doors of opportunity.

This is the true magic of showing up—you never know who you will meet or where those connections might lead. Meeting one person naturally leads to meeting the next, creating a ripple effect that mirrors the treasure map of life. Along this journey, I am collecting beautiful gems in the form of friendships and partnerships from around the world. Together, we shine brighter and create a more profound impact. I feel deeply blessed to have discovered these "gems" simply by showing up and embracing the opportunities life presents.

From Wake-Up Call to Purpose: Creating a Movement to Empower Stories and Legacies

Before diving deeper into the power of showing up, let me share a bit about my journey. I'm Dr. Angelica Benavides, also known as Dr. B., The Ultimate Legacy Builder. Today, I'm driven by a passion to help others, particularly women, share their stories and leave a lasting legacy. I believe storytelling has the power to inspire, uplift, and transform lives, and my mission is to empower women to reclaim their confidence and step fully into their greatness.

It wasn't always this way. Believe it or not, I was once incredibly shy. Growing up, I missed countless opportunities because I felt like I didn't belong or wasn't good enough. Even when I did show up, I would often slip away early or stop showing up entirely, afraid of being seen or judged.

Then came my wake-up call: cancer. It shook me to my core and forced me to confront the fact that life is fleeting. It was in those moments of facing my own mortality that I realized I didn't want to waste another second doubting myself or shrinking away from opportunities. I made a decision—I would show up fully in life and embrace every opportunity, not just for myself but to help others do the same.

This revelation led me to create a movement dedicated to helping people show up for themselves, to tell their stories, and to live, lead, and leave a lasting legacy. I wanted to ensure that others didn't wait for a wake-up call to start living fully. Through my work, I've helped women and survivors from all walks of life to embrace their power, reclaim their voices, and share their stories with the world. Together, we're building a legacy that will inspire generations to come. Showing up isn't just about being present— it's about showing up for your own life and creating the impact you were meant to make.

The Power of Showing Up: A Magical Experience

So, what is it about showing up that makes such a difference? The truth is that showing up puts you in the right place at the right time. Whether you realize it or not, countless connections are waiting to happen. You may meet someone who knows someone who can unlock a door for you three levels deep into your network. The power of showing up lies in the ripple effect—you show up for one opportunity, and it leads you to another, and another, creating momentum in your life and your career.

For example, my involvement with LOANI and GSFE has opened doors I never expected. It started with one "yes," and now I find myself surrounded by women who uplift each other and encourage growth. Each event, each interaction, adds a new layer to the treasure map of my life.

When you show up, you allow the universe to meet you halfway. You place yourself in the flow of opportunity, and suddenly, things begin to happen. You build relationships that help you grow, personally and professionally. You meet people who challenge you, support you, and inspire you to reach higher. Showing up is a magical experience because it's about stepping into the unknown with confidence that something beautiful will come out of it.

Missed Opportunities: When We Don't Show Up

On the flip side, think about the countless opportunities we miss when we choose not to show up. How many times have we declined an invitation or passed on an event, only to later realize that we missed out on something significant? It's so easy to say "no" when life feels overwhelming, when we're exhausted, or when we believe we don't have the time. Often, we convince ourselves that we can't afford it, financially or otherwise. But the truth is, when we truly want something, we find a way to make it happen.

When we don't want it badly enough, we make excuses.

It's time to stop making excuses and start recognizing that life is all about how you handle Plan B. Rarely do things go exactly as planned, but showing up—despite the challenges—can make all the difference. I've learned that life rewards those who take action. Showing up is a commitment, not just to others but to yourself. It's a declaration that you are worth the investment of time, energy, and resources. Failing to show up because "you don't have the time" or "you can't afford it" often costs you far more in the long run than you realize. Opportunities don't always come twice, and the connections you might make or the lessons you might learn by simply being present are invaluable and irreplaceable.

Ultimately, the only thing standing between you and the life you desire is your willingness to show up and take action.

The Treasure Map of People: Building Relationships

One of the greatest treasures on the map of life is the people we meet along the way. Whether it's a mentor, a colleague, or a friend, each person has the potential to shape our journey in profound and unexpected ways. Showing up is the key to forging these invaluable connections, and it's often through these relationships that we discover the very opportunities we've been searching for.

I have to confess that the most precious gems I've collected in life are the incredible people I've met simply by showing up. Even when I didn't have the time or resources, I aligned myself with my highest purpose and found a way to make things happen. And when I did, the magic unfolded. Through showing up, I've built extraordinary relationships across the globe—friendships that have enriched my life in ways I never anticipated.

I've been blessed to meet people from all corners of the world who have since become dear friends and extended family. I've had the privilege of visiting them and sharing unforgettable experiences, like spending time with my friend Amelia in Norway, Mint in Thailand, Dr. Elizabeth in Davao, Ambassador Gloria in Mexico, and Dr. Jaya in London. And the list goes on. Showing up has truly created a treasure map of people, each one adding value, love, and depth to my journey. These relationships are not just connections; they are treasures that have made my life richer and more meaningful.

Closing the Circle: Saying Yes to Yourself

In the end, showing up isn't just about being there for others—it's about showing up for yourself. It's about recognizing that you deserve the opportunities life presents to you and that you are capable of making the most of them. When you say yes to opportunities that align with your values and vision, you are saying yes to your growth, your success, and your legacy.

I am deeply passionate about helping others, especially women, share their stories and build their legacies. The power of showing up is a crucial piece of this puzzle. It's how we find the confidence to step into our greatness, the resilience to overcome challenges, and the vision to create lasting impact.

In my own journey, I've learned that when you show up—fully, authentically, and with an open heart—the universe responds. It brings the right people into your life, the right opportunities into your path, and the right lessons for your growth. So, say yes to the next invitation, the next event, the next project. Show up, and watch the treasures unfold.

Conclusion: Life as a Treasure Map

As I reflect on my own experiences, I am grateful for the moments I said yes and showed up. Each opportunity has been a treasure, leading me further down the path of personal and professional growth. The power of showing up is undeniable. It's the key to unlocking the hidden treasures of life—the people, opportunities, and experiences that shape us into who we are meant to be.

So, I encourage you to look at your life as a treasure map. Follow the paths that align with your purpose, say yes when the right opportunity arises, and always show up. You never know what treasures are waiting for you just around the corner.

Dr. Angelica Benavides

Dr. Angelica Benavides, also known as Dr. B., The Ultimate Legacy Builder, is a global private publisher, author, and founder of the Alive and Beautiful Foundation. With a passion for helping women and survivors of life's challenges reclaim their power and share their stories, Dr. B. empowers others to leave lasting legacies through impactful storytelling. As an international publisher, she helps people become comfortable with using AI prompting to create books, content, courses, and more, combining traditional storytelling with cutting-edge technology. Through her foundation, she uplifts cancer survivors and fosters entrepreneurial growth, all while encouraging women to embrace their greatness and build their own lasting legacies.

Connect with me

https://blinq.me/6XdEPTRPdsS5664TXbOI?bs=db

Special Gift

🎁 Free Gift Just for You!

As a thank you for reading, I'd love to invite you to join my exclusive AI Workshop—completely free! 🚀

In this workshop, you'll learn how to leverage AI to boost your creativity, speed up your writing, and supercharge your success in business. Don't miss out on this opportunity to dive deeper into the world of AI!

👉 Click here to claim your free spot! https://ai-drivensuccess.drbglobal. net/

I can't wait to see you there! Let's unlock the power of AI together. Use coupon code: aiworkshop.

THE IMPACT OF 'SHOWING UP'

By Ambassador Dr. (h.c). Avic Ronquillo-De Castro

Showing up for others means that you are there for someone when they need you. You show kindness by helping others and not just thinking of yourself. You give people the respect they deserve.

The two core components to "showing up" are knowing ourselves and engaging in conscious preparation. Showing up is a combination as a whole, as a resolution, motivation, behavior, attention and choices.

Importance of "Showing Up"

We put ourselves into a place where we open the door to new conversations, solutions, opportunities, experiences, and relationships.

Showing Up requires intelligence, intuition, empathy, generosity, confidence and a willingness to be.

It is a level of visibility to which reliability, empathy, care, intentionality, thoughtfulness and a tangible feeling of "just being there" that is consistently demonstrated by someone.

First Rule of Success

If you want to succeed, you 've got to show up and participate.

When you show up, you tell others and yourself that you're serious about your goals. Being consistent is key. People start to trust and rely on you because they know you will be there when you are needed.

Benefits of 'Showing Up'

Being present in both big and small gatherings or events is important both 'in the moment' and long-term showing unconditional attention and support is a basis for strong and vital relationships.

Appreciation of yourself, your achievements and your impact on others leads to stronger bonds and greater joy.

Dressing Up in Showing Up

We dress up in order to show the honor and respect demanded of a particular activity or because these are community affairs, and we want to appear at our best when seen by others.

Dressing up is important in 'Showing Up' to boost our mood. It can enhance our productivity based on what we wear. For example, to wear formal outfit can enhance focus, attention to detail, and critical thinking.

These are the benefits of dressing up properly in 'Showing Up' at any event or meeting:

a. You are more confident that dressing up has proven to have the ability to boost your mood and overall confidence.

b. You gain respect and recognition.

c. You might move further in your career.

d. You become more social.

e. You are prepared to meet anyone.

"Showing Up" can encompass a variety of topics depending on the context, whether it's about personal development, professional growth, or creative expression. Here are some key themes you might consider discussing:

Authenticity: The importance of being true to oneself and the impact it has on relationships and creativity.

Presence: How being fully present in the moment enhances experiences and connections with others.

Vulnerability: The role of vulnerability in building trust and deeper connections.

Commitment: Discussing the significance of showing up consistently in personal and professional contexts.

Overcoming Fear: Strategies for facing fears that prevent us from showing up fully.

Mindfulness: Techniques for cultivating mindfulness to enhance presence and focus.

Resilience: How showing up during difficult times can build strength and character.

Accountability: The importance of holding oneself accountable in both personal and professional realms.

Creativity and Expression: How showing up impact's artistic endeavors and the creative process.

Community and Support: The role of community in encouraging individuals to show up for themselves and each other.

Self-Care: Balancing the act of showing up for others while also taking care of oneself.

Goal Setting: The importance of setting intentions and goals to guide one's efforts in showing up.

Feedback and Growth: How receiving and giving feedback can enhance our ability to show up effectively.

Role Models: Discussing individuals who exemplify the concept of showing up and what we can learn from them.

Impact of Technology: Exploring how technology can both help and hinder our ability to show up in meaningful ways.

Time Management in Showing Up

Showing up on time is a soft skill that can be improved through time management. Here are some time management tips that can help you be on time:

a. Prioritize: Prioritizing tasks helps you focus on what's most important and get rid of unnecessary tasks. This can help you be more productive, especially when you are busy.

b. Plan: Planning helps you see all the tasks you need to do and how they relate to each other. This can help you plan your course of action.

Write down them and see every minute to be used on a task or meeting.

c.   Set Time Limits: Set time limits for tasks and activities. If you are showing up at a meeting, set a 2 hour to 4-hour window schedule and/or include travel time to go to the destination or event location.

d.   Learn to say No: Saying No is a critical time-management skill that helps you protect your time.

e.   Organize: Keep your space clean and organized so you can find things easily and put them away once you are done or accomplished a finished task.

f.   Time Block: Time blocking involves dividing your day into blocks, with each block dedicated to a specific task or group of tasks.

g.   Daily Schedule: Keep yourself a journal or a calendar where you write down all your meetings and events to go either in person or online for showing up.

h.   Automation: You can set an automation on repetitive tasks, tackling difficult tasks first, batching similar tasks, and avoid multi-tasking.

Creating a "Showing Up" meeting checklist

Creating a "Showing Up" meeting checklist can help ensure that you're prepared and make the most of your time in meetings. Here's a simple yet effective checklist to consider:

Pre-Meeting Preparation

1. Agenda Review

   o Read and understand the agenda.

   o Note any topics you need to contribute to.

2. Background Research

   o Gather relevant information or data.

   o Review previous meeting notes if applicable.

3. Questions and Points

   o Write down questions or points you want to address.

   o Prioritize your points based on importance.

4. Materials and Resources

   o Prepare any necessary documents, presentations, or reports.

   o Ensure all materials are accessible (digital or printed).

5 Technical Setup

   o Test your technology (camera, microphone, software).

   o Have backup options ready (e.g., phone numbers for dial-in).

Day of the Meeting

1. Timing

   o Set reminders for the meeting time.

o Join the meeting 5-10 minutes early.

2. Environment

o Choose a quiet, well-lit space for the meeting.

o Minimize distractions (turn off notifications, close unrelated tabs).

3. Dress Code

o Dress appropriately based on the meeting context.

During the Meeting

1. Engagement

o Actively listen and take notes.

o Contribute to discussions when appropriate.

2. Body Language

o Maintain eye contact and use positive body language.

o Nod or show acknowledgment when others are speaking.

3. Time Management

o Be mindful of the agenda and keep contributions concise.

o Avoid side conversations that may distract others.

Post-Meeting Follow-Up

1. Notes Review

 o Summarize key takeaways and action items.

 o Clarify any uncertainties while the information is fresh.

2. Action Items

 o Assign deadlines to your tasks.

 o Communicate with team members as needed.

3. Feedback

 o Reflect on the meeting's effectiveness.

 o Consider areas for improvement for future meetings.

Having this checklist handy can streamline your meeting experiences and ensure you're consistently prepared. Adjust it to fit your specific needs and work culture!

Written by: Ambassador Dr. (h.c.) Avic Ronquillo-De Castro

Please contact me at: mrdcentrep@gmail.com

Ambassador Dr. (h.c.) Avic Ronquillo-De Castro

Amb. Dr. Avic Ronquillo-De Castro (h.c.) is a successful entrepreneur, administrator, and accounting specialist with a passion for managing, coordinating, and accounting.

Amb. Dr. Avic is an international social media digital marketing partner & event Host. She has helped many businesses establish their online presence and reach their target audience through social media marketing.

She is also a book author & keynote speaker and an entrepreneur.

Amb. Dr. (h.c.) Avic's dedication to her work has made her a respected figure in the business community. She continues to innovate and grow her business, always striving to provide the best possible service to her clients. Today, Amb. Dr. (h.c.) Avic is an accomplished entrepreneur with a thriving business. Her experience in management, coordination, accounting, event planning, and social digital marketing makes her a valuable asset to any business looking to grow and succeed.

WORK HISTORY:

CURRENT:

Entrepreneur, Author, Speaker, Fitness & Sports Coach

Accounting Specialist - Winchester, CA

- My New Hub, Inc. - Administrator

Int'l. Social Media & Mktg. Partner- RM Realty, Philippines

Chief Financial Officer-Godly Encouragement Ministries Church- Chino Valley, CA

Megalite Corp CA - CEO/CFO 2003-2010

Volleyball Clinician COACH- USYVL, Lake Elsinore/Murrieta, CA 2014

EDUCATION:

Computerized Bookkeeping & Accounting 1992-NRI, McGraw-Hill CEC, USA

AA Secretarial 1981 & BSBA Accounting- 1986- University of the East- Caloocan, Philippines -1986

American Institute of Professional Bookkeepers –Member

Friends_ Next Level (Facebook group)- Social Group Administrator & Founder

Global Society of Female Entrepreneurs- Member

Global International Alliance University (GIAU) – Honorary Doctorate of Humanitarianism graduate 2024

LOANI Miracle Women Awardee 2024

All about Showing Up Vol. 3 Book-co-author 2024.

VOICE OF PEACE Book– co-Author 2024

Coming Off Mute-The Power in Finding Your Voice- co-Author 2024

Power of Networking Book- co-Author 2023

RKMPIII- Ambassador of Kindness & Happiness 2024

Women of Achievement West Coast Rising Star Leader Finalist Awardee-2023

LOANI-Ladies' of All Nation, Inc.- International Filipino Leader Awardee-2023

LOANI Global Executive Member 2024-2025

BPMI Ladies Clubs Global-Global Iconic Changemaker Awardee-2023

Fitness Instructor- ZIN (Zumba International Network) instructor/ member

Showing Up: The Key to Inner Fulfillment

By Ambassador Belinda Foster

Have you ever awakened in the early morning before dawn and watched the sunrise? It is such a beautiful experience to witness. It is glorious and magnificent in its transformation as it moves from navy skies to periwinkle blue shining bright with the sun's beams eloquently painting the morning. A new day.

Just as the sun rises in the morning, we are given a new opportunity to discover more about life, people, our world and our purpose. We are unique as human beings because we have the innate power to set goals. The goals that we set sometimes are based on things we say we want to accomplish. For example, we may want to purchase a new pair of shoes. It takes the effort to show up to make it happen. We get up and we go to a shoe store and try on shoes until we find the right pair that feels just right and fits our style. Goals like these are achieved by taking the time to act upon them in this way.

The power of showing up is essential to our daily life experience and journey as we evolve in our path to self-discovery. We are born with a bright light and open mind to explore creativity. As a child, we played with toys and watched cartoons that were colorful with imaginary stories that came to life that made us laugh or pay attention to the characters created by animators. An animated film didn't just happen to be. It took a group of people to show up to make it happen. Artists, voiceover actors, animators, editors and all the professional people who come together to produce a unique work.

What is our purpose? What road do we travel? Where do we find ourselves in this world? It is a process that is unique for each and every person's journey. We can think logically and make a list of goals we want to accomplish from a logical perspective. Then, there is the other way of setting goals. A way that is illogical. A way that is based on our inner hopes and dreams.

There is nothing like the experience of getting a good night's rest. As we sleep by day or night, there are moments where we have dreams. The essence of dreaming is something that we may control depending on thinking about a place we want to travel and imagining it in our minds while we are awake. When we go to sleep, there is a different type of dream experience. It is something that we usually can't control. As we dream in our sleep, we can find ourselves walking into our own visual space, a movie that is predesigned and even selected as we drift off to sleep. Sometimes these dreams at night are so real it seems like it is an actual life experience.

We can feel that way about a dream while we're awake. These types of dreams occur when we look at a beautiful sunset that we admire, and we feel a sense of peace from it that takes us into a daydream of walking along the shores of a Hawaiian beach where we see ourselves. We experience the daydream as if it is a real experience. We suddenly have the desire to plan a trip to Hawaii. We set this as a dream goal, and we pursue it with focus and joy.

Another example is that you may attend a tennis match and enjoy watching the players play. You see yourself as a tennis player from watching the

match. You take the steps to sign up for tennis lessons at a local YMCA. The first day that you show up is the beginning of your journey to pursue your dream to play tennis.

Showing up can also mean connecting with others who are living the dream that we see for ourselves. When we connect with others this way, it is absolutely profound. We are so connected as members of the human race in this way; and just as we see ourselves in others who emulate the talents that we have inside of us, sometimes we're not even aware that that talent is there until we see it in someone else.

Setting goals is part of our livelihood as human beings. We pursue our dreams through stepping out in courage and conviction. It is when we pursue our dreams with this type of focus that we pursue knowledge of how to achieve our goals. When we experience using that gift or talent, we experience the joy of using it. This brings inner fulfillment. It is even more profound when we use our gifts that we develop through showing up to help others in need.

Showing up to benefit others in society helps us to realize that our gifts and talents that we love and enjoy doing have a true purpose. It is when we get up and attend an art museum and find our home in the space of the art that this purpose is realized. It is when we go out to an art supply store and purchase canvases, brushes, paints, and attempt to create our first work of art that our purpose is activated. Showing up has different levels of fulfillment in our lives in this way.

You may find yourself spending hours sitting on a porch looking up at the stars or enjoying the beautiful view of nature through the canvas of a magnificent painting. You may find joy in showing up at the zoo to view animals on display. You may find that you are born to write about them. You take that moment to show up for a writing workshop where you are on your way to the vision of who you are born to become. Showing up is the activation of your pursuit of happiness toward your purpose. You find yourself because you showed up to attend a class again and again until you master that talent or craft; and if you're consistent enough in showing up, you discover that showing up means that you connect in moments with people who showed up to arrive at a mastery level for the new purpose of feeding you the knowledge that they received. It is truly a give and take type of thing that occurs when we show up for one another. Giving to others is one of the most meaningful ways of showing up. In moments like these, the giver shows up to share what they got out of their experience and suddenly the student learns something new and thus, grows in their own development process.

When you are consistent in showing up toward your dream, you realize the process is one that takes patience and due diligence. When you pick up materials such as the canvas, the paint, and the charcoal and begin to draw or create art that is astounding you arrive at a new space of understanding of your communication skills with others. Art is a silent art of communication where others show up to simply look and marvel at the human messages reflected in the artwork as expressed by the artist.

The process of creating your artwork is step one of showing up. Do you just let the artwork sit there in your art room or do you envision sharing your work with someone who you just met? It is in moments of the human connection where we have the opportunity to show up and share a little bit of ourselves to inspire and even enlighten others. Let's say you take your artwork and decide to donate that artwork to a charity; and you may say to yourself 'I am going to show up and talk about what it was like to draw this painting.' In this type of showing up, you're sharing your experience, and you find the joy in doing that. Someone who showed up is seeing your artwork and they purchase it, carrying your story with them. Artists and

art collectors show up for mutually beneficial purposes. Art collectors show up at art shows because they have a passion for it. Artists discover moments that they define on canvas that lead to their own new experience of life and understanding of the human experience.

Whether you paint art on canvas or daydream of places you want to travel, you have the innate power to show up through your imagination or through real awakened moments and embrace your space and talent.

One of the most important benefits of showing up is that we connect with others. Sometimes we connect with friends and family. Sometimes we connect with new people that we meet for the first time. We find ourselves meeting up with people who share similar goals with us by simply pursuing our goals. We take English classes and meet others who are interested in English and writing. Showing up in this way is great because we grow in our abilities with others who are on a similar path. We can share and receive feedback with others that are pursuing goals in the same world of interest that we have. Whatever it is that you do best, you discover you have associates and friends that you build with and that you're not alone in your pursuit of your dream. You soon discover you are changing, growing, and living your dream. You're walking in your dream, and you continue to do so. You get better and better at what you do by simply showing up and applying yourself. More importantly, you're connecting with more people and sharing your gifts with others on your journey. You never know who you are inspiring when you are living your truth.

Through your natural passion for living life, you discover how to experience optimum happiness. There is a joy from giving to others and showing up sometimes it can also mean you just may show up to support someone else in their lives or meet a need in their lives.

In showing up, we discover that there is a big world out here. There are opportunities to meet new people each and every day. As we meet people, we grow in our understanding of the floral variety of the human race. When you think about it, it is in our moments of congregating with other people that we find support and new possibilities.

Feelings of loneliness and uncertainty vanish when we step out to show up for a lunch meeting with friends or a restaurant outing with family. It is in these moments that we realize that we don't have to take life so seriously each and every moment. We don't have to be in work mode 24/7. Variety is the spice of life. And this includes taking time to gather and meet in settings where we can simply enjoy the moment. There are other ways that we are needed in this journey as well.

There are times when we gather to have fun. There are other times when we gather to make a difference in someone's life. Sometimes we have to show up when we need to rescue someone or defend someone who is being bullied or who is being mistreated. In those moments, we identify the needs of others and pull from our own inner courage to try and help someone in need. These are tougher moments because sometimes you have to just step out on faith and realize that you have to position yourself as that person who stands up for that person; and maybe there are other people that don't see the need to help, and they simply walk away. Showing up is a choice that we make each day in each situation that we face or experience.

You speak up on behalf of someone being pushed around because you know that person doesn't deserve to be bullied. In those moments of showing up, it takes a special type of courage, it takes the courage of just being a caring human being. I think that this is so powerful. We show up for different

reasons over time. Sometimes we change what we are looking to achieve based on phases of our self-awareness and environmental conditions.

I remember walking into the airport and being greeted by a man behind a podium. When he took his break. I saw him enter a portable wheelchair and prepare to transport himself to the food court of the airport. What I sensed was inspiring. He didn't need much assistance as he had mastered using a motorized wheelchair. He was self-sufficient and had adapted to his chair throughout his travels. Although he was in a chair, he expressed his joy for life with others on the job, and that was what stood out from interacting with him.

What was nice is that he inspired me about the power of giving. His smile and light reminded me of the wise saying, let your light shine. When we show up and share our joy, we find true happiness in our daily living experiences. We grow as we show up and meet new people. It is important to know that when we show up in this way, the sun comes shining through. It's the power of showing up that helps us to find the doors that we must go through in order to explore our purpose. And as we discover our own creative expression through art, language and style of living, we see ourselves grow and develop from showing up and walking a little further down our path toward success.

Success is achieved in each moment when we walk in our inner truth. Showing up provides the key to the door where we must walk through toward the path of making our dreams happen. We can talk about our dreams, but it takes getting dressed for the occasion and stepping out in style toward a specific road and path and not looking back in order to get there.

Showing up is not a random choice. It is a targeted effort based on a clear focus on the values you carry, the talent you have, and the vision you see for yourself.... You soon find where you belong in walking on this type of path. Take your time each day to put the connection with humanity first.

Making money is what we are taught to do as a necessity of living. We can settle for second best if we choose by taking a job that pays the bills. That is not the ultimate purpose of showing up. Just as you can land a job you don't like, you can also step out on faith and pursue a creative vision for something that no one else has achieved...a vision that you see for yourself, and it is possible and can definitely be done.

There is a universal truth in showing up.... always remember that it's in showing up that we grow as human beings ...it's showing up that we learn that we are not alone in this world... and it's in showing up that we walk through the doors to make our dreams come true.

Ambassador Belinda Foster

Belinda Foster is the founder of AWJ Platinum PR, a Los Angeles-based full-service marketing and multimedia firm.

As a seasoned expert in Public Relations and Marketing, she is best known for engaging and strategizing major campaigns in the entertainment.

industry for both indie and major projects across the television, literary, film, fashion, sports, and music to name a few. She also works with private sector businesses in PR and marketing with respect to consumer engagement for business development.

In addition, Belinda Foster is a professional writer, radio host, and producer. She has worked with legends including Melvin Riley, Morris Day, John Amos, and Dr. Cherilyn Lee, who has appeared on CNN, the CBS Early Show, FOX National news, and other major outlets.

www.awjplatnum.com

It's all
About
Showing
Up

Adjust Your Crown Queen
By Briana Rice

"Would you show up if you knew you would be crowned Queen?

Follow me as I detail a serendipitous set of events that led to one of the biggest individual wins of my lifetime!

We often hear the cliché that you have to be in the right place at the right time, but I literally saw this manifest before I took the crown as Miss California African American 2024 and Ms. Woman of Achievement International 2024.

Like many women, I've watched beauty pageants on TV, always delighting in the gowns, the exquisite physiques, and the way contestants stood and spoke with such confidence. I admired them but never saw it within myself.

I became a beauty pageant queen because it felt divinely orchestrated by God Himself.

Luckily, a few key events fell into divine alignment. The first was meeting my pastor and friend, Dr. Tyra Lee. I reached out to her after seeing a Facebook ad for an event planner course. I'd been planning events for years, but after experiencing a traumatic brain injury, I knew I needed a refresher if I ever hoped to get back to work.

After hearing my story, not only did Dr. Tyra Lee allow me to take part in the course through her nonprofit, She Is Foundation Network, she also gave me a partial scholarship to help with the fees, knowing I was in a devastating season of disability.

Dr. Tyra Lee hosts an annual award and fashion show where guests receive awards for their accomplishments, and I received an award for completing the event planning course. Much to my surprise, I also received a Humanitarian and Community Life Changer Award.

I rarely talk about my good deeds, because I believe giving back to the community is simply what we're supposed to do. But I've supported women who've endured human trafficking. I've quietly stepped in to help those who were homeless, offering them shelter and psychiatric assistance. I'm a certified Tantra teacher and Sound Healer, and many of my clients have shared stories of domestic violence, suicide, depression—challenges people often keep hidden. I've supported them, encouraged them to find peace, and kept everything confidential.

Sharing these experiences with my pastor and friends, receiving this recognition was truly a blessing. These are not things I post about on the internet—I believe in preserving people's dignity when they're at their lowest.

At this same awards ceremony and fashion show, I locked eyes with Marlene Martin, my now pageant director, and across from her sat the most elegant woman I'd ever seen, Alicia Couri. She embodied everything I saw as a queen—a refined woman who sat confidently in her worth.

Marlene Martin approached me and asked if I'd ever considered pageantry. I was bewildered. I saw elegance and beauty in her, but here she was, seeing the same in me. I immediately started crying.

The tears I shed were not just from shock but from feelings of unworthiness. Living with an invisible disability, I had let negative comments make me feel unworthy and unlovable.

Surprisingly, Marlene saw something in me, but I was overwhelmed by the idea of having less than three weeks to prepare for the pageant. I was also preparing to launch my wine festival, Blackberry Merlot, just a week after the pageant.

I prayed to God for clarity, thinking He would open doors to make the festival a success. Blackberry Merlot isn't just a wine event; it supports causes close to my heart, including traumatic brain injury awareness, suicide prevention, and women's empowerment.

I also had just finished a 90-day fast, recommended by a dear friend, Reproductive Health Specialist, Elena Lakay. The fast was designed specifically to prepare myself mentally and physically to heal from my invisible disability and to naturally treat a recent fibroid diagnosis. So, I felt more in tune with my natural intuition and wisdom than ever before.

Even though I was reluctant, within two weeks I contacted my pageant coach, Vincent Lappas. We worked tirelessly to craft a speech that would honestly share my experience living with an invisible disability, where I felt my life, my passion, and my career had come to a screeching halt. But I decided to push forward, crafting my platform: 'Life and Empowerment After a Traumatic Brain Injury.'

My goal was not just to promote the Blackberry Wine Festival but to turn my pain into purpose, using my testimony to empower others.

When the pageant day arrived, two weeks later at the Queen Mary in Long Beach, I was fraught with nerves. Despite lingering feelings of unworthiness, I knew I had to give it my all. Even if I didn't win, I could still stand as a testimony of resilience, showing that not only was I physically beautiful, but there was beauty, love, and light within my heart.

The Achievement pageant spanned three days, where we not only paraded in gowns but attended seminars that taught us the power of affirmations. I gave my speech, and I witnessed other women bravely step forward with their talents, fitness presentations, and shared wisdom.

For the pageant, I chose the title Miss California African American because I wanted to embody the beauty and resilience of African American culture. In my country wisdom segment, I quoted the director of the Smithsonian African American Heritage Museum, who said, 'To be African American is to embody values like resilience, optimism, and spirituality.' I added that these values fuel my mission to promote life and empowerment after a traumatic brain injury.

When the time came for the final announcements, I stood quietly, clapping for each queen as their titles were called. I was ready to clap for whoever would win the title of Ms. Woman of Achievement. Much to my shock and surprise, they called out Briana Rice. I immediately grabbed my stomach in disbelief, tears streaming down my face. In that moment, I realized those voices of unworthiness weren't mine. They belonged to someone trying to break my confidence, to make me forget I already had everything it took to be a queen.

Walking onto the stage to be crowned, I felt deeply humbled. This wasn't a moment of winning over others—it was an affirmation that everything I had done in my life, from graduating college to traveling through 43 countries, starting my own business, and serving my community, had prepared me for this.

This moment proved that showing up is the key. It's about standing in

your truth and recognizing the power of showing up for yourself and your community.

It was time for me to adjust my crown! I am so grateful that I showed up as a Queen.

Briana Rice

Meet Briana Rice, a developmental biologist and Ms. California African American 2024 and Ms. Woman of Achievement International 2024.

Briana is also passionate about wellness and reproductive health. She a developmental biologist and is a certified Tantra teacher, womb healer, and Sound Healer.

Briana is the visionary behind the love and light movement and Co-producer of the wine festival Blackberry Merlot.

She won with the platform "Life and Empowerment after a Traumatic Brain Injury". She uses her platform to encourage women living with invisible disabilities. Briana Rice curates' luxury travel experiences and upscale events.

Briana's mission is clear: Using affirmations to guide individuals on their journey from trauma to complete healing, both mentally and physically. She empowers them to manifest their desires by meticulously planning and hosting luxurious travel events and retreats.

Fostering Diversity and Inclusion

By Professor Caroline Makaka, PhD

It's truly enriching to step outside our comfort zones. Meeting people from diverse backgrounds broadens our perspectives. Engaging with others who have different life experiences opens our minds. It allows us to learn and grow from each other's unique stories. Embracing these connections creates a more understanding and compassionate world.

The pursuit of peace transcends borders and languages. It is a universal desire, woven into the fabric of every society. Through understanding and respect, we can bridge cultural divides. Let us celebrate our differences while working together towards a harmonious world.

By embracing diversity and fostering empathy, we can pave the way for a more harmonious world. Through open dialogue and collaboration, we can overcome differences and work together towards shared goals.

Showing up is often the hardest part, but it's also the most rewarding. Taking that first step opens doors to possibilities you might not have imagined. Don't be afraid to ask for what you want and need, even if it feels daunting. The courage to ask can lead to unexpected opportunities and connections. You never know what doors a simple question might unlock. Remember, your voice matters, and your willingness to engage can make all the difference.

Sometimes the hardest part is simply making the first move. Taking that initial step, however small, can be incredibly empowering. Showing up, being present, and engaging demonstrates your commitment. It's a testament to your willingness to try, to learn, and to grow. Remember, even the smallest actions can create ripples of positive change.

Great opportunities don't always announce themselves loudly. Sometimes they appear quietly, requiring a keen eye to spot them. Being prepared and ready to step forward is crucial. Showing up with enthusiasm and a willingness to learn opens doors. Embrace these moments, for they can lead to amazing things.

Imagine a world where diverse traditions weave together like vibrant threads in a tapestry. A global community celebrating its rich heritage, where differences are embraced and celebrated. Picture a world resonating with the music of unity, a symphony of shared experiences and dreams. In this world, understanding blossoms, and respect deepens, fostering a sense of interconnected messages among all.

Let us strive to create this tapestry of harmony, where every thread contributes to the beauty of our shared humanity.

A global community celebrating its differences, finding strength in unity. Shared experiences and understanding bridge cultural divides, fostering empathy and respect. This harmonious blend of perspectives enriches lives, fostering innovation and progress. Together, we stand stronger, united in our shared humanity.

Cultural exchange programs foster understanding and empathy between people from different backgrounds. By sharing traditions, perspectives, and experiences, we develop a deeper appreciation for the world's diversity.

These programs break down barriers and challenge stereotypes, promoting tolerance and respect on a global scale. Through these meaningful interactions, cultural exchange programs contribute to a more peaceful and interconnected world. Ultimately, by bridging cultural divides, we create a more harmonious and understanding global community.

In Conclusion

Learning new ideas and advice is a fantastic way to grow as a person. It broadens your horizons and helps you see the world from different angles. You can discover innovative solutions and approaches that you may never have considered before. Embrace the opportunity to expand your knowledge and understanding, as it can be truly enriching. Keep an open mind and never stop seeking new information and perspectives.

Life can be challenging, but we don't have to face it alone. Offering a helping hand or a kind word can make a world of difference.

Let's show up and support each other. Every act of kindness contributes to a brighter tomorrow.

Working together allows us to combine our diverse skills and perspectives. Through collaboration, we can achieve more than we ever could individually. By supporting and learning from one another, we create a positive and productive environment. When we work together, we build strong relationships and a shared sense of accomplishment. Let's strive for success as a team. Let our collective efforts create ripples of compassion that reach far and wide.

When we support each other, we build stronger communities and brighter futures. We rise by lifting others, fostering a sense of belonging and shared purpose. Let's remember the power of unity and always strive to be pillars of support for one another.

Let's focus on spreading love and understanding. When we work together towards this common goal, positive change is possible.

You can help to make the world a better place.

You can help to create a more compassionate world. To do this, you have to remember that your actions have consequences and that you must take responsibility for them in order to bring about positive change.

Let us strive to build bridges of understanding across cultures and continents. Through open dialogue and collaboration, we can overcome differences and work together towards shared goals. Let us nurture a spirit of peace within ourselves and extend it outwards to all corners of the globe. Together, we can create a future where peace prevails, and all people can thrive.

Professor Caroline Makaka, PhD

Professor Caroline Makaka is a woman of many talents and an expert in many industries. She is a lady with a vision and a mission to shape the future of the world through courage, strength, resilience, hope, tenacity and transformational power to create a better world.

She is a Professor of Global Leadership and the Founder/President/CEO of LOANI - Leaders of All Nations International and the Creator of the We Are the Change World Movement.

Global Chairperson of Global International Alliance (GIA)

International Advisor for Global Society for female Entrepreneurs. (GSFE)

Prof: Caroline Makaka has dedicated herself to sustainability and corporate social responsibilities.

As a Professor of Global Leadership, her role is to foster an inclusive and collaborative environment within international organizations and institutions, academic associations and non-profit international organizations by building bridges across that transcend geographical boundaries, fostering cultural exchange programs, connections, and collaborations between individuals, communities, and organizations from diverse backgrounds where they can navigate and thrive in multicultural environments, both locally and globally, more importantly, broaden their global horizon and fostering a more equitable and inclusive society.

Her expertise spans a wide range of skills, including Philanthropy, Global Leadership, Global Cultural Exchange, Charities, International Project Management, Global and Social Leadership and Development, Business Management, Human Resources, Counseling, Equality and Diversity, Women and Girls Empowerment, Youth Empowerment, Sustainable Development, and Economic Development.

Special thanks to one of the most powerful and wonderful world-inspiring leaders who brought us all together.

Lady Amb. Dr. Robbie Motter, founder of Global Society for Female Entrepreneurs.

She is a woman of positive influence, a woman of sterling qualities, an exceptional kind of leader and a valuable asset to humanity.

Lady Amb. Dr. Robbie Motter

She is one amazing woman who has gone above and beyond to transform so many people's lives and made such a huge impact in many lives by inspiring them to become a better version of themselves.

She is a wonderful, kindhearted, resilient, generous, influential leader with a heart of gold.

A leader who has embraced her leadership role in this world and made a significant impact on our communities and our lives.

She is a beacon of unity, reminding everyone of the strength found in shared humanity.

A peace leader who continues to inspire generations after generation because of her desire to create a better and peaceful world for herself, the people around her and the future generations.

Her passion is to empower, inspire, mentor, educate and to connect women to be successful entrepreneurs.

Lady Amb. Dr. Robbie taught many of us the importance of showing up and the power of asking.

Professor Caroline Makaka, PhD
President
Leaders of All Nations International (LOANI)
info@loaniglobal.org
+447478281693
Instagram: @loaniglobal
Facebook: LOANI
www.loaniglobal.org

It's all
About
Showing
Up

I SHOWED UP

By Ambassador Dr. (h.c.) Charmaine Summers

I have been on an incredible journey for the last 61 years. My name is Ambassador Dr. h.c. Charmaine Summers, proudly born and raised in Orange County, California. I grew up in a loving home filled with encouragement, thanks to my parents, Patrick and Lucille Tocher, along with my three siblings. Their unwavering support formed the foundation for my aspirations, giving me the courage to chase my dreams.

At a young age, I was introduced to the sport that would change my life: Golf. My father Patrick, an avid golfer, put a club in my hand before I could even walk. Our family outings to the golf course became treasured memories, we often encountered amazing people who shared stories, laughter and life lessons-connections that shaped my character and outlook on life.

Following my marriage, I was blessed with a beautiful daughter, Crystal Summers, who graduated from Chapman University and went on to pursue her passion as a professional international tennis player. I couldn't be prouder of her accomplishments.

A Passion for Golf

As I continued playing golf throughout my life, I pursued my passion with determination. I competed on the Pro Western Tour, soaking in the experience and gaining invaluable insights along the way. Eventually, my journey led me to open the Orange County Academy, where I had the privilege of sharing my love for the game with the younger generations.

My experience and dedication brought success, allowing me to open a second academy. This took root at the Newport Beach Golf Course, where I found immense joy in coaching children. Working with young golfers felt instinctive and fulfilling-it was clear that this was my passion, I thrived on their enthusiasm and innocence and in nurturing their skills. I also discovered my own growth both personally and professionally.

A New Chapter in Menifee, California

Life then led me to Menifee, California, where I sought new opportunities to continue my teaching journey. One fateful day, I SHOWED UP to play at Cherry Hills Golf Course, little did I know this routine visit would alter the course of my life. While there, I had a chance meeting with the owner, who, impressed with my background hired me on the spot as the General Manager, my heart raced with excitement: I accepted the position, and thus began a new, thrilling chapter in my life,

Giving Back to the Community

With this new role came a desire to give back to the community, I was fortunate to cross paths with Nicole Farrell, who had an incredible background in being a DJ. One of our memorable ventures was hosting a karaoke night that turned out to be an absolute blast and became a once-a-week event that was always filled with great talent. Those evenings not

only sparked joy but also opened doors to meet incredible individuals from my community.

Nicole invited me to a meeting for the Global Society for Female Entrepreneurs (GSFE), I remember that day vividly - I SHOWED UP! Attending that meeting was a pivotal moment in my life, as it introduced me to Ambassador Lady Dr. h.c. Robbie Motter. From the first moment I met Robbie, there was an undeniable connection. She radiated positivity and warmth, and I felt instantly inspired. Under her guidance, I began to explore new creative avenues, including singing, which brough back so many memories as my father loved music, I also started performing and writing. This vibrant moment blossomed into a new passion and purpose,

Achievements and Recognition

As I delved deeper into my creative pursuits, I was honored to be recognized for four books as a US and International award-winning author. My efforts did not go unnoticed: I was awarded a Presidential Award from a US President, for my work in the Community. My city recognized me as the Citizen of the Month for my work with Seniors. There were numerous other accolades from diverse dignitaries worldwide. However, one of the most meaningful titles bestowed upon me was that of Ambassador of Happiness and Kindness – a role that resonates deeply with my vision of the world.

Additionally, I was granted an Honorary Humanitarian Doctorate recognizing my commitment to uplifting others. Each achievement, while significant, represents a chapter of growth and the impact of SHOWING UP consistently, allowing for transformative experiences.

The Power of SHOWING UP

Reflecting on my journey, it's evident that SHOWING UP has influenced my life at various levels. The connections I've fostered and the opportunities I've seized all stem from that simple act of presence. I am immensely grateful for every encounter and chance that has brought me to this stage in my life - a stage I embrace with open arms.

To anyone reading this, I urge you to embrace the power of SHOWING UP and ASKING. The unknown can be intimidating, but the rewards are often greater than the risks. You never know where a single decision to SHOW UP might lead – be in unexpected friendships, career advancements, or personal growth. Life has a way of rewarding our courage, and magic often resides just on the other side of fear.

So, take a moment, gather your courage, and step forward, SHOW UP for yourself, and others, and do not hesitate to ASK for what you desire. In doing so, you may unlock doors you never knew existed. Let your journey unfold and watch as the universe collaborates with you to create beautiful experiences.

Ambassador Dr. (h.c.) Charmaine Summers

Ambassador Dr. (h.c.) Charmaine Summers played on the Pro Western Women's Golf Tour. She is a Golf Instructor, Singer/Performer, Event Planner, Award Winning Author and the Director of the Lake Arrowhead GSFE Network. Charmaine is also a Wife, Mother, and Grandmother.

She can be reached:

Email: orangecountygolf@yahoo.com

Phone 714-350-3626.

SHOWING UP Can Be So Amazing

By Ambassador Dr. (h.c.) Chebra Dorsey "Ochea"

It's so amazing when I SHOW UP, those words resonate deeply within me, embodying the resilience and determination that have shaped my journey. My name is Ambassador Dr, (h.c.) Chebra Dorsey, known to the world as "OCHEA": a celebrity designer whose life has been a tapestry woven from passion, creativity, and unexpected challenges. My story is one of transformation, illustrating how we often find strength in the most unlikely of circumstances.

A World of Dreams and Aspirations

Before my life took this dramatic turn, I was immersed in the vibrant world of Fashion and running my Boutique in Lemon Grove, CA., and in designing as well as doing Fashion Shows. As a designer, every day was an opportunity to express my creativity, to fabricate dreams into tangible pieces that adorned the bodies of individuals, seeing to make their mark or to just feel beautiful. Yet, despite the success, I kept being told that I needed to write a book, I struggled with self-doubt when I thought of writing and being an author, it seemed unattainable, I kept making excuses, burying my aspirations alongside my fashion work.

A year before the dog attack, I began drafting a book titled "What Are You Wearing? The Inspirational Spiritual Side of Fashion was meant to be not just a reflection or not just fashion, but so much more. My anxiety about writing held me back. I started strong but faltered midway, shoving the writing aside as life's demands took precedence. The idea of being an author felt foreign to me, a dream that was just always out of reach.

The Turn of Fate

Then, in an unexpected twist of fate, everything changed. One early morning, I was out for my morning walk, lost in thought about my next design and enjoying the beautiful flowers when I was attacked by a dog who escaped from his yard, The experience was harrowing: I sustained five bites, and the medical team stitched me up with twenty stitches in total. It was one of the worst moments of my life. I felt vulnerable, scared and heartbroken, I spent four agonizing months bedridden, with nurses attending to my wounds and physical therapy sessions becoming my new reality. It's incredible how quickly life can pivot, throwing you into a storm unprepared, Yet, amidst the pain and helplessness, I realized something profound; I had a choice, I could either wallow in despair or harness my energy toward completing my book.

The Turning Point

During those long months of recuperation, while lying in bed with my leg propped up and a machine humming beside me, I made a decision, I would not let my injury define me or hold me back. Instead, I would channel my

pain into purpose. It was the darkest day of my life that ignited a fire within me, pushing me to write on paper to finish the book I had started a year prior.

Every word I wrote became a testament to my resilience. I poured my heart into the pages, each page reflecting not only fashion but also the journey of self-acceptance and healing. Writing and also finding co-authors for my book became my sanctuary, a sacred space where I could transcend my physical limitations and embrace my voice.

SHOW UP for Yourself

As I continued to write, I began to understand the importance of SHOWING UP for myself. It dawned on me that my journey mirrored so many others. We encounter obstacles, self-doubt, and fear, yet the key to overcoming them is often simply to SHOW UP. To lean into your passions, despite the challenges that life may throw your way.

On the day I sent my completed book, a rush of emotions washed over me, I felt exhilarated yet terrified. What if the world didn't receive my words well? What if my vulnerability was met with ridicule? But deep down, I knew I had to take the leap. I had faced physical pain: conquering the vulnerability of sharing my thoughts with the world seemed a worthy challenge.

The Launch

When the day finally arrived for the book's launch, I was a bundle of nerves and excitement. I sat waiting to see the results, watching the clock tick down to the moment I would share my creation with the world, and then it happened it was published and hit various categories and achieve #1 US and International status on Amazon US and Amazon UK. It was exciting to see other online bookstores like Barnes N Noble, Walmart and other places pick up the book and I remember the day I heard it was in the Harvard Book Store at Harvard and so many other places. The response was and continues to be overwhelming, all this recognition left me elated and in tears, I couldn't believe it, the very act of SHOWING UP had altered the course of my life in ways I never imagined.

Reflections of my Journey

Looking back on the dog attack, though traumatic was a catalyst of something remarkable, It forced me into a period of introspection, revealing not just my vulnerabilities but also my capabilities. and reminded me that sometimes the universe has a way of nudging us into paths we are meant to tread, even if that means experiencing pain and discomfort along the way.

I now carry the phrase "SHOW UP" as a mantra in all aspects of my life, it reminds me that whether in writing, designing, or facing challenges head-on, the most crucial step is to SHOW UP as your authentic self. Life will throw hurdles your way, but how you respond defines your journey.

The Importance of Community

Success is rarely a solo endeavor. I was fortunate to have an incredible

support system of friends, family, my GSFE and LOANI sisters and my Publisher Havana Book Group that encouraged me to pursue my writing dream. Their belief in me, even when I struggled to believe in myself, was invaluable. It reinforces the idea that we are stronger together, Community plays a pivotal role in our journeys, providing encouragement, feedback, and the love we need to keep pushing forward.

I also did not let my leg injury stop me on an opportunity I had to go to London where I received a Humanitarian Honorary Doctorate degree, on this same trip I had the opportunity to speak in Parliament and to receive the "I am Superwomen Award" plus I had the opportunity to meet and network with women from all over the world.

Embracing The Future

Today, as I reflect on my journey on my life as Ochea, the celebrity designer and now an award-winning author- I feel a sense of gratitude and resolve, I am committed to SHOWING UP, not just for myself, but for those who look to me for inspiration. I understand the power of storytelling and hope to continue sharing my experiences to encourage others to break through their barriers.

In many ways, What Are You Wearing? The Inspirational Spiritual side of Fashion, is just the beginning of my story, I envision a future where I can weave together themes of resilience, hope and style-tying them into new projects, I am so excited to know that this book is heading to be on the book shelf of the Oldest Library in the World in Egypt and also now is in Australia and is making its way all over the world.

Conclusion: The Legacy of SHOWING UP

Life is filled with unexpected events, both good and bad, and the key lies in how we respond. SHOW UP for yourself, embrace your journey, and do not shy away from sharing your story. You never know who you might inspire along the way.

So, it's so amazing when I SHOW UP, no matter what I am doing, I embrace the beauty of vulnerability, resilience, and the richness of life experiences. As I continue my journey, I strive to create not just through fashion but also through words, confirming once again that SHOWING UP can lead to extraordinary outcomes. You have the power within you; just remember to SHOW UP and seize it. Remember the challenges may be daunting, but they also open doors to opportunities you never imagined possible, embrace your journey and remember to SHOW UP is to truly live.

Ambassador Dr. (h.c.) Chebra Dorsey

Ambassador Dr. (h.c.) Chebra Dorsey is an award-winning Celebrity designer and an Award-Winning Author, who has received hundreds of prestigious awards for her work from all over the world.

She can be reached at: 619-736-0645, 619-985-3804,

Facebook/chebradorsey, Instagram: Ocheafashion, ocheafashionproduction or ocheafashionboutique

It's all
About
Showing
Up

Prioritizing Self-Care: The Foundation of Empowered Living

By Ambassador Dr. (h.c.) Cheri Reynolds

In an increasingly demanding world, prioritizing your well-being is not just a nice-to-have; it is an absolute necessity. The hustle and bustle of daily life can easily overshadow our personal needs, resulting in burnout and overwhelming stress. Let's clarify one crucial point: self-care is not selfish—it is essential.

When you invest in your own well-being, you essentially equip yourself to show up more fully for others in your life.

In today's fast-paced society, particularly for women, the pressure to juggle a myriad of responsibilities can be daunting. We often feel guilty for carving out time for ourselves, worrying about the consequences on our families, jobs, and obligations. However, neglecting self-care leads to diminished functioning in our roles. Irritability, fatigue, and disengagement become commonplace when we fail to attend to our own needs.

Conversely, dedicating time and resources to self-care revitalizes us, transforming us into more vibrant, energized, and efficient individuals. So, let's explore what authentic self-care encompasses. It goes beyond mere pampering; it integrates nurturing various aspects of your life, including physical, emotional, mental, and spiritual dimensions.

Emotional Self-Care

Emotional self-care is about recognizing and acknowledging your feelings, allowing yourself the freedom to experience them. This might manifest through journaling, confiding in a trustworthy friend, or seeking professional help when necessary. Women are often burdened by emotional weight, and it is crucial to release these emotions in healthy, constructive ways.

Consider establishing a routine that engages you in reflection. Ask yourself: How am I feeling today? What do I need? How can I provide myself with the emotional support I deserve? Creating space for these reflections fosters emotional resilience and awareness.

Mental Self-Care

Mental self-care emphasizes the importance of continuous learning and personal growth. Engaging with podcasts, books, and seminars can stimulate your intellect and broaden your perspective. Surround yourself with individuals who inspire and challenge you to think differently. Seek workshops or classes that spark your curiosity or explore online courses to enhance your skills.

Investing in your mental health not only empowers you but also elevates your ability to contribute meaningfully to the world around you. Embrace the process of learning as vital to your overall well-being.

Spiritual Self-Care

Spiritual self-care may be one of the most transformative forms of self-care. Whether through prayer, meditation, connection with nature, or other

spiritual practices, nurturing your spirit offers profound benefits. It links you to something greater than yourself and imparts a sense of peace and purpose.

Prioritize activities that resonate with your soul. Whether it involves volunteering, immersing yourself in nature, or engaging in creative pursuits, allow yourself to discover and nurture the spiritual side of your being.

Establishing Boundaries

One of the most vital aspects of self-care is the ability to set and maintain boundaries. Societal expectations often position women as caregivers, leading to overcommitment and eventual resentment. Understanding and practicing the art of saying "no" without guilt is essential.

Evaluate your commitments and determine whether they align with your personal values and goals. If they do not, consider gently stepping back. Establishing boundaries enables you to devote your energy and time to what truly matters.

The Ripple Effect of Self-Care

When you show up for yourself, you create a ripple effect that extends to those around you. Your enhanced energy and positivity can uplift not only your presence but also influence the environments you inhabit. When we prioritize self-care, we become role models for others, demonstrating the importance of nurturing oneself.

Moreover, when you approach life with a well-balanced mindset— grounded in self-awareness and self-care—you inspire others, particularly other women, to prioritize their own needs. This cultural shift encourages an understanding that self-care is not a luxury but rather a foundation for healthier relationships—both with us and those around us.

Conclusion

Prioritizing self-care involves a conscious choice to make your well-being a priority. It's about acknowledging that you are deserving of time, space, and energy. By focusing on emotional, mental, and spiritual self-care, along with establishing boundaries, you not only become a better version of yourself but also create a more balanced and fulfilling life.

In doing so, you pave the way for a future where self-care is viewed through the lens of necessity rather than indulgence, actively breaking the cycle of guilt and overwhelm that so many women face. Let's collectively embrace self-care as a non-negotiable part of our lives, sparking a revolution in how we approach our own well-being and, by extension, our communities.

Ambassador Dr. (h.c.) Cheri Reynolds

Cheri Reynolds is an Entrepreneur with Great Expertise in marketing and connecting with like-minded individuals! She aligns with Positive Energy bringing it to the table in her leadership roles. Currently she is the Director of the Oceanside GSFE.

CEO Cheris Energy Solutions partners with Powur PBC Solar.

Influencer PRO with Shoply decentralized Commerce

In the past she was an Ambassador with the Chamber of Commerce in Riverside and Hemet.

She is a mom of 2 and Grandmother of 5 and her WHY is to leave a legacy for her Grandchildren and her 2 Great Grandchildren

Dr. (h.c). Cheri Reynolds can be reached at 909-238-5790 email cherisenergysolutions@gmail.com, Instagram@i_lovemotherearth.

Showing Up: The Doors of Opportunity

By Ambassador Dr. Cherilyn Lee

In life, we often underestimate the power of simply showing up. It sounds deceptively simple, yet it has the potential to unlock countless doors, leading us to opportunities we might never have encountered otherwise. For me, this journey began two decades ago when I met Lady Dr. Robbie Motter, a moment that would forever alter the trajectory of my life.

I remember that day vividly. I was a strong woman, a determined entrepreneur with a clear vision for my future. Yet, like many, I grappled with insecurities and the overwhelming fear of stepping out of my comfort zone. However, when I walked into that room and saw Lady Dr. Motter, a beacon of inspiration and empowerment, something shifted within me. Her presence radiated warmth and encouragement, and it was clear that she was dedicated to uplifting others. It was in that moment that I realized the importance of showing up—not just physically, but with an open heart and a willingness to engage.

When Lady Dr. Motter invited me to join the Global Society of Female Entrepreneurs (GSFE), I felt a mix of excitement and apprehension. It was an opportunity to connect with like-minded women who shared similar aspirations and challenges. I approached this new chapter with the confidence of a leader, knowing that I had already established myself as a force in my field. I came to the group with my own strengths, my own journey, and my own drive to succeed.

By choosing to show up, I opened the door to a world filled with possibilities. The GSFE became a sanctuary for collective growth, where I could learn, share, and thrive alongside extraordinary women who, like me, were passionate about their entrepreneurial journeys. Each event was a chance to network, exchange ideas, and gain insights from industry leaders. I immersed myself in this environment, soaking up knowledge and inspiration while also contributing my unique perspectives and experiences. I discovered that my voice mattered, and my experiences had value—not just for me, but for everyone in the room.

As I continued to show up, I was invited to participate in several book projects that would become international bestsellers. Titles such as "Love Your Haters," "Peace," and "Voices of Peace: A Global Perspective" stand out as significant milestones in my journey. Contributing to these works allowed me to share my story and connect with a wider audience eager to engage with themes of resilience and empowerment. This experience reinforced the truth that by simply being present and participating, we can create ripples of impact that extend far beyond our immediate circles.

The success of these books was exhilarating, but it was just the beginning. With each project, my commitment to showing up was recognized in remarkable ways. In 2024, I was honored to be named one of the Top 50 Humanitarian Leaders. This accolade was not merely a title; it represented the culmination of years of hard work, dedication, and the willingness to show up for causes that mattered. The recognition was humbling and a testament to the power of community and support from those around me.

Beyond my personal achievements, I was also chosen to serve as a Director

of the Global Society of Female Entrepreneurs. This position was an incredible honor and an opportunity for me to contribute even more to an organization that had already given me so much. As a Director, I leveraged my skills and experiences to help shape initiatives that empowered other women and fostered connections. It was fulfilling to guide the direction of an organization dedicated to uplifting female entrepreneurs, igniting my passion for advocating for women's rights and entrepreneurship.

My involvement with the GSFE was not just about personal growth; it was also about fostering a spirit of collaboration and mutual support. Every member brought their unique talents to the table, creating an environment where we all thrived. The heartfelt connections forged within the group were invaluable. We celebrated each other's successes, offered guidance during challenging times, and provided a network of encouragement that propelled our businesses forward. The sense of camaraderie was palpable, as we cheered each other on in our respective journeys.

As I continued to engage with GSFE, I conducted powerful workshops that highlighted my expertise as a holistic healthcare practitioner. One of the standout components of my nonprofit work is the three-minute cardiovascular metabolic screening, a transformative tool that empowers individuals to take charge of their health. These workshops are designed not only to educate but also to inspire participants to embrace healthier lifestyles. By sharing my knowledge on various health issues and leading engaging discussions, I have created an environment where participants feel empowered to make informed decisions regarding their well-being.

The achievements I experienced were amplified by the incredible women I met through GSFE. The organization provided a nurturing environment where members rallied around one another, offering encouragement, resources, and collaboration. The support I received was invaluable—not only for my personal growth but also for my business. I found mentors within the group who guided me, shared insights, and connected me with opportunities I would have never accessed alone.

As I continued to engage with the Global Society and its members, I witnessed the power of community. Women supporting women is a force that cannot be underestimated. We cheered each other on, celebrated successes, and offered guidance during challenging times. It was a reminder that we are not alone on this journey; we have a network of support that amplifies our voices and empowers us to take bold steps. The realization that our collective strength could elevate us all was both inspiring and empowering.

One of the most significant milestones in my journey was receiving an honorary Doctorate degree. This achievement was a direct result of showing up and actively participating in my community and the organizations I valued. It symbolized my commitment to my profession and my dedication to making a positive impact on the lives of others. The recognition was more than just a title; it reinforced my belief in the importance of contributing to society and uplifting those around me.

My role as a Director allowed me to foster an environment of collaboration and growth within the GSFE. I initiated programs that connected seasoned entrepreneurs with newcomers, creating mentorship opportunities that proved invaluable. By facilitating workshops and seminars, I encouraged members to share their expertise and experiences, fostering a culture of learning and support. The bonds formed in these sessions were powerful, as women shared their journeys, struggles, and triumphs, creating a tapestry of resilience and empowerment.

Showing up has also taught me the importance of giving back. As I gained confidence and experience, I felt a deep desire to contribute to the growth

of others. I began mentoring aspiring entrepreneurs, sharing my knowledge and insights to help them navigate their own journeys. It was a fulfilling experience, witnessing their growth and success as they, too, embraced the power of showing up. I also began to host workshops and seminars within the GSFE, creating spaces where members could learn from one another, share their stories, and foster connections that would propel them forward.

The impact of showing up extends beyond professional growth; it has shaped my personal life as well. I have formed meaningful relationships, deepened my connections with loved ones, and discovered a newfound sense of purpose. I have learned to cherish moments of vulnerability and authenticity, recognizing that they create the foundation for genuine connections. The support from the GSFE members has been a source of strength, providing reassurance during challenging times and celebrating milestones together.

As a holistic healthcare practitioner, my practice has flourished as a result of the connections I've made through the GSFE. The organization provided me with a network of like-minded professionals, many of whom became clients, collaborators, and friends. The insights I gained from fellow members enriched my practice, allowing me to integrate new perspectives and approaches to wellness. Each client interaction became an opportunity to show up for others, guiding them on their healing journeys and empowering them to take charge of their health and well-being.

Reflecting on my journey as a holistic healthcare practitioner, I recognize that my approach is rooted in the principles of showing up. By being present for my clients, I create a safe space for them to explore their challenges and aspirations. I have learned that each interaction is an opportunity to make a difference, to uplift, and to inspire healing. The relationships I have built through the GSFE have not only enriched my professional life but have also deepened my understanding of the interconnectedness of mind, body, and spirit.

As I continue to navigate this journey, I remain committed to showing up for myself, my community, and the causes I believe in. The doors that have opened for me have not only transformed my life but have also allowed me to contribute positively to the lives of others. The experiences I have gained and the connections I have forged are a testament to the power of showing up and embracing the opportunities that arise.

In closing, I urge you to consider the power of showing up in your own life. Embrace opportunities, confront your fears, and take that leap of faith. You never know what doors may open or who you may inspire along the way. Your journey is unique, and by showing up, you have the power to shape your path and create a life filled with purpose and connection.

The journey may be challenging, but the rewards of showing up are immeasurable. Together, we can create a world where every individual feels empowered to share their voice, pursue their passions, and make a meaningful impact. Let us all choose to show up, to engage, and to uplift one another.

The practice of holistic healthcare has deepened my understanding of the interconnectedness of mind, body, and spirit. By showing up for my clients, I have been able to guide them on their healing journeys, empowering them to take charge of their health and well-being. This aspect of my work has reinforced my belief in the importance of being present, not only for oneself but also for others.

As I continue this journey, I am excited to see what new doors will open and what connections I will forge. Each step I take reinforces the belief that showing up is not just a one-time event; it's a continuous commitment to

growth, connection, and empowerment.

Through the years, I have learned that the journey of showing up is not solely about personal success; it is also about creating a legacy of support and inspiration for future generations. By empowering others to find their voices and encouraging them to step into their power, we contribute to a cycle of upliftment that transcends individual achievements.

Ultimately, the essence of showing up lies in the willingness to engage with life fully, to embrace the opportunities that come our way, and to uplift those around us. As we continue to navigate our paths, let us remember that the act of showing up can create profound change—not just in our own lives, but in the lives of others as well.

Ambassador Dr. Cherilyn Lee

Dr. Cherilyn Lee, PhD, CHNP, Certified Health Coach, and Certified Functional Nutrition Coach is a trailblazer, philanthropist, international speaker, author, renowned global holistic practitioner, and the Founder and President of the NuWellness Development Foundation (NWDF) (501(c)(3)).

Dr. Lee has been bestowed four United States Presidential Lifetime Achievement Awards by President Obama, President Trump, and President Biden and has received numerous awards and recognition from government branches at every level, from the US State Department to the Los Angeles City Council, for the humanitarian work she provides under the NWDF. In addition, to her non-profit, she has a holistic wellness center at 4221 Wilshire Blvd in Los Angeles.

Contact:

Dr. Cherilyn Lee

Email:drlee@nuwellnesshealthcare.com

Phone:888 903 2145

It's all
About
Showing
Up

The Courage to Ask

By Ambassador Reverend Dr. (h.c.) Christine Park

When approached to write this chapter, I thought long and hard about my experiences and what words of wisdom I could offer. I realized that showing up is the easy part; asking on the other hand is exceedingly difficult.

I have infinite stories of showing up throughout my lifetime. For instance, I showed up at Head Start, PTA and IEP meetings and ended up an Advocate for Children, especially for those with learning disabilities. I showed up at numerous Conventions and Conferences and ended up filling in as a speaker a time or two. I would show up at, and sponsor customer events as a business owner and reap the rewards of a stronger customer base. I showed up at a karaoke event, after being placed on oxygen 24/7, and now I sing at various events. I showed up at a GSFE meeting and now I am an active member and Director of the GSFE Menifee Network, sharing my experiences and knowledge with a global sisterhood. I showed up when asked to write a chapter in a book, and as of this writing, I am a three-time, number one international bestselling author with aspirations to write my own books. I showed up as a speaker and now have a growing catalog of motivational presentations. These are just snippets of instances of showing up. My showing up experiences are infinite because I continue to show up every day.

As I expressed earlier, Showing Up is the easy part - Asking on the other hand, is more difficult. Let's dive further into the asking part.

Our lives are filled with expectations and rules of society, the act of asking for what we want can often feel intimidating. We are conditioned to question our desires and hold back, fearing judgment or rejection. Yet, it is through this act of vulnerability, this very admission of need, that we uncover unlimited possibilities of opportunities and connections. Let's explore the courage required to ask, the changes in how we think that are necessary to overcome our fears, and the life-changing power that arises when we decide to show up and ask.

Fear is a powerful emotion, one that often dictates our actions and decisions. The roots of this fear can stem from various sources. For many, childhood experiences where asking for help or expressing needs resulted in disappointment or ridicule can create a deep-seated apprehension. The conventions of society can amplify this pressure—ideas about self-sufficiency, independence, and the stigma of needing help can lead us to view asking as a weakness rather than a strength.

However, the refusal to ask for what we need can often lead to stagnation. Opportunities slip through our fingers, relationships falter, and potential remains unrealized. The cost of silence can be staggering, preventing us from growing personally or professionally. Embracing the power of asking allows us to step beyond these limitations, reminding us that our voices matter.

Asking for something—be it help, a favor, or an opportunity—can be a powerful confidence booster. Consider the stories of individuals who, despite their initial trepidation, ventured out of their comfort zones to ask for what they desired. Each time they did, their confidence grew, paving the way for greater risks and rewards. Whether it was a student requesting

a mentoring relationship or an employee seeking guidance from a superior, the act of asking has the potential to change lives.

When one person has the courage to ask, it can create a chain reaction. By witnessing the bravery of others, we may feel inspired to voice our own needs. This shared experience fosters a sense of community and mutual support. Knowing that others have faced similar fears can encourage us to step forward and ask as well.

Reframing the act of asking is crucial in overcoming the fear associated with it. Instead of viewing asking as a sign of desperation or weakness, consider it an expression of self-advocacy and strength. Each no should not be seen as a personal failure but rather as a steppingstone toward eventual success. This change in perspective empowers us, positioning us as active participants in our own lives rather than passive observers.

Building confidence takes practice. Begin by asking for small things in your daily life—a friend's opinion, assistance with a task, or advice on a decision. These small requests can serve as a training ground for larger asks in the future. Each time you show up and ask, you reinforce your ability to advocate for yourself, reducing fear and opening new doors.

Engaging in mindfulness can help ground us when fear threatens to overwhelm. Take a moment to breathe deeply and center your thoughts. This practice allows us to step back and recognize that rejection is a natural part of life; it does not define our worth. By cultivating self-compassion, we acknowledge that everyone faces rejection at some point, and we can choose to learn and grow from our experiences rather than let them hold us back.

In professional settings, the value of asking cannot be overstated. Whether it's reaching out for mentorship, inquiring about job opportunities, or asking for constructive feedback, these actions often lead to significant growth. People are generally willing to help, but they are not mind readers, they need to know you're seeking their assistance. The simple act of asking can help you build valuable networks and create paths that might otherwise remain blocked.

In personal relationships, openness about our needs can lead to deeper connections. When we articulate our desires, whether for emotional support or shared responsibilities, we invite others to do the same. This mutual exchange fosters healthier, more fulfilling relationships, as honesty paves the way for understanding and empathy.

The act of asking is indeed a powerful tool for transformation. Each time we muster the courage to ask, we not only enhance our own lives but also contribute to a broader culture of openness and support. The journey begins with showing up, being vulnerable, and confidently articulating our needs. As we practice this vital skill, we open ourselves to a world of possibilities, reminding ourselves that asking is not just a request—it's a declaration of our value.

Ask yourself:

1. What is one thing you've been hesitant to ask for, and what would asking for it mean to you?

2. Can you recall a time when your willingness to ask led to a positive outcome? How did that experience shift your perspective?

3. How can you support others in their journey to ask for what they need?

As we embrace the courage to ask, we not only advocate for our needs but also inspire those around us to do the same. Let us step forward, ready to show up and ask for what we truly desire.

Ambassador Reverend Dr. (h.c) Christine Park

Christine Park is a woman who has worn many hats throughout her life. She values family more than anything else and is a mother, grandmother, and great-grandmother. Originally from northwestern Pennsylvania, Christine earned her cosmetology degree from Penn State Cosmetology and attended Penn State University and the Art Institute of Pittsburgh. For several years, Christine advocated for early education, particularly for children with learning disabilities. She later became a successful businesswoman owning multiple businesses across Ohio.

Christine holds cosmetology and teaching licenses in Pennsylvania, teaching licenses in Ohio and security licenses in 19 States. In addition to her business success, Christine is also an ordained Minister with an honorary doctorate in Divinity. Her dedication to her profession led her to being named Woman of the Year.

She is an active member of the Global Society of Female Entrepreneurs and director of the Menifee network. Christine is also a speaker, international best-selling author, poetess and loves to sing to her heart's content. Her passion for empowering women in business was recognized with a Miracle Woman Award and she is also an RKMPII Ambassador of Kindness and Happiness and has received numerous other awards.

Currently residing in Sun City, California, Christine is working on several writing projects to share her knowledge and experiences with others. With a lifetime of achievements, Christine Park continues to inspire and motivate those around her.

Reach out to Christine via email at: menifeegsfe@gmail.com

Facebook: GSFE Menifee Network

Instagram: @menifeegsfe https://instagram.com/menifeegsfe

Tiktok: tiktok.com/@menifeegsfe

It's all
About
Showing
Up

Showing Up – It Is All in The Asking
By Crystal Perez

It was during a discussion that the topic was "who would dedicate this song to you? I had to read the prompt a couple times... am I sure I am reading this right? To put it briefly the lyrics were, "because you loved me." So, I considered who would say to me, "Crystal, you were there for me along the way and I am basically better off from it, because you loved me." I then came to the disheartening realization that many of us could not fathom being the person being described in the song. Being that person for another to look to, being that person to lean on, that person encouraging someone to keep going...because that person loved them. Their minds immediately went in the opposite direction of the question "yes, yes...I have a person in my life that comes to mind. I am so grateful to the ones who were there for me and loved me. I can think of what that person did for me right away." But the thought of being that person, that rock of a human being for someone else was just not in their grasp.

I immediately thought, this can't be true. Certainly, we all show up for people and in turn we have individuals that show up for us. Some more than but still a give and take during life. I sat with this emotion of why it was so hard for us to say that we [ourselves] are an inspiration for people in our lives. Someone who is always there and showing up. Sometimes the voice inside our heads says, "I am just not that special to make that huge of an impact on others." Maybe, it has become an expectation to show up in general. We are expected to do things and be there for our children. We must be there for our spouse and our aging parents and the friend that is always having boyfriend drama; don't forget the groups we are in, work, our siblings, pets and the mailman for god's sake... don't forget the neighborhood watch, or charity work, church and whatever else life has to throw at us. I feel we have been conditioned as women that we are never doing enough therefore how can anyone ever think of us and say, "Thank you, you gave me strength, you pushed me to try harder, you aided me when I couldn't go on, you supported me, you lent me a helping hand, you wiped my tears, you cheered me on, you gave me a safe place, you read me bedtime stories, you inspired me...because you loved me".

When I first thought of myself as a person who was showing up for others, I was like YES! Yes, I have. I have done so many things for so many people, I am a rock star mother and a kick ass spouse, don't forget a work horse! I wholeheartedly love my community. I serve my God. Nurtured and loved my babies. Lived up to my marital vows. Helped bury our loved ones. Through tremendously difficult times in my life when I was not only physically but also mentally struggling, I put a smile on, I put others first and kept pushing through. I can think of several individuals that would say or could say I inspired them. I was there for them to lean on. I helped them in their time of need, I am who they are because I love them and believe in them. Shout it from the roof tops... me, me, me! I am so proud of myself.

Then the little voice in the bottom of my soul crept up and said: [conversation with self-]

"Hey, you... yeah you... you are being quite the conceited self-righteous little girl there aren't you? EW where did that come from? Am I? No, no I did not

mean it that way... wait what? Tsk tsk "Welllll, you ARE supposed to do all that for your family, friends and community." "Of course, I am" "Has anyone ever come up to you and told you that you are the reason 'their wings could open and fly'? "That is ridiculous ..." "umm not in so many words," "Stop being silly" "no...I guess...um then I am not all that great then, am I?" AND on top of this vanity, it is absurd that I would think of doing all this for myself as well as for everyone else is just plain selfish. Plus, I am just doing what I am supposed to do and at the end of the day... it's probably not enough.

Ultimately, it starts with appreciation of self, our achievements and acknowledging our impact on others. It is just hard to get there for some of us. Let's show up for ourselves by practicing self-love.

To be brutely honest some take more than they give; feeling it is up to the world to constantly give them help. They need to receive numerous accolades and require a lot of energy. Please keep in mind time is our most limited resource so when we show up, we are giving a portion of our life that we can never get back. Alternatively, there are many people that feel extremely grateful and with such admiration but do not know how to express it or express it in different ways and remember they may not be able to write a hit song about you. (giggles)

As for me it has always been about showing up although I probably did not refer to it as that. I was taught as a child that we always do for everybody in our community and each other as family [friends being family too]. It was just something that we did. Never late, saying yes to every event, always lending a helping hand, listening to other's heartache, giving advice and compassion. Things like that. Fortunately, my husband was raised the same way... always giving everything he has... to everybody else. I ponder within that mindset our personal requirements may get lost in the shuffle. Neglecting ourselves and overlooking our human need to be taken care of.

In our desire ask for help...We give so much to everybody else and that is the roll we chose in life.

Luckily, I only have a couple of examples of being taken advantage of [probably not intentionally]. I had a friend once that I thought to be a close friend, but it always seemed one sided. She expected everyone to make a big fuss about her birthday but never remembered mine [or anyone else's for that matter]. She wanted me to join her "business" but would make rude comments about my career passions. I was always expected at all her events but not once in several years, did she ever come to mine. She would be bizarre to my children and even my animals making weird comments, but her animal was expected to be the "star" of the show. It was strange to say the least and I had to end the connection. I just couldn't be a part of a one-sided relationship. With her or anyone else. I came to realize it of course had nothing to do with me, but it bothered me that it took so long to finally stand up for myself. It bothered me because I valued the relationship and time I gave away to the friendship. What in me made me think... I just need to show up for her and not let her down even though I was being let down. This example is not to shame this person but to be mindful of something in us that lets us be taken advantage amongst the goal of being there for others. Hopefully, we can have a deep conversation about what has happened or maybe I will never get answers to my questions.

People may be lost on how to show up for others and sadly are most likely not showing up for themselves either. It really starts with making a commitment to yourself and to others, persevering through obstacles, not making excuses, witnessing and being present, understanding that small events are just as important as big events, knowing that showing up may mean different things and have different styles for different people, showing unconditional attention and support, giving yourself grace and practicing compassion.

Sometimes, I felt showing up was a chore and it became a daunting task to show up... a dread... even a harsh resentment. I have come to realize I needed help too. I needed to implement healthy boundaries as well and I needed to show up more for myself. And that little annoying voice that says "I can't possibly ask... I am not weak... but are the people who ask you... are they weak? No of course not! Okay then, you are not making sense." Who put this burden on your shoulders? What made you feel that you are not allowed to crumble?" I wasn't asking and I was subconsciously blocking my receiving. I have come to find I was utterly wrong. The most profound personal practice you will ever discover is in the asking.

This past year has been a moment in time of reflection for me. Not just looking back on recent events but my entire life I have reflected on the people that have reached out to me. Old and new friends have encouraged me. Professionals have teamed up for me. People have inspired me. Friends that have prayed for me. Strangers that have smiled at me. Family that has cried with me. My husband that has truly lived up to and surpassed his wedding vows to me and I cannot forget my fur baby that has unconditional, pure love for me. All this and more... but do you know what? I was fearful of being dismissed. I am not fearful of asking or accepting anymore. I know if I ask, I shall receive with humans as well as the entire universe.

I sit and wonder how this unworthiness and insecurity built in me. The feeling that I must always be of service and never let anyone down but at the same time I am undeserving of having that connection and love in return. The shame of celebrating myself and the service that I give whole heartedly. The shame of patting myself on the back. It's so strange when I think about it, and the admission that it is so difficult being the Matriarch. Foreign when I write it down and read my own words of sadness.

I guess at the end of the day we may never hear the words of gratitude from others that we long for. Some don't feel gratitude for what we have done for them... but know that most will. There will be individuals that will ask us for help and there are times when we need to be the ones that are doing the asking. People are human and we all struggle. The feeling of being there not just for someone else but for us too is amazing and God smiles on us all.

There is such a vital importance of Showing Up for others and ourselves. Having that sense of accomplishment within. Seeing facial expressions of joy and relief to have someone like us in their corner. The confidence it brings. The feeling of being proud, amazed, and at peace with ourselves. The emotions of harmony and connection within our community. This is the groundwork of strong and fundamental relationships.

I guess my message to myself and hopefully someone who needs to hear it is: Showing Up is a main ingredient of creating the life that we all aspire to have. Reflect on all the wonderful people who have shown up for us and always keep them in our hearts giving gratitude for those special angels that bless our daily life. Know we are angels in return. Don't let the fear of dismay or unworthiness creep in. Keep giving. Keep going above and beyond. Keep asking. Keep showing up!

Crystal Perez

I am a Native Californian, wife, mother, grandmother, aunt, sister, sister-in-law, niece, cousin, entrepreneur, friend but most importantly I am Crystal. I have over 20 years of experience in corporate accounting and 4 years in Real Estate and Mortgage lending. My passion is being active in

my neighborhood, holistic medicine specializing in stress management and herbology. I also adore painting and writing. Recently I have launched my wearable art fashion line. Choosing this unique career path for myself has always been an ambition of mine because I strive to flourish in my community by combining creativity, health, and an abundant lifestyle to facilitate individuals in turning their dreams and mine into realities.

Crystal Perez

424-205-2364

perezcl25@gmail.com

https://www.facebook.com/profile.php?id=100054896919606

It's All About Showing Up
By Dr. Dana and Dr. Nick Haselum

We are Dr. Dana and Dr. Nick Haselum, authors, life coaches, motivational speakers, and humanitarians, committed to researching and sharing practical strategies for personal growth and development. Our expertise lies in providing actionable insights and tools to help individuals cultivate essential skills for success. Through our Mindset Mastery program, we work with both corporate and private clients to significantly enhance their productivity and achieve their goals.

As current Chairpersons for Equality, Diversity, and Inclusion at Ladies of All Nations International (LOANI), we are dedicated to promoting positive change. Additionally, we host various events and the popular online series, REALationship Talk, where we engage audiences with thought-provoking conversations.

Our passion is to inspire and empower others by fostering meaningful insights and encouraging personal growth. Whether through our coaching sessions, writing, or public speaking engagements, we are dedicated to helping individuals realise and reach their full potential.

Flight over fear - Dana's Story

I was in my early twenties, and the world felt like a very hostile place. My heart had been shattered in the space of a few short years, and the pieces didn't seem to fit back together anymore. Love had become synonymous with pain. Trust, with betrayal. The scars of previous abusive relationships ran deep, and I had decided to swear off love altogether. The idea of opening up to someone again was terrifying, almost unimaginable. But little did I know, life had its own plans.

Growing up in a small village in Trinidad, I had always been full of life—bright-eyed, adventurous, and hopeful. But after years of enduring manipulation, gaslighting, physical and emotional bruises, I was no longer that same girl. I felt jaded, untrusting, and burdened by an internal war between wanting to love again and being paralyzed by fear. The final breakup had been the tipping point. The physical and emotional abuse had crushed me, and the idea of entering a new relationship was nothing short of horrifying.

I convinced myself that it was better to be alone, better to avoid the possibility of more pain. But despite my reservations, life threw a curveball in the form of a mutual friend, who introduced me to this young British chap named Nick. At first, I resisted. The thought of putting myself out there again was terrifying. I wasn't ready for another disappointment, another heartbreak. But eventually, I relented—not because I was eager to meet someone new, but because something inside me whispered that maybe, just maybe, I needed to take this leap of faith.

Nick and I began chatting, and our conversations were long and meaningful, yet effortless. We lived in different cities, which I found to be a relief at first. The physical distance allowed me to feel safe. But over time, as we chatted for seven long months, I found myself feeling something I hadn't felt in

years—comfort. Our conversations made me laugh, think, and, slowly but surely, begin to heal.

But it wasn't all smooth sailing. In those early months, I was constantly terrified. My fears of abandonment, betrayal, and getting hurt again resurfaced often. Every time my phone buzzed; I worried it would be the text that would unravel everything. I didn't know how to trust anyone anymore. Yet, he was patient. He didn't rush me or push for more than I was ready to give. Instead, he made me feel seen, understood, and, most importantly, safe. But even so, opening my heart again felt like the scariest thing I had ever done.

I had to ask myself, Did I want to live in fear for the rest of my life, or was I going to show up for myself? The answer wasn't easy, but deep down, I knew that if I didn't take a risk, I'd be trapped in a cycle of fear forever. I didn't want to live that way. So, despite the walls I had built around my heart, I decided to confront my fears head-on.

Then came our first real date—a date that would change everything. Nick invited me to join him on a trip around Europe. It sounded crazy. Who agrees to spend 21 days with someone they've only known long-distance? My immediate reaction was panic. But deep down, a voice whispered, this is your chance to see if you're ready for this.

I took a deep breath and said, "Yes."

We started in Barcelona, wandering through the stunning architectural wonder that is the Sagrada Familia. I remember standing inside the basilica, looking up at the intricate design of Gaudi's masterpiece and feeling overwhelmed. In that moment, I wasn't just looking at a piece of art; I was confronting the layers of fear, doubt, and pain I had carried with me. He stood by my side, and for the first time in years, I felt a glimmer of peace.

Paris was next, where we stood beneath the Eiffel Tower as the sun set, casting a golden glow over the city. It was breathtaking, but I couldn't fully appreciate it because, inside, I was still struggling. Every part of me wanted to retreat, to protect myself. Yet he remained steady, kind, and understanding.

We travelled across all Europe, through Antwerp, Amsterdam, and Zurich. In Interlaken, we did something I would have never dared to do on my own skydiving. It was the ultimate metaphor for my life. As I stood on the edge of that plane, my heart racing, I realised that this was exactly how I felt about love: petrified to leap into the unknown yet knowing that I had to take that jump if I ever wanted to feel alive again. So, I jumped. And when the parachute opened, the world unfolded beneath me in the most spectacular way. I was free, weightless, and completely alive.

Our journey continued through Rome, Athens, and finally London. On the last night of our trip, we took a walk through the streets, the iconic skyline of London glowing softly in the distance. He turned to me, and for the first time, I saw a vulnerability in him that mirrored my own. He got down on one knee and proposed. My breath caught in my throat, and time seemed to stand still.

It wasn't just the proposal that overwhelmed me—it was the realisation that despite everything, I had chosen to show up for myself. I had allowed myself to trust, to open my heart, and to leap into the unknown. Saying yes to Nick wasn't just about agreeing to marry him—it was about saying yes to life, to love, and to the possibility of happiness. It was about recognizing that I was stronger than my fear.

Eight years later, we are happily married. My life has taken a path I never could have imagined back when I was too scared to even consider dating again. I now travel the world as a motivational speaker, sharing my story of

resilience, fear, and overcoming the odds. I tell people that had I not chosen to show up for myself, my life would be unrecognisable today.

Nick and I have built a beautiful life together, but the most important lesson I've learned is that showing up for yourself—despite the fear, the pain, and the uncertainty—is the greatest act of courage. Had I not taken that leap, I would have never known the depth of love and joy that awaited me on the other side.

Nick's story

It all started with a question. One seemingly simple, yet powerful question: "What if I could inspire others through public speaking?"

For as long as I can remember, I've had a desire to share my ideas with the world, to take the things we see every day but often overlook and shed new light on them. There's something powerful in connecting with others, in sharing stories and perspectives that change how people view the world. But like many people with big dreams, I didn't know where to start. The thought of standing in front of a crowd, articulating my thoughts, felt intimidating, almost impossible. I knew what I wanted, but I didn't know how to make it happen.

The turning point in my journey came through my wife Dana, who has been an accomplished public speaker for many years. Watching her captivate audiences with her words, move people with her message, and inspire change in ways that left me in awe, I couldn't help but feel a sense of longing to follow that same path. But as much as I admired her skill and passion, I doubted whether I could ever reach that level. After all, she made it look so effortless. I wasn't sure I had the same talent.

I shared this desire with her. I told her how much I wanted to speak, how I wanted to inspire others and share my unique insights on life—things people tend to overlook or take for granted. And in her usual supportive way, she simply smiled and said, "You can do it. You just have to start."

It sounds so simple, doesn't it? *Just start*. But the truth is, that's the hardest part—taking the first step. She encouraged me to ask for opportunities to speak, no matter how small or informal the settings. "If you wait for the perfect moment, it will never come," she said. "You have to create the opportunity yourself."

So that's exactly what we did. Together, we joined a small speaking group—a modest gathering of people who were just as nervous and eager to improve as I was. It wasn't glamorous, and it wasn't the big stage I had dreamed of, but it was a start. I still remember the first time I stood in front of that small group, my palms sweaty, my heart racing. I doubted myself the entire time, wondering if anyone would care about what I had to say.

But I spoke. And that was all that mattered.

In those early days, I focused on the simple things—the everyday insights and strategies that we often overlook for the greatest results. I talked about perspective, how changing the way you view a situation can change your entire approach to life. I spoke about resilience, about finding strength in the moments when you feel weakest. And with each talk, I noticed something: I wasn't just speaking to an audience; I was also speaking to myself.

We began giving talks together, and that's when the real magic happened. While we had different styles and messages, our journeys seemed to complement each other in ways I hadn't anticipated. Her experience and confidence balanced my fresh perspective and enthusiasm. We bounced ideas off each other, developed our messages, and shaped our talks into

something that resonated with our audiences. We weren't just speaking anymore—we were building something together.

As we gave more talks and grew more comfortable in our roles, our audience began to grow. What started as small gatherings of a few curious listeners soon expanded into larger events, with more people eager to hear what we had to say. With each speaking opportunity, I gained more confidence and found my voice. The more I shared, the more I realised that people *did* care about what I had to say—that my insights had value, and my message had the power to inspire.

One of the most important lessons I've learned in this journey is the power of asking. If I had waited for someone to invite me to speak, or for the "perfect" opportunity to come along, I'd still be waiting. Instead, by asking for those initial opportunities, by showing up to speak in small, informal settings, I opened doors I never even knew existed. Each time I asked for a chance to speak, I was saying to the universe, "I'm ready. I'm here. Let's go." And the universe responded.

It wasn't always easy. There were moments when I felt discouraged, when the turnout for an event was smaller than expected, or when I stumbled over my words. But every time I questioned whether I was on the right path, Dana was there to remind me why I started. She pushed me when I needed it, encouraged me when I doubted myself, and celebrated every small victory along the way.

As my public speaking career began to grow, so did my passion for helping others. I realised that this wasn't just about me—it was about the people I could reach and the impact I could have on their lives. Through our talks, Dana and I began to see firsthand how our words could inspire change, spark new ideas, and empower people to take action in their own lives. It was an incredible feeling, and one that only deepened my commitment to this path.

Looking back, I can't imagine what my life would be like if I hadn't taken that first step if I hadn't asked for the opportunity to speak. It's hard to believe how much has changed since those early days, when I doubted whether anyone would even listen. Now, I've had the privilege of speaking at countless events, from small community gatherings to larger conferences, each one a new opportunity to inspire and be inspired in return.

And the best part? Dana and I get to do this together. Our journeys may have started in different places, but they've converged in a way that makes us stronger as a team. Her wisdom, experience, and calm confidence balance my energy, passion, and hunger to grow. Together, we've built something that's greater than the sum of its parts, and I know that this is only the beginning.

Had it not been for the simple act of asking, of stepping out of my comfort zone and showing up, life would have taken a very different course. But because I asked, because I took that first leap, I'm now living a life filled with purpose, passion, and the incredible privilege of inspiring others.

And for that, I am eternally grateful.

Contact us via

Email: dana2inspire@gmail.com

Facebook: https://www.facebook.com/Dana2Inspire/

Instagram:

https://www.instagram.com/travel_spice_danah/

It's all
About
Showing
Up

Journey into the Dark
By Deirdre Selby

A Dark Retreat

I heard the words, and my heart and soul knew I was going. I knew going deep into the dark on a spiritual retreat was a must and would require me to show up for myself in a way I never had. It would have me asking for guidance on a deeper level than I ever had before. My team would be there for me, I knew that!

Darkness casts a shadow not just on our sight but on our souls.

So, I set off on a Dark Retreat in Oregon, spending seven nights in a cozy little hobbit hut, completely shut off from light for six of those nights. My hosts cared for my basic needs, such as food and warmth, so I could double down and focus on my inner journey.

My journey to get ready for the darkness was a long one. As we all do, I learned from a very young age that the darkness is a scary place, that evil, sinister things hide within the dark, it is a place to be afraid of and to avoid at all costs. How did I arrive at this way of thinking?

Let me rewind a little.

The darkness of my youth was not external darkness, it was a darkness of the soul. I am the result of a marriage that should never have happened. My mother, a survivor of lifelong abuse, unknowingly chose a partner mirroring her tormentor. My father, an outsider himself, mirrored the behaviors he'd endured. Violence from before birth, darkness was my ancestral heritage.

My father's rage was a sickening storm, violence that spilled over from way before I was born. My mother, pregnant and violated, took a blow to her stomach in her second trimester. I was the embryo that took that blow.

Fortunately, I survived, but the anger etched itself into my core. It took root in me alongside a gnawing emptiness; I didn't know who I was or that I deserved better.

The pure helplessness of the choices that I had every day fed the darkness of my rage, even as I watched helplessly as dinner flew across the kitchen. My throat hit my stomach, the ability to speak was lost, and feeling blows raining down upon me was safer than not knowing what was happening to my mother behind closed doors.

Anger was my constant companion, until at about age 16, I came close to losing control and causing major physical damage to my younger brother in one of our many physical altercations. The darkness beat me into retreat. I found a way to put a permanent lid on my rage, but in doing so, I unconsciously killed all my emotions.

The numbness was like a slow death, a gaping hole I learned to fill with food. Later, I sought validation in the fleeting attention of men who would happily use my body as I lay there feeling nothing. But their admiration felt hollow, a cheap substitute for the love and connection I craved.

After reaching 200 pounds before I was 20, I knew something was wrong. Not because of how I felt, but because of how I looked, and I began asking

for help. Experimenting with one kind of therapy after another, dismissing the ones that held me accountable and responsible—not for my past, but for my choices. My beliefs stood firm. I was the victim of my circumstances! I wanted absolution, a place to lay the blame for all the darkness, anger, and shame.

However, I finally understood. External darkness was a mere absence of light, easily remedied. But the darkness within, fed by my denial of responsibility for my choices, lingered like an infected wound. It intensified until it suffocated me, consuming every shred of light and leaving behind a hollow shell. I believed I'd become a shapeless, big fat mass of darkness, a burden to myself and everyone around me.

Little did I know how much darker it would get. My son was born when I was 38, and with him the depression and darkness hit hard. Sitting on the floor with my infant son laying in my lap, tears running down my face, I was afraid to touch him! Antidepressants and anti-anxiety medications failed.

Finally, I reached the end of the line and attempted to take my own life and failed.

Now, there was no choice now but to deal with the ever-present emotions. The darkness, now taking the form of depression and anxiety, was front and center, and shoving it down, burying it as I had done for so long, was not an option. I had to confront it head-on.

My first step was a decision.

If I were going to live, I was going to create a life worth living.

To do this demanded me to ask for and to accept help. With all medications gone, the bleakness of my life hit full force! It was clear I needed to learn other means of coping.

My call for help was answered in several ways, one of which was returning to transcendental meditation, a coping strategy I watched my mother use, which I had temporarily adopted in my youth. Meditating allows you to look within. It is a safe place that encourages focus, so the mind does not run away with you, hunting down all the worst-case scenarios.

After that, I turned to journaling, which allowed me to write about the darkness inside and provided safety to express what I would never say aloud.

Now my darkness had an outlet, but did not immediately turn into light. Instead, I began to find a whole new level of my soul. Hidden in the darkness were beautiful insights and messages. Eventually, that same "evil" darkness uncovered some rare and unique spiritual gifts which have become a highlight of my life.

Life continued with its varying challenges. My son was diagnosed on the autistic spectrum, so I was faced with a choice: should he be medicated? Deep in my gut, I knew this would deaden his spiritual gifts, evident from a young age. He had no veil between this world and the next.

Or do we train these gifts, embrace his essence, and accept that he is not broken? He has not come into this world imperfect and flawed, but perfect, exactly as he is supposed to be!

My son Sean and I asked for and ended up working with spiritual teachers. He, to explore his gifts and I to follow the road out of the darkness, or as it turned out to be, into the darkness. As Sean recognized and nurtured his connection, he learned how to create boundaries and see the divisions between this world and alternative dimensions.

I found within my inner darkness very different, yet similar abilities.

My new spiritual way of thinking came from the idea that life happens for me, not "to me" accepting that old, rejected responsibility piece from way back in my teenage years was tough. This is true, even when it does not feel like it, and became a cornerstone of my new belief system.

Buried underneath all the trauma, pain, and darkness was my soul's purpose. Unwittingly, I had chosen this hard road because I had high-level lessons to master. An easy life only occurs for those who are not ready for higher level learnings, this belief made my trials easier to bear. My reason for coming into this life was finally being revealed to me. This revelation was a crucial foundation but wasn't the final step.

It was like finding a rough gem. The real work – cleaning, cutting, polishing, and setting – was yet to begin.

Nothing can be done to me, without my permission on a spiritual level. Everything is done for me.

A whole new light shone down on my childhood. I had been beaten up in my home, bullied in my school, molested, and mistreated. I had spent 20 years in therapy to release this pain, and still, I did not learn how to feel my feelings.

As gut-wrenching as it was, none of this abuse existed without my permission on a soul level. But why had I agreed to this? Embracing my darkness brought me to the lessons I now had to face.

Here was the true entry onto my path of darkness. Many call this shadow work. The actual difference between my path and theirs is they seek to bring light upon the shadow to reduce its size. I strive to embrace and understand what transpired in the darkness and hold onto the strength that lies in this amazing place. I work to bring this rod of steel, this backbone, into the present moment, always there, always accessible, and open, releasing the inner warrior as my inner powerhouse.

However, this requires one to be open to the fact that they are never the victim: they only play the role in an age-old dance. We have chosen in prior incarnations to take part in one of three roles in an ever-changing play being reenacted with the same sparks. The same souls reincarnate together repeatedly, trading back and forth the roles of Perpetrator, Victim, and Savior.

In this life, being the Victim and the Savior were my two favorite roles. I took care of my mother; I stood between her and my father. I beat my brother; here I was, the Perpetrator.

As I really looked deeply into these dark and murky depths, I saw how I gloried in playing all the roles. It kept an odd sort of balance. But it is possible to take personal responsibility for my choices, to release these roles, and live a life from a different script. After all, I was miserable. This was not the life I wanted to be living. It was time to make a change.

Again, I asked for help, showing up for myself, this time in the spiritual community. I acknowledged the time I consciously chose to place my emotions on hold. I asked for the keys to release them. These were revealed to me when I found my inner child living in a cage guarded by a giant wolf (one of my spirit guides) who would not let me near. I met the inner bullied schoolgirl. And the inner me who was still the extremely overweight adult who would not let anybody close. I befriended each of them in turn, as well as many more, over years and years of deep inner work.

Now, in my 60s, the darkness is no longer a scary place inside or out. And now it was Dark Retreat time! I did the work. I was ready. I had six more

months to prepare before my booking, and I asked my spiritual team what they recommend I do to prepare?

Learn to BE, I was told.

What the F*** does that mean? Learn to BE!

I start watching videos, listening to people who have gone into the dark. Their stories do not resonate; somehow, I know mine will be unique to me.

What is this BE? Mine is a life of DO, not be. And I got a blindfold mask that allowed me to experience absolute darkness. I taught myself to write in the dark; a flow of consciousness at first, writing about BE and feeling.

This is different; I am not planning what I will do next, but simply paying attention to what is, the sights, the sounds, and the textures in my world.

There are four areas of life: the physical, the mental, the emotional, and the spiritual. Each is affected by the dark to a different degree and in very different ways. I ask my spiritual team for help; they are always there and step up to guide me.

And boy, did Spirit bring challenges at this time, a 500-mile move, taking this city girl into the country, selling a house, buying a house. The loss of my BooBear, even at age 19, yet kittenish in spirit. The emotional gains and losses gave me many opportunities to access deep into the magic of my shadow, my inner strength, and my darkness.

January arrives, and it is cold! We trekked through the snow and mud to get to my little hobbit hut. I regret the timing a little, but it won't matter once I go into the darkness, close the door, and turn out the lights.

I signed up for the healer, who came the next day. Scott, the owner, suggests I turn out the lights the first night as a trial run to get into the right frame of mind. I do so and keep busy, oh so busy, in the dark. I am journaling and playing my brass bowl and drum, even my meditation has a measure of activity. I learned to eat in the dark. I count the steps to the bathroom, the box where he puts the food, and anything to keep my mind occupied.

But in the dark, there is only so much to do.

Food is delivered once each day in the late afternoon. There are no electronics, and your phone is left outside. Not only is the goal to disengage, but all these devices bring in light.

I ran out of things to do; it was a long night before I finally fell asleep. I didn't know if I had slept long or short when I awoke, which bothered me. I knew the healer would arrive around 11, and I was free to turn the lights on or leave them off. My time in the dark officially began after our time together concluded. I felt like I was waiting, waiting in the dark. I looked outside, and it was light; I decided to enjoy the outdoors and called my husband to chat one last time.

What was my goal for my time in the dark? That was her question, the healer's question. I had not really thought about it. I knew I was drawn to the dark; I HAD to be there. While she did her energetic work, I focused on this; I was there to increase my connection to myself. This was important; this was the BE!

I turned off the lights for the next six nights, five full days, and began a glorious period of connection to me and my guides. My BooBear (my beloved cat) was by my side the entire time. I never knew whether I slept during the day or at night.

I traveled throughout the multiverse, meeting alternative aspects of myself, chatting with angels, working with my ancestors and guides, and journaling. I filled an entire book, some writings to clear my thoughts,

some channeled that I never fully realized until I read them later. I danced, I chanted, I drummed, and I connected to ME!

I asked for connection from my time in the dark, and I showed up for me. This has allowed me to show up for those I love, my clients, and those in the spiritual realm.

My darkness gives me strength. And as it turns out, it always has.

Deirdre Selby

Deirdre Selby, Career Educator and Owner of Soul Enhancements, has been working with her spiritual gifts for her entire life. She is the creator of the 5D Living, Now Experience, a Reiki Master, Chi Gun Practitioner and Crystal Healer, being highly intuitive to otherworldly energies she encourages you to embrace your shadow side to tap into your gifts. Her philosophy is that the only way to change our world is to always come from love.

The Deadly Grip of Fentanyl
By Ambassador Dr. (h.c.) Dorothy Wolons

In the year 2023, a silent and deadly killer has emerged, wreaking havoc on the young generation across the globe. Its name is fentanyl, a synthetic opioid that is fifty times more potent than heroin. The impact of this lethal drug has been devastating, leaving a trail of destruction in its wake.

In the early 2020s, fentanyl began to flood the streets, disguised as a less potent substance. Its cheap production and high profitability attracted drug dealers, who saw an opportunity to maximize their profits. Unbeknownst to the users, a single dose of fentanyl could prove fatal.

The impact of fentanyl on the young generation has been catastrophic. It has seeped into every corner of society, ravaging communities, and leaving families shattered. The allure of a quick high and escape from reality has enticed many young people to experiment with this deadly substance.

What makes fentanyl particularly dangerous is its potency and unpredictability. A minuscule amount can lead to overdose and death. Young people, seeking a thrill or relief from the pressures of life, have fallen victim to its grip. The alarming rise in overdose deaths has left medical professionals and law enforcement agencies scrambling to find solutions.

Not only does fentanyl pose a significant risk to those who actively seek it, but it also lurks in other illicit drugs. Counterfeit pills, laced with fentanyl, have become a common occurrence. Users, believing they are taking something less potent, unknowingly ingest a lethal dose.

The impact on families and communities cannot be understated. Parents have lost children, siblings have lost siblings, and friends have lost friends. The despair and grief that follow are indescribable. The young generation, once filled with dreams and aspirations, now faces a grim reality overshadowed by the constant threat of fentanyl.

Efforts to combat the fentanyl crisis have been met with mixed success. Education and awareness campaigns have been launched, highlighting the dangers of this deadly drug. Harm reduction strategies, such as access to naloxone, a life-saving overdose reversal medication, have been implemented. However, the battle against fentanyl continues to be an uphill struggle.

As the world grapples with the devastating impact of fentanyl, it is clear that a comprehensive and multi-faceted approach is needed. Stricter regulations on the production and distribution of opioids, increased support for addiction treatment programs, and a focus on mental health services are crucial in addressing the underlying issues that contribute to drug abuse.

In the face of this crisis, it is essential for society to come together and support the young generation. By providing resources, compassion, and understanding, we can help those affected by fentanyl find a path to recovery and prevent further tragedies. The fight against fentanyl is far from over, but with collective efforts, we can strive to protect the future of our young generation.

My story begins, never thought I would find myself in this position. As a proud mother, I had always imagined a bright future for my son, Jordan. He was a big part of my world, my Bubbie. But on that fateful New Year's Eve, everything changed in an instant.

The day had started with so much excitement and anticipation. We were all parting the house to go our separate ways to celebrate. Jordan, being the social butterfly that he was, had plans to attend a sober party with his friends later that evening. I couldn't have been prouder of the man he had become. Struggling with addiction was hard, but he was determined, six months clean and on the right path. He had bought a car, was leasing an apartment, one week away from becoming a certified SMOG technician and enrolled in college. To become a Master Automotive technician.

As I left the house to go to the mountains to celebrate the new year, I passed his bedroom and said Happy New Year, he replied to Happy New Year mom, I love you" I said, "Love you too," never did I ever imagine those would be our last words. Little did I know, my worst nightmare was about to become a reality.

It was close to midnight when my phone rang. The shrill sound pierced through the phone, my daughter Jurnie screaming something is wrong with Jordan. He is not answering from the bathroom.

A joyful atmosphere, instantly silencing the room. My heart pounding in my chest. Her voice on the other end was of panic, I knew we had to get home, this wasn't good. Rafael and I stayed on the phone while my daughter called 911. Rafael called a friend who was nearby to rush over and knock the door down. The ambulance arrived and half the police department were there when we got home.

"Ma'am, I'm a police officer. I'm sorry to inform you ....your son, Jordan.

He was found unconscious and unresponsive; they did their best. As I rushed to the door, they would not let anyone inside.

Time seemed to stand still as those words echoed in my ears. My world came crashing down around me. I couldn't breathe, couldn't think. Everything blurred, and the sounds around me became distant echoes. My son, my beautiful boy, was gone.

In the days that followed, I was consumed by grief. The pain was unbearable, and my heart felt like it had been shattered into a million pieces. I blamed myself for not being there, for not protecting him. How could I have let this happen? I was his mother, and it was my job to keep him safe.

As the shock slowly wore off, I found myself transitioning from a proud mother to a grieving one. The weight of loss pressed upon me, suffocating me with each passing day. I couldn't escape the guilt, the what ifs that plagued my mind. I would never get the chance to see Jordan grow into the amazing man, or father I knew he would become.

But amidst the darkness, I found solace in the memories we shared. I held onto the laughter, the love, his pictures, his love of music and the joy we experienced together. I knew that I had to honor his memory by raising awareness about the dangers of drugs, especially the deadly grip of fentanyl. No other mother should have to experience the pain I now carry.

Losing Jordan was a devastating blow that forever changed the course of my life. But through the pain, I have found strength. I am determined to turn my grief into action, to make a difference in the lives of others. My son may be gone, but his spirit lives on within me, guiding me to fight for a world where no mother must endure the loss I have suffered.

2 years prior Jordan was living on the streets, a 24-year-old male in Indio, California, especially during scorching temperatures exceeding 100 degrees,

is an incredibly challenging and harsh reality. The relentless heat takes a toll not only on physical health but also on mental and emotional well-being. The lack of shelter and basic amenities intensifies the struggle to survive each day.

Despite these circumstances, my son "Tall Jordan" was a remarkable individual who left a lasting impression on everyone he encountered. His charismatic personality and warm presence made him a familiar face in the community. Whenever I would visit Indio, whether it was in grocery store parking lots or other public spaces, the homeless individuals would come up to me, knowing that I was there to see Jordan. I was his mom, and safe to talk to. Within a short time, he would appear, seemingly connected to a network of communication that transcended the absence of phones or other traditional means of contact.

Our visits were infrequent, occurring only once or twice a month, but they held immense significance. We would spend time together, going to the movies, having dinner, or simply strolling through places like the 99 Cents store. Given his limited belongings, he never asked for anything extravagant or costly, as his backpack could only accommodate the essentials. Yet, his gratitude for even the smallest gestures was palpable.

Throughout his journey, I never gave up on my son and always longed for him to come home. The turning point came on my birthday in June when one of our visits he expressed his desire to return home. Overjoyed, I immediately headed back home (Menifee) from Indio with my son. During the car ride, we filled the air with songs, as music was a significant part of his life. His eclectic taste spanned from Frank Sinatra, old-school classics to even punk rock, which brought us closer together. It was the best car ride ever!

Upon returning home, Jordan made the courageous decision to quit fentanyl cold turkey. This was an immensely challenging process for him, characterized by ten days of excruciating physical and emotional pain. The withdrawal symptoms included screams, tears, and blistering sores as his body fought to rid itself of the drug's grip. Witnessing his resilience during this tumultuous period only deepened my admiration for his strength.

For a brief period, we had some stability in our lives, as we found a good place to stay. However, the grip of addiction is relentless, and after six months, Jordan experienced a relapse that shattered our world once again. Addiction is a formidable adversary, capable of dismantling even the most hopeful of recoveries.

Despite many setbacks, I remained steadfast in my love and support for my son. I continued to seek avenues for his recovery, understanding that his battle against fentanyl requires ongoing dedication, compassion, and professional intervention. Our journey together had been marked by both triumph and heartbreak, but I refused to give up on him. I held onto hope, believing that one day he would conquer his addiction and find the peace and stability he so deserved. But that fatal New Year Eve addiction won, and he was somehow triggered to try it one more time. I question everyday What triggered him? He was on top of the world, so many things were happening for him, and us.

All gone in an instant. Changing our family forever.

A Mother's Memorial I never thought I would be sitting here, writing about the loss of my precious son. It's a pain that no parent should ever have to endure. Jordan, my beautiful boy, was taken from me too soon, a victim of the drugs that plague our community. During my grief, I knew I had to do something to bring awareness to the devastating impact of drugs in our city. I wanted to honor my son's memory and make sure that his story

would not be forgotten. That's when the idea of a memorial bench came to me. I decided that the perfect place for Jordan's memorial would be John V. Denver Park, 28050 Encanto Drive, in the City of Menifee California. It was a place close to his heart, where he used to attend his AA and NA meetings at Unity Hall, just a block or two away. I wanted his memorial to be a source of comfort and support for those struggling with addiction, a reminder that they too can fight this battle. With a sense of determination, I reached out to the city. I had never seen a memorial bench in any other park, but based on a referral from a friend, I called the city and set up a meeting. To my surprise, they mentioned a program they were considering. We saw this as an opportunity to partner together and make Jordan's memorial a reality. Through this partnership, Jordan became the first recipient of one of these benches in the City of Menifee. I am deeply honored that his memorial not only features the serenity prayer but also includes his picture. The city recognized the urgent need to combat the use of fentanyl in our community, and they saw this memorial to raise awareness. The power of asking was evident throughout this process. Sometimes, all it takes is the courage to ask for what you want. In my case, it resulted in a beautiful memorial for my son. Though he will never see it or come home, we now have something tangible to remember him by. And I hope that this bench will also serve as a source of strength for others in the park, reminding them that they too can overcome their battles. Losing a child to drugs is a pain that no parent should ever have to bear. But through this memorial, I hope to bring awareness to the drugs that are tearing apart our community. Let us come together and fight against the devastation caused by addiction. It is time for us to support one another and provide the resources necessary for recovery. In memory of Jordan, let us honor his life by standing up against drugs. Let this bench be a symbol of hope, resilience, and the power of unity. Together, we can make a difference and create a community free from the grip of addiction.

On December 6, 2023, the Menifee City Council recognized Ms. Dorothy Wolons for donating a beautiful bench at John V. Denver Park to honor her son, Jordan Hughes.

Jordan, a long-time Menifee resident, passed away earlier this year. To memorialize his life, Jordan's family and friends raised funds to donate a park bench that includes his photo and a custom engraving of the serenity prayer to the City of Menifee. John V. Denver Park was selected for the memorial bench as Jordan's family and the Denver Family are close friends.

#JordanHughes13

We have witnessed the incredible strength and resilience of a grieving mother who, in the face of unimaginable loss, found the power to ask for change. Through her partnership with the City of Menifee, she successfully brought awareness to the fentanyl crisis and secured a bench in a city park, serving as a powerful symbol of the struggles of addiction that plague our communities. This chapter serves as a reminder that by showing up and asking for help, we can make a difference and bring about positive change in our community.

Ambassador Dr. (h.c.) Dorothy Wolons

Dorothy Wolons is a dynamic individual who was born and raised in Detroit, Michigan. Currently residing in Menifee, California, Dorothy has embraced her surroundings and has become an integral part of the community.

Dorothy's professional journey began in the field of finance, where she spent the early years of her career as a Collections Manager, after graduating from Wayne State University. Her passion for helping others led her to inspire and educate certified students in the collection field. However, seeking new challenges, she eventually transitioned to running a national sales team before venturing into entrepreneurship. Dorothy successfully owned and operated two of her own retail stores, showcasing her exceptional business acumen.

Further exploring her potential, Dorothy found her calling at the Menifee Valley Chamber of Commerce, where she served as the CEO and Director for an impressive tenure of 10 years. During her time in this esteemed position, she accomplished remarkable feats and garnered invaluable experience in the chamber industry. Dorothy's dedication and commitment to the community she served were truly commendable. She regularly volunteered and actively participated in numerous gratifying organizations, including being a member of the GSFE (Global Society for Female Executives).

Dorothy's personal life is also filled with happiness and fulfillment. As a devoted mother and loving grandmother, family holds a special place in her heart. She cherishes her time spent with her children, grandchildren, and her partner Rafael. In addition to her family commitments, Dorothy has also achieved recognition as an international best-selling author, demonstrating her exceptional writing skills.

Beyond her professional and personal accomplishments, Dorothy also carries the title of an ordained minister. Her faith and spirituality have guided her throughout her life, providing her with a strong moral compass and a genuine desire to help others.

After the death of her son, she is dedicated to creating a peaceful world she is deeply passionate about combating the fentanyl crisis that plagues our streets. Dorothy firmly believes that every child deserves a safe environment to grow and thrive, free from the clutches of this deadly drug. Through her unwavering commitment and advocacy, she strives to raise awareness, promote prevention, and support initiatives that aim to eradicate the presence of fentanyl in our communities. She stands united in the fight against fentanyl, working towards a future where our children are safe and protected.

With a wealth of experience, commendable achievements, and a heart full of compassion, Dorothy continues to make a positive impact on the world around her.

Dorothy Wolons
#JordanHughes13
MOM
Grandma
New Hub Auto Service
Advanced Emission Specialist
Rippin Disc Golf
GSFE-Globalsocietyforfemaleentrepreneurs.com
Fabulous DIVA
International Best-Selling Author
Minister

Cell: (951) 240-0219
Dorothy.Wolons@yahoo.com
Dorothy Wolons
29075 Glencoe Lane
Menifee, CA 92584

It's All About Showing Up:
The Power of Asking

By HRM Queen Eden Soriano Trinidad

Introduction

"Oh, that you would bless me indeed and enlarge my territory, that your hand would be with me and that you would keep me from evil so that I may not cause pain." — 1 Chronicles 4:10

The journey of life is filled with opportunities, challenges, and I've come to know the profound power of asking, especially when that request is directed towards the Almighty Living God. This prayer has been my constant, a heartfelt plea for growth and protection. And remarkably, God has answered. You can explore my journey and achievements further on my website, (https://www.edensorianotrinidad.com).

This prayer has not only shaped my life but has also opened doors I never imagined possible.

I will share the transformative experiences that came from asking, showing up, and embracing the unexpected.

The Power of Prayer

Prayer has always been a cornerstone of my life. Each day begins with a heartfelt conversation with God, where I lay my hopes, dreams, and challenges before Him. This practice of daily prayer is more than just a routine; it is a sacred time where I seek guidance and strength. Over the years, I have seen prayers answered in ways that were sometimes subtle, other times overwhelming. For instance, there were moments when I faced daunting challenges—whether managing a school or navigating personal struggles—when my prayers for wisdom and clarity were met with unexpected solutions. I've learned that asking is not merely about voicing needs; it's about cultivating a relationship with the Divine. Each answered prayer deepened my faith and reinforced my belief in the power of asking.

Embracing Opportunities

One of the most significant opportunities arose when I was appointed as the Prime Minister of Birland. This position, while an honor, carries a weight of responsibility that is both exhilarating and daunting. Birland, situated in the BirTawil land between Sudan and Egypt, is a unique humanitarian initiative focused on providing support and refuge. It was born out of a vision for peace, kindness, and humanitarian aid—a vision I wholeheartedly embrace. The path to this role was not straightforward. It involved countless discussions, negotiations, and a shared belief in the possibility of creating something new. My appointment came about through a network of individuals who believed in the vision we collectively shared. They saw potential where others saw obstacles, and it was through their encouragement that I took on this mantle.

Connecting with Dr. Robbie Motter

My journey took a pivotal turn when I met Dr. Robbie Motter. The encounter was serendipitous; her vibrant energy and commitment to empowering women resonated with me instantly. Dr. Robbie not only invited me into the Global Society for Female Entrepreneurs (GSFE) but also became a mentor and friend. Her impact on my life is immeasurable. She embodies the essence of mentorship—someone who not only guides but inspires action. Through her, I learned the importance of collaboration and community. She consistently emphasized that our individual journeys are interconnected, and together we can create waves of change.

Visa Journey:

A Leap of Faith Applying for a U.S. visa felt daunting. The process was riddled with uncertainty, especially with so many responsibilities demanding my attention at home. I vividly remember the day of my interview, a blend of hope and anxiety coursing through me. When I arrived at the embassy, my name was not on the master appointment list. A moment of panic surged within me as I whispered a prayer for clarity and peace. But just then, the officer confirmed that my name was on the computer. In that moment, I felt a profound sense of divine intervention. When asked why I wanted to travel to the U.S., I simply replied, "I have to fulfill the invitation of Dr. Robbie Motter." After what felt like an eternity of scrutiny, the officer smiled and said, "Welcome to the USA." It was a surreal moment, a testament to the power of faith and persistence.

Experiencing the USA Landing in the U.S. was like stepping into a new world. The vibrant energy, the diverse culture, and the sheer scale of everything were overwhelming yet thrilling. My first days were a whirlwind of activities, filled with events, introductions, and experiences that opened my eyes to the beauty of this country. Traveling through Southern California was a highlight. Each city held its own charm, from the stunning beaches of Santa Monica to the bustling streets of Los Angeles. I was particularly struck by the warmth and hospitality of the people I met. Their kindness was a reminder that no matter where we are from, we all share a common humanity.

The Tribute to Dr. Robbie Motter

The tribute held for Dr. Robbie's 88th birthday was a celebration of her incredible life and contributions. As I stood among friends and fellow GSFE members, I felt a deep sense of belonging. Each story shared reflected the profound impact she had on so many lives, including my own. During the event, we awarded recognition to various individuals, and I had the honor of presenting awards to recipients. The joy in the room was palpable, a testament to the power of community and gratitude. That night, as we celebrated Dr. Robbie, I realized the importance of honoring those who uplift and inspire us.

Meeting Influential Figures

My time in the U.S. also allowed me to meet remarkable individuals who have made significant contributions to society. Meeting Mayor Bill Zimmerman was particularly special. As I walked into Menifee City Hall, I felt both excited and nervous. This was my first official meeting as a Queen, and it was surreal to be welcomed so warmly. We discussed potential collaborations and the importance of humanitarian efforts in building communities. His genuine interest in Birland was encouraging, and we

exchanged ideas on how to raise awareness for our cause. Such encounters reaffirmed my belief that leadership is about building relationships and fostering collaboration for the greater good.

A Dream Come True: Disneyland

When I mentioned my wish to visit Disneyland, I had no idea what was in store. Dr. Robbie sprang into action, reaching out to Dr. Maria Zulmara, the "Disneyland Queen." Despite my initial hesitations, I found myself at the gates of one of the most magical places on earth. The experience was nothing short of enchanting. Each ride, each character I met reignited a sense of childlike wonder in me. The joy on my face as I rode the Pirates of the Caribbean was genuine. I realized then that the magic of Disneyland transcends age; it serves as a reminder to embrace joy and wonder in our lives.

The Celebration of Birland's Anniversary

Celebrating the 9th Founding Anniversary of the State of Birland was a milestone I will cherish forever. Initially, I thought a simple picnic would suffice, but Dr. Robbie envisioned something grander. With her unwavering support, we organized a formal event that celebrated not just Birland's founding but the collective efforts of everyone involved in its creation. As guests arrived, I was overwhelmed by the love and support from newfound friends, and community members. The beautiful venue was adorned with decorations that reflected our mission and vision. I took a moment to thank everyone for their contributions, and as I spoke, I felt a deep sense of gratitude for the journey that brought us all together.

Dr. Robbie: The Road Runner of California

During my month-long stay with Dr. Robbie Motter, she truly became a whirlwind of energy and inspiration. With her at the helm, we traveled to over 40 cities in California, each visit unfolding new opportunities and insights. It was exhilarating to hop in the car and set off to the next destination, whether for networking events, community gatherings, or simply to explore the unique charm of each city. Every trip felt like an adventure. Dr. Robbie's passion for connecting people was infectious. She would introduce me to influential figures, entrepreneurs, and community leaders, each encounter was a chance to learn and grow. I remember our visits to coastal towns, where we shared meals at quaint cafes, discussed our dreams, and planned future collaborations. Each city had its own distinct vibe—some bustling with energy, others calm and reflective, but all enriched by the warm welcome we received. Every day was a memorable moment with her. We drove through the picturesque landscapes of the California countryside. The rolling hills, dotted with vineyards and wildflowers, were breathtaking. As we traveled, Dr. Robbie shared stories from her own journey, each tale infused with wisdom and humor. Her ability to make every moment meaningful made the long drives fly by.

A Day on Lake Arrowhead

Amidst our whirlwind schedule, one of the highlights was our boat tour on Lake Arrowhead. This stunning alpine lake, surrounded by towering pine trees, was the perfect backdrop for a day of relaxation and reflection. As we glided across the shimmering water, I felt a sense of peace wash over me, a welcome contrast to the bustling pace of our travels. The boat was filled with laughter and camaraderie. Dr. Robbie, ever the entertainer, shared stories about the area's history and its significance with the community. We

stopped at scenic points, taking in the breathtaking views and capturing memories with our cameras. As we floated on the lake, I had the chance to connect with others on the boat—entrepreneurs and visionaries who were as passionate about making a difference as I was. Conversations flowed effortlessly, each exchange rich with ideas and dreams. It was during this serene moment that I realized the importance of balance; while ambition drives us, moments of tranquility fuel our souls. The day culminated with a shared picnic on the boat, where we enjoyed delicious snacks and toasted to our adventures. I felt a profound sense of gratitude for the connections we were forging and the experiences we were creating together. The boat tour on Lake Arrowhead became a symbol of the harmony between work and play, reminding me that life's journey is as much about the people we meet as the destinations we reach.

Reflections on Generosity and Kindness

Throughout my travels, I encountered countless acts of generosity that left an indelible mark on my heart. Whether it was a warm meal shared with new friends or the support of those who believed in my mission, each gesture reaffirmed the importance of kindness. These experiences reminded me that our individual actions can ripple outwards, inspiring others to contribute to the greater good. As leaders and changemakers, it is essential to foster an environment of support and compassion, encouraging those around us to thrive.

A Warm Welcome at Every GSFE Meeting

Throughout my stay in the USA, particularly in my engagements with the Global Society for Female Entrepreneurs (GSFE), I was met with an overwhelming sense of respect and admiration. Each meeting I attended was not just a gathering; it was a celebration of shared dreams, goals, and aspirations. As Dr. Robbie Motter's guest, I felt like royalty, welcomed with open arms and warm smiles. At every GSFE meeting, members took the time to introduce me with great reverence. It was heartening to hear their words of encouragement, as they recognized my role as the Prime Minister of the State of Birland. Their respect extended beyond mere titles; it was rooted in a genuine appreciation for my mission and vision for humanitarian work. As I stood before them, I often felt the weight of my responsibilities, but also the strength of the community surrounding me. Every introduction was accompanied by a burst of applause, creating an atmosphere of encouragement that spurred me on. I was often invited to share my insights about the State of Birland and our goals. It was a platform where I could articulate our vision of a humanitarian country, one that prioritizes kindness and compassion, and I seized every opportunity to do so.

Elevating the State of Birland

The GSFE meetings were pivotal for raising awareness about the State of Birland. With each presentation, I aimed to illuminate our aspirations and the unique challenges we faced as we established this new humanitarian country. I spoke passionately about our commitment to fostering peace, kindness, and cooperation, and the members were genuinely receptive, engaging in meaningful dialogue that reinforced our shared values. One of the most impactful moments came during a gathering in Riverside, where I had the chance to raise the Birland flag. The act of raising the flag was symbolic; it represented hope, unity, and the promise of a brighter future. As I held the flag high, I felt a surge of pride and determination.

The applause that followed was a testament to the support I felt from the community. At that moment, I knew that Birland was not just a dream; it was a burgeoning reality, backed by people who believed in its mission. Photography opportunities at these events became a cherished tradition. Each time I held the Birland flag, I was greeted with cheers, and cameras flashed around me. These moments were captured not just as personal milestones, but as representations of the support and solidarity from the GSFE community. They served as visual reminders of our shared commitment to create positive change in the world.

A Warm Reception in Every Setting

Beyond formal gatherings, even our outings to restaurants were filled with moments of recognition. As Dr. Robbie and I dined in various establishments, I was often greeted with curiosity and warmth. Staff and patrons alike would stop to inquire about my work and the State of Birland. Dr. Robbie, ever the gracious host, would introduce me with pride, highlighting my role and the humanitarian mission I represented. These interactions were invaluable. Each conversation became an opportunity to educate others about Birland and the unique vision we had for this new country. I relished the chance to share stories about our initiatives and how we were striving to foster a community built on compassion and collaboration. Many were intrigued and expressed their desire to learn more, providing an organic platform for raising awareness. The respect I experienced throughout these engagements left a profound impact on me. It reinforced the idea that genuine relationships and a sense of community can fuel progress. The support I received extended beyond mere acknowledgment; it created a ripple effect, inspiring others to think about how they could contribute to the vision of Birland.

Building Lasting Connections

By the end of my stay, I realized that every handshake, every conversation, and every introduction had woven a network of support around the State of Birland. I was not just a visitor; I was part of a larger movement, surrounded by individuals who understood the power of unity and collaboration. The impact of these gatherings stretched far beyond the events themselves. Each encounter opened doors to new partnerships, collaborative initiatives, and friendships that would help propel our vision forward. As I reflected on my experiences, I felt a deep sense of gratitude. The respect and admiration I received fueled my determination to advocate for Birland, knowing that I was supported by a community of like-minded individuals who believed in the power of kindness and humanitarianism.

The Journey of Self-Discovery

This journey was not only about external experiences but also a profound journey of self-discovery. As I navigated new environments and faced challenges, I learned more about my strengths, values, and aspirations. Each encounter, whether challenging or uplifting, contributed to my growth. I began to understand that leadership is not just about titles; it's about impact. It's about showing up for others, advocating for change, and embodying the values we wish to see in the world. This realization has shaped my vision for Birland and my role within it.

Concluding Thoughts

As I conclude this reflection, I want to emphasize the central theme of my journey: the power of asking and showing up. Each opportunity that

arose stemmed from a willingness to embrace the unknown, to ask for help, and to take action. I encourage everyone to embrace their own journeys with faith and courage. The world is filled with possibilities waiting to be explored, and by asking and showing up, we can create meaningful change in our lives and the lives of others. My hopes for the future remain bright, as I continue to work towards the vision of Birland and the impact we can make together. ---

God has truly enlarged my territory, and I am forever grateful for people like Dr. Robbie Motter who helped make these dreams a reality. I could fill pages with stories from my two-month adventure in the U.S., but the essence is clear: when you ask and show up, the world opens up in miraculous ways.

https//www.edensorianotrinidad.com
https//www.birlandstate.org
http//www.birland.net
X Account: @BirlandPM
Email: edensorianotrinidad@gmail.com

HRM Queen Eden Soriano Trinidad

Queen Eden Soriano Trinidad is a distinguished global figure renowned for her multifaceted contributions to peace, education, and humanitarian efforts. Her impressive background includes:
President of the Royal Kutai Mulawarman Peace International Institute, Inc. (RKMPII): Founded in 2021, this institute promotes world peace through education, creating roles such as Peace Envoys and Ambassadors of Kindness and Happiness to spread joy and peace worldwide.
Prime Minister and Queen of Birland: Leading the Kingdom of Birland,

Africa's 55th country, which is recognized for its humanitarian focus.

Secretary General of the United Global Kingdoms: In this role, she coordinates global initiatives for peace and human rights with the objective to give dignity to the lost Indigenous kings.

High Commissioner for Human Rights of Parliament: Her appointment, officially registered with the UN ECOSOC ESANGO, reflects her commitment to human rights.

Royal Chaplain General: This designation from the International Association of Licensed Chaplains and her life-long role as Chaplaincy Practitioner from All Nations University in South Africa highlight her dedication to spiritual and moral leadership.

Accomplished Poet and Author: She has written and translated poetry, co- authoring international bestsellers like "Expert World Leaders" and "Voices of Peace."

Educator and Philanthropist: Queen Eden pioneered the Lucio Abrigo Memorial Learning Center Inc. in San Agustin Iba, Zambales, Philippines, which provides quality education to underprivileged children. The school, started in 1991, continues to support students despite financial challenges.

Her tireless efforts have earned her numerous accolades globally, reflecting her deep commitment to humanitarian causes, peace, and cultural enrichment.

For more information, visit:

[Harvest Christian University] https//www.harvestchristianuniversity. education/universityambassador)

[InternationalOrganizations](https://uniagsfmi.com/blog/vicerectorados-internacionales/)

[Birland State) (https://birlandstate.org)

You can also contact her via email at edensorianotrinidad@gmail.com or follow her on X (formerly Twitter) at @BirlandPM.

It's all
About
Showing
Up

Discovering Hidden Treasures Through Mentorship

By Ambassador Dr. (h.c.) Elizabeth "Liz" Mejia-Celis

Life is a beautiful journey. It has its highs and lows, but it's through these peaks and valleys that we are able to learn and grow into the best version of ourselves. These valleys are disguised opportunities, and it's up to us to see what's hidden and rise from the ashes like a phoenix with renewed strength, hope, a sense of renewal, and the determination to let go of what was and focus on what will be.

Throughout our life we meet many people and share many experiences. Some people only stay in our life for a little while and others may stay for a lifetime. The first people we look up to are our parents and then our teachers. They both teach us right from wrong, about values and morals, how to behave, how to read and write, how to communicate, and how to become compassionate and kind human beings among many other things. As we become adults, our parents, teachers, grandparents, and best friends become our role models. They give us the best advice to help us face the real world.

My mentors are filled with real life experiences. They share their wisdom to help others along the way. I became an entrepreneur in 2005 when I had my last child. As a mother of four, I needed more freedom and more income to sustain my family. I never worked in the corporate world. Instead, I was more involved in the artistic fields. I worked as a photographer for 12 years before I ventured on my own to launch my business.

Being an entrepreneur is not easy. Our families criticize us sometimes for not having a 9 to 5 job with a fixed income. However, being self-employed has its advantages and disadvantages just like a full-time job does. It's all about balance.

The advantage is that you have complete freedom to set your schedule. As human beings, there are no limits as to what we are capable of achieving. The only limits are the ones what we set for ourselves. The disadvantage is that if we do not work hard enough to make our business grow, we may stumble along the way and lose our focus. For entrepreneurs, focus, determination, and mentorship are extremely important.

The first mentor I had was a life coach. Her name is Sandylu Guerrero of Life's Choice Coaching with Sandylu Guerrero. Her last name means warrior and that is what she is — a true-life warrior. She took her pain and turned it into a purpose to help others get through life's challenges. Sandylu helped me shed false beliefs I had about myself.

Through the women's association I am part of, Global Society for Female Entrepreneurs (GSFE), I have found mentorship with different people who have assisted me with business coaching. For example, Tyara Lee helped me with my marketing needs and introduced me to my current business coach, Sheila Andres from Realize Your Vision, who has helped me tremendously to structure my business. Alongside my mentors, networking has become the key that has opened many doors for me.

Through my life's journey of healing and discovery and through GSFE, I also met two of my spiritual mentors. They have both played a crucial role

in my life. One of them is Tomasa Macapinlac, a shaman who has achieved mastery of the Inca tradition. Under her tutelage, I took a nine-month course called, "Live Your Soul's True Destiny." This experience led me to discover more about myself and heal deep wounds that were affecting my business and personal life daily.

I am also grateful that through GSFE I met Virginia Earl. She is a writer and editor and has her own spiritual business. I have learned so much from her Akashic Record Readings. She is a certified Akashic Records Readings consultant and the owner of Seven Mystic Rings, a spiritual healing business in Murrieta, California.

The Akashic Records is a library in a different energy field that contains the records of each human being's soul from the beginning of time to the present. This library stores a compilation of every action, feeling, and thought that every individual has ever experienced on Earth since their soul was conceived. Not many people know about this, but I was lucky to find her.

Virginia accessed my Akashic Records and all the questions I had were finally answered. I always thought I was just making things up; I was surprised when I found out that wasn't the case. One of the many things she told me was that I needed to find my purpose and to surround myself with influential and powerful women as she strongly believes that one's destiny is influenced by the people around us. She also encouraged me to write my first book chapter, "Gaining My Wings to Fly, A Metamorphosis "From Pain to Freedom," which was published in "Love Your Haters," an Anthology compiled by Angela Covany.

Currently, I am working with Gina Kegel, a restorative ascension energy healer who works with The Emotion Code. She helps people release trapped emotions that are stuck in their body and that if ignored lead to physical, emotional, energetic, and psychological diseases. She is an expert at releasing blockages and trauma. With Gina, I have released trapped emotions in numbers unheard of. During each session we release sextillions of trapped emotions, and I know because I can see the results in the quality of my life.

My spiritual mentors have been a key factor in breaking the emotional blockages I carried for decades. My experiences with bullying as a child, my failed relationships and experiences of loss have shaped my life in many ways.

To be able to move forward in life and grow as human beings, we must be willing to see all aspects and versions of a story — the good, the bad and the ugly. We sometimes carry so many fears and insecurities that stop us from becoming the best versions of ourselves. Surrounding ourselves with the right people and finding the right mentors who are qualified to help us specifically in the areas we need is especially important, invaluable and life changing.

Finding Robbie Motter for me has been the biggest blessing in my life. I met her over 10 years ago while doing a fundraiser for one of her networks in the Los Angeles area. The director of her network was Alina Estrada. Alina loved working with me. She loved my work and saw the value in offering my services to her entrepreneurial members so they could update their business photos. Robbie is great at staying connected and connecting with people.

In 2020, while the pandemic was going on Robbie founded her own non-profit to assist women entrepreneurs. She invited me to her Long Beach networking chapter, and I showed up. Robbie always spoke very highly of me and my work, and she introduced me to many ladies who eventually turned into my clients.

She also invited me to her conferences and other major events. At the Long Beach network, I met Marlena Martin, director of Woman of Achievement Pageantry. Marlena loved my spirit and personality, and she invited me to participate in her upcoming pageant. I was shocked by her proposition. In my late forties, I never thought of competing in a pageant. I was curious and flattered and said yes. I had no idea what I was getting myself into. I had to prepare a speech and talk about my talents, which made me feel speechless as I was not good at public speaking.

My talent is in my photography expertise. When I spoke with Marlena, she suggested that I display my work, so I did just that. I selected three nature images for my display, and I wrote a brief description about each one.

During the pandemic, I found refuge in nature more than ever as I felt like a prisoner in my own home. I chose some shots I took during my escapes into nature because I thought they were in alignment with what was going on all around us. I knew I wasn't the only one who saw nature as a way to escape from everything. The loneliness, sadness and isolation we all felt was real. Feeling a connection with nature was a way to find some normalcy and sense in our daily lives. There was so much confusion and uncertainty in all our lives during that time.

After the pandemic, mental health and awareness was very needed. I had to decide on a platform and share a cause. So, I took this opportunity to make mental health awareness my cause and intertwine it with nature's beauty, benefits, and hidden symbolism open to interpretation. As nervous as I was, I moved forward with my talent presentation.

Although images speak for themselves and are open to interpretation, I decided to touch on the hidden symbolism of each image. As I presented my three photos, I relaxed and spoke from my heart. I took my audience on a journey as I described each one of my images.

The first one was about a cactus plant surrounded by spring poppies, with a ray of colors from orange to yellows and greens. I represented my culture as Ms. Elite Mexico-America, and those pictures depicted the vibrant colors of the Mexican culture. The yellow and orange colors are warm and inviting. The cactus is green and prickled, representing the pain we sometimes carry.

The second image depicted the Manhattan Beach pier with its infinite life force. The ocean is infinite in its waters with a never-ending flow. The waves come and go in a constant and uninterrupted giving and receiving motion. The pier resembles a gateway, a portal or door to an infinite realm of beauty with its waves crashing and creating a wonderous masterpiece.

The third image was about a sunset representing new beginnings. No matter what happens during your day, you always have a new opportunity to start fresh and make a difference the next day.

I encouraged the audience to close their eyes and use their senses. I asked them to visualize their feet touching the cold sand while they listened to the sound of the waves, breathed in the fresh sea breeze and felt the warmth of the sun caressing their faces. I finished my presentation by saying, "If life does not turn out the way you would have liked, re-adjust your focus and take another shot." Meaning, never

give up. As long as we're breathing, there's always tomorrow offering renewed hope.

My presentation turned into a speech, which was something that I was dreading to do due to my fear of public speaking. However, in life you must take chances. I went in blindly without any expectation whatsoever, and what I gained was courage and was amazed at myself. Thankfully, because of people like Marlena and Robbie who believed in me and saw

something in me that I didn't, I was able to get out of my comfort zone, do the unexpected, take another step to overcome some of my self-limiting beliefs, break barriers and boast my self-confidence.

I won first place in the talent competition. Although I did not win the crown, I walked away with an incredible experience. I was immensely proud of myself for showing up and saying yes to this opportunity. Robbie Motter always says, "Showing up is like a treasure map. You never know who you'll meet or the treasures you will find," and I have discovered this to be true. I found my own treasures through this unforgettable experience.

I have met some of the most amazing people through Robbie and her organization. GSFE motivates, uplifts, educates, and supports its members. We are never in competition with each other. Instead, we compliment and complete each other, which is what makes Global Society of Female Entrepreneurs so unique and amazing.

Eventually, through life's trials and tribulations there are certain things that we are able to see through a clear lens. The lens isn't blurry anymore. It is crystal clear. It is then that we come to realize that the people who truly love us unconditionally and want the best for us will be there for us no matter what.

They're the ones who will support us, cheer us on, and be glad for us wholeheartedly with each new milestone we reach. These are our people — the ones who want more for us and not more from us. These are the people we feel we have a bond with, are in alignment with us and vibrate on the same energetic frequency we do. The moment they show up in our lives, they stay and ride the train of life with us until the end. These are my people! These are some of life's hidden treasures and the people I look forward to creating everlasting memories!

The Train of Life

Life is like a journey on a train... with its stations...with changes of routes... and with accidents!

At birth we boarded the train and met our parents, and we

believe they will always travel on our side. However, at some station our parents will step down from the train, leaving us on this journey alone.

As time goes by, other people will board the train, and they will be significant, our siblings, friends, children, and even the love of your life. Many will step down and leave a permanent vacuum. Others will go so unnoticed that we don't realize they vacated their seats.

This train ride will be full of joy, sorrow, fantasy,

expectations, hellos, goodbyes, and farewells. Success consists of having a good relationship with all passengers requiring that we give the best of ourselves.

The mystery to everyone is: We do not know at which station we ourselves will step down. So, we must live in the best way, love, forgive, and offer the best of who we are. It is important to do this because when the time comes for us to step down and leave our seat empty, we should leave behind beautiful memories for those who will continue to travel on the train of life.

I wish you a joyful journey on the train of life. Reap success and give lots of love. More importantly, thank God for the journey.

Lastly, thank you for being one of the passengers on my train.

— Unknown Author —

Ambassador Dr. (h.c.) Elizabeth "Liz" Mejia-Celis

Liz Mejia-Celis has been an independent professional photographer since 1993. Her specialty has been family portraits, headshots, branding and glamour shots. For almost three decades she has enjoyed bringing out the best in people. With her travel studio, Photo Styles by Liz, she has brought out smiles, joy and laughter. Her photography emanates confidence, self-empowerment, self-esteem, and self-love.

In 2022, she was awarded an honorary doctoral degree in humanitarianism in London. She has also received various awards from GSFE and represented her country of origin at the 2021 Woman of Achievement Pageant as Ms. Elite Mexico-America where she won 1st Place in the talent competition with her nature photography display.

Liz is an international best-selling author, and you can find her contributions in "Love Your

Haters," "Top 100 Influential Women," "Christian Women Who Blossom" and "What Are You Wearing? The Inspirational Spiritual Side of Fashion."

She also teaches how photography relates to real life, and she strongly believes that for an image to be created it needs contrast, light, balance, and several adjustments to achieve a perfectly crafted masterpiece, a real life parallel she holds dear to her heart.

Liz may be reached via email: photostylesbyliz@gmail.com or her cell phone (323) 804-0092. You can also go to www.photostylesbyliz.com, or follow her on IG: @photostylesbyliz, or

Facebook: Liz Mejia-Celis. To save her contact information, scan the following QR Code.

ALL THE REASONS

By Gloria Favela Rocha

Growing up in a small rural farming community of North San Diego Co., amongst avocado orchards and citrus groves, was the playground for this little tom boy. Being the only girl of 7 siblings made for much imaginative play. We spent our days riding bikes, building forts, climbing trees (my personal favorite), building go carts and running around endlessly on the farm. I also wasn't aware there was a difference between a girl and a boy. My brothers always included me. I grew up adventurous and curious. There was a lot of love in this family.

The addition of a younger brother with special needs was a great reason to pull together and help with Sammys care. He became the nucleus of the family. And since I was the only girl, I helped my mom as much as a young girl could. Sammy was certainly worth all the extra efforts. He was always ready to hug and kiss us all. Around the age of 4, my parents decided that an operation to repair a hole in his heart would help him strengthen his body. While the doctors were operating on him, they discovered that his esophagus was too narrow to withstand the heart surgery. They placed a tracheostomy in hopes to expand his airway.

This also meant that he needed to stay longer in the hospital. Those days were long and difficult since he and my mama had to stay behind. Sammy would rush to the elevators to block our leaving him. We all cried. He came home with the tracheostomy, and I was able to learn how to clean it out with a little vacuum of sorts. Our little Sammy was the last thing we would see when leaving for school in the mornings, he would run to my bedroom window to send us a last wave goodbye. His sparkling, big blue eyes smiled at us.

March 27 is a day that is burned in my memory, and also the last time I saw him standing at my window. When I came home, he was napping as

usual. My mama asked me to wake him for dinner. When I walked in to get him, his beautiful lips and hands were blue and purple. Our lives changed forever. We all had a hole in our hearts. Long gone were the birthday wishes for toys. Gone were the happy Christmas lists. Sammy was the only thing I wished for. I felt different from all the kids at school. Like an alien without a ship. I didn't care much for the same things that teenagers cared for.

My first year of college, my family suffered another loss. One of my older brothers was traveling back from a motocross exhibition, when the motorhome he was driving, lost its brakes going down a steep hill. They went off the road to swerve away from traffic and the motorhome crashed and exploded. I was already very sheltered and protected, this made my parents' fears even greater. I wasn't allowed to venture far from home. I decided to study closer to home. I took an oil painting class, and it sparked something in me I hadn't ever witnessed. The birth of colors. My teacher, Charlotte Saunders, asked me one day after class, to go see a project she was working on. To my surprise this Gray-haired lady climbed up a 2-story ladder to paint the top of a saguaro cactus. After that day, she asked me to become her apprentice. 3 years of studying her every move. I listened to her Color theory. Her storytelling through imagery was magical. After those

years of learning, my master artist set me free. Charlotte told me I no longer needed her. It was bittersweet. I started my own company and lucky for me I became very busy. I painted children's murals, restaurants, and private homes. Then I expanded, even further, into commercial painting with my contractor's license in toe. The family business flourished as we grew into painting hospitals and large buildings. What a wonderful busy time. One day as we were painting hallways, I noticed a dreary Gray, unused exterior patio. I quickly drew up a mural that made this space friendly and welcoming. I put the sketch on the supervisor's desk and walked away.

Several weeks later, he approached me and asked for a more detailed.

sketch for that area. We brainstormed a project that included the vistas of that site a century ago. Historical Mural of Escondido, Ca. honoring its

farming roots, nurses, and the first Dr. of this little charming town. It

measured a whooping 250'x18 at its tallest point. I painted my heart out for an entire year. I was in heaven! The patients and staff became involved in the imagery I painted. The train depot, ice factory, family ranches, packing houses, downtown streets with their Victorian facades, were showcased in the mural.

From there I was asked to paint another large mural in the rehabilitation area that was a semi-indoor, outdoor area with a track for the patients use in therapy. This one was to include the local wildlife, landscape, and landmarks in the surrounding mountains. Bears, Mountain Lions, Owls, Roadrunners, Bobcats, were a few of the images that were depicted. The ceiling, walls, columns, and track area were all included in this project. Ceiling was 7000 sq. ft. walls over 300'x 10'. The patients that came for physical therapy 3 times a week saw the story unfold again. They would sit on the scaffold next to me, paint occasionally, but mostly reminisce about their healing journey. One patient shared that while watching me paint, her very severe pain would subside. Another nurse shared with me that she worked on their bodies while I worked on their souls. This made me weepy. And from that point forward, I knew I had to do more to help in any way I could. I went to a hospital in San Diego that had a well-established art for healing program and so began my training with them. 1½ years later, I was ready to come back to my community to start our own program. I was scared but with the help of the Doctors, Nurses, and Therapist I charged forward. The acute rehab was my first classroom.

One by one, we worked with the patients. Most of them were recovering

from brain injuries. Losing mostly the mobility in their less dominant hand. We listened to music, painted, and laughed. Sometimes, they didn't want to return to their rooms and so they stayed the hours with the other patients. They shared their stories, comforting one another. I got to witness miracles. What an honor for me to be present. Some spoke for the first time since their injury, yet others cried to see what beauty they were still able to create. My heart expands far beyond what's possible when I'm with them. Almost a decade into this journey, 3 hospital classes in, I am still in awe of them. The blind choose to come paint with me, time and time again. The speechless sing, word per word while their fingers push paint. They have taught me that we are far greater than our bodies. We are limitless Spirit.

The latest mural that I completed is Las Marias, Mother Mary, Mary Magdalena, & Mary de Cleophas. Some of the female greats in Biblical History.

We are all the Marias, dedicated, faithful, loyal, passionate, creators of life.

Gloria Favela Rocha

Gloria Favela Rocha is a 30yr professional muralist/paint contractor/art instructor that lives the mountain foothills of San Diego.

Gloria was professionally trained in oil paints and acrylic in her 20s. Became an apprentice to a muralist for 3 years before starting her own company. She also started an arts for healing program at her local hospitals in Escondido to give back to her community 8 years ago.

Gloria has exhibited in Distinctions Gallery, Escondido Arts Partnership, and in Chicano Park. Restoring 3 murals recently and heading as the female lead artist on the massive 7 story Anastacio Hernandez Mural, an enormous honor for her. 70 + murals over 30 years and counting. Painting aboard has also been a major accomplishment as well. She also painted the 1st permitted intersection mural in San Diego and helped set up guidelines for future such projects.

Gloria has been interviewed by KPBS, Palomar Live, as well as international news organizations including newspapers and magazines over the years.

Artist Gloria Favela Rocha

www.rochapaint.com

Premier Mural and Painting Services | Valley Center, CA | Rocha Murals & Paint
Contact Rocha Murals & Paint at (760) 525-2830 for top-notch mural and painting services in Valley Center, CA. Specializing in both residential and commercial projects, we offer custom murals,

painting, and carpentry services tailored to enhance your space.
www.rochapaint.com

Instagram: glorioustravels
Facebook: Gloria Favela Rocha
Email: muralglory@hotmail.com
rmpinc@yahoo.com

It's all
About
Showing
Up

From Punjab to the World: The Extraordinary Journey of GM. Dr. Jasbir Singh

By GM. Dr. Jasbir Singh

A Boy from Punjab with Big Dreams

GM. Dr. Jasbir Singh was born in Kapurthala, Punjab, a small but vibrant town where his childhood was deeply rooted in tradition and local values. His early life was simple—like most children in small towns, he attended a local school, played with friends, and had a routine that revolved around family, education, and community. But as he grew older, something unusual began to take shape within him—a burning fascination with martial arts.

His love for martial arts began unexpectedly. It was during a family movie night when he first saw Bruce Lee on the screen. Lee's speed, agility, and mastery of combat were like nothing GM. Dr. Singh had ever seen before. The way Lee carried himself, with confidence and precision, struck a chord in the young boy's mind. At that moment, GM. Dr. Singh knew martial arts was more than just a form of self-defense—it was an art form that required intense discipline, focus, and mental toughness. He was determined to master it.

In the small town of Kapurthala, martial arts training was not easily accessible. However, GM. Dr. Singh's journey began with his first martial arts teacher, Amardeep Singh Patial, who introduced him to the basics. As his passion grew, he sought out further opportunities, eventually learning Taekwondo under Grand Master Shin Byeong Hyun, a 9th Dan from Kukkiwon, South Korea. GM. Dr. Singh's dedication was relentless, and he continued his pursuit of martial arts, rising through the ranks to achieve a 5th Dan from Kukkiwon, South Korea and 7th Dan from the World Karate Federation.

Despite the challenges of a limited environment, his drive pushed him to excel. GM. Dr. Singh realized that martial arts were not just about fighting techniques; it was about building character, developing mental resilience, and maintaining a sense of humility even as one grew stronger. This philosophy shaped his teenage years, influencing his school life and his interactions with others. He became known for his discipline, focus, and dedication to martial arts.

However, as much as GM. Dr. Singh loved his hometown and the life he had in Punjab, he felt that his journey was just beginning. Deep down, he knew that martial arts could open doors to something greater. He wasn't content with just being good at the art—he wanted to use it to make a difference, not just for himself but for others as well. His dream was growing bigger by the day, and GM. Dr. Singh began to realize that his future lay beyond the borders of Punjab.

Becoming a Master of Martial Arts

As GM. Dr. Singh moved from adolescence into adulthood, martial arts had become an integral part of his identity. His dedication to the practice was relentless - he trained every day, learning new techniques, pushing his limits, and continually seeking ways to improve both physically and mentally. By the time he reached his early twenties, GM. Dr. Singh had mastered several forms of martial arts, earning respect in his community and among his peers.

He became proficient in various disciplines and earned district level then state level and eventually global recognition, representing India in world games such as the World Kickboxing Championship in Italy, World Taekwondo Championship in Paris, where he achieved 2nd place, World Karate Championship in Thailand with a silver medal, and gold medals in both the International Karate Championships in Nepal and Bangladesh.

GM. Dr. Singh also received his Ph.D. and professorship in martial arts, further solidifying his place in the martial arts community. Along with numerous hall of fame awards from countries such as the UK, Korea, China, India, Japan, Germany, Singapore, Indonesia, and Thailand, GM. Dr. Singh's accomplishments extended beyond competitions. He became the 7th Dan in the World Karate Federation and graduated as an International Master in Kukkiwon, completing the International Referee Course from South Korea.

But becoming a master was not just about perfecting combat skills. It was about understanding the deeper values that martial arts taught - discipline, self-control, humility, and respect for others. These principles became his guiding forces, not just in training but in every aspect of his life. Martial arts taught GM. Dr. Singh that real strength came from within. It was about staying grounded, even in victory, and understanding that the journey of self-improvement never truly ends.

Through his rigorous training, GM. Dr. Singh realized that martial arts were not just about personal growth; it could also be a vehicle for empowering others. As he became more skilled, he started teaching martial arts to young people in his town. He saw how learning these techniques helped them build confidence, develop discipline, and find focus in their lives. This inspired him even more - martial arts wasn't just a personal pursuit; it was a way to uplift others.

Despite his growing influence in his community, GM. Dr. Singh felt a strong urge to do more. He had reached the peak of what he could achieve locally, but he knew that martial arts had a much larger role to play on the global stage. His vision had grown beyond Punjab, and he knew that if he wanted to truly make a difference, he had to take a bold step—a leap of faith that would change the course of his life forever.

He had always admired the stories of those who pursued their dreams relentlessly, even when it required stepping into the unknown. It was with this mindset that GM. Dr. Singh made the decision to leave Punjab and move to the USA. He knew the path ahead would be challenging, but he believed that the power of martial arts could transcend borders, cultures, and languages. His journey as a master of the art was only just beginning.

The Bold Decision to Move to the USA

Leaving the familiarity of home and moving to a completely foreign land was one of the most significant decisions of GM. Dr. Singh's life. The USA was a place of immense opportunity, but it also presented countless challenges. He left behind his family, friends, and the comfort of his hometown, armed only with his martial arts skills, a burning ambition, and the hope that he could make a meaningful impact on a global scale.

When Dr. Singh first arrived in the USA, the reality hit hard. The cultural differences, financial pressures, and the overwhelming task of establishing himself in a new country were daunting. The path was far from easy. He took up various jobs to sustain himself while continuing to train and hone his martial arts expertise. It was a humbling experience, but GM. Dr. Singh had learned from martial arts that perseverance is key, and every setback is an opportunity to learn and grow.

In the early days, GM. Dr. Singh faced rejection after rejection. Breaking

into a new market, especially as an outsider, required more than just skill - it demanded resilience, networking, and a deep belief in the value he could bring to the table. Yet, he kept showing up, kept pushing forward, knowing that it was all part of the journey.

GM. Dr. Singh's journey in the U.S. taught him valuable lessons - not just in martial arts but in life itself. It reaffirmed that showing up, day in and day out, is what makes the extraordinary happen. The challenges he faced were real, but they only strengthened his resolve to make a lasting impact through his craft.

Creating Global Impact: Founding International Police Forum

With his roots firmly established in the U.S., GM. Dr. Singh recognized martial arts' potential to enhance global security, particularly in training armed forces and law enforcement agencies. This realization led him to create the International Police Forum (IPF), where he conducted numerous training sessions for armed forces around the world. The forum combined martial arts with modern policing techniques to develop skills essential for maintaining peace and safety.

With this vision in mind, GM. Dr. Singh founded several organizations focused on using martial arts to benefit society, particularly in the realm of public safety and defense. But his most significant achievement came with the establishment of the International Police Forum. This organization became a platform for collaboration, training, and the exchange of ideas between law enforcement professionals around the world.

The International Police Forum was born from the belief that martial arts, combined with modern policing techniques, could enhance the skills of law enforcement officers globally. It wasn't just about physical training—it was about instilling the mental and emotional strength needed to deal with high-pressure situations, protect communities, and uphold justice.

Through the forum, GM. Dr. Singh had the privilege of working with police forces, military personnel, and security agencies across various countries. The impact of his work was undeniable officers were not only improving their combat skills but also gaining a deeper sense of discipline, empathy, and ethical responsibility. Martial arts, in this context, became a tool for peacekeeping and conflict resolution, helping officers navigate their complex roles in an increasingly challenging world.

The creation of the International Police Forum was a milestone in GM. Dr. Singh's life. It represented the culmination of years of hard work, dedication, and an unwavering belief in the power of martial arts to transform lives. What started as a passion in the streets of Punjab had now grown into a global movement, shaping the future of law enforcement and public safety.

GM. Dr. Singh's efforts garnered lifetime achievement awards from both the IPF and the World Sports Martial Arts Council. In recognition of his work, he received accolades from Joe Biden and Donald Trump in 2023 and 2024, solidifying his influence on a global scale.

Empowering Humanity: Uniearth Humanity and Peace Foundation

The Uniearth Humanity and Peace Foundation is the culmination of GM. Dr. Singh's life's work and reflects his unwavering commitment to empowering others and creating lasting global change. Launched in the mid-2000s, the foundation focuses on humanitarian efforts, promoting peace, education, and sustainable development. GM. Dr. Singh's vision for the foundation was simple yet profound: to build a better world by empowering individuals and communities, no matter their background, to achieve their full potential.

Under his leadership, the foundation has undertaken numerous projects

around the globe, ranging from providing educational resources to underserved communities, to disaster relief efforts, and peacebuilding initiatives in regions affected by conflict. GM. Dr. Singh has partnered with international organizations, governments, and grassroots movements to ensure that the foundation's efforts reach those who need it most.

One of the foundation's flagship programs is its youth empowerment initiative, which aims to give young people the skills and tools they need to become leaders in their communities. Through a combination of martial arts training, leadership development workshops, and mentorship programs, the initiative has helped thousands of young people across the world discover their potential, build confidence, and take an active role in shaping their futures.

GM. Dr. Singh's focus on youth empowerment stems from his belief that young people are the key to a more peaceful and prosperous world. He often says, "If we can teach our youth the value of discipline, respect, and responsibility early on, we are not just creating future leaders, but we are also preventing future conflicts." His programs emphasize not just physical fitness but also mental fortitude, ethical decision-making, and a sense of responsibility toward one's community.

A Global Ambassador for Peace

GM. Dr. Singh's legacy as a martial arts master, humanitarian, and peace ambassador is vast. His work continues through the World Sport Martial Council, which he leads with over 550 members globally. He remains dedicated to using martial arts as a force for good, showing that the discipline, perseverance, and respect it teaches can transform lives and communities around the world.

As he looks to the future, GM. Dr. Singh remains focused on empowering the next generation of leaders, inspiring others to show up for their own lives, and using their talents for the greater good.

As the founder of the Uniearth Humanity and Peace Foundation, GM. Dr. Singh has earned recognition as a global ambassador for peace. His work has taken him to the halls of the United Nations, where he has been invited to speak on the importance of grassroots empowerment and the role of martial arts in conflict resolution. His message has resonated with diplomats, humanitarians, and leaders from all walks of life: real change begins at the individual level, with the cultivation of discipline, empathy, and respect for others.

GM. Dr. Singh's legacy as a martial arts master, a peacebuilder, and a humanitarian is far-reaching. Through his life's work, he has demonstrated that the values of martial arts—discipline, humility, perseverance, and respect—are universal and can be applied to solve some of the world's most pressing challenges. His journey from a small town in Punjab to the global stage is a testament to the power of passion, hard work, and the belief that one individual can make a difference.

As GM. Dr. Singh looks toward the future, his focus remains on empowering the next generation of leaders, not just in martial arts but in every field. His foundation continues to grow, expanding its reach and impact across the globe. Through his work, GM. Dr. Singh hopes to inspire others to show up for their own lives, pursue their passions with dedication, and use their unique talents to contribute to the greater good. In his words, "The extraordinary happens when you show up, again and again, with an open heart and a determined mind."

Expanding Horizons: Beyond Martial Arts into Holistic Empowerment

As GM. Dr. Jasbir Singh's reputation in martial arts grew, so did his

understanding of the broader applications of the discipline. Martial arts had taught him invaluable lessons about perseverance, focus, and personal growth, but he realized that the same principles could be applied to other areas of life as well. This epiphany became the driving force behind his next big mission: to use the core values of martial arts not just for individual empowerment, but for creating societal change.

In the 2020s, GM. Dr. Singh started collaborating with various educational institutions, integrating martial arts training into the academic curriculum. He believed that martial arts could complement traditional education by fostering emotional intelligence, resilience, and leadership skills in students. GM. Dr. Singh's innovative programs gained traction quickly, as educators and parents alike saw how students became more disciplined, confident, and focused through martial arts. His approach was holistic, teaching students not just to excel physically but to also become compassionate, well-rounded individuals capable of handling life's challenges.

This success opened up new opportunities for GM. Dr. Singh to expand his influence. He began delivering seminars and workshops across the globe, traveling to countries like Canada, Australia, and the United Kingdom to share his philosophy. What distinguished GM. Dr. Singh's teachings from those of other martial arts masters was his emphasis on the mental and spiritual aspects of the art. For him, true mastery meant achieving balance—between body and mind, ambition and humility, and power and compassion.

The Importance of Showing Up

At the heart of GM. Dr. Singh's extraordinary journey lies one fundamental principle: showing up. Whether it was as a young boy in Punjab, practicing martial arts in the streets, or as an adult in the U.S., facing countless challenges and rejections, he never stopped showing up. His success, he believes, was not born out of talent or luck, but out of perseverance and the willingness to put in the work, day after day.

GM. Dr. Singh's story serves as a powerful reminder that success is not about avoiding failures or setbacks—it's about pushing through them. It's about having the courage to keep moving forward, even when the road is tough. From being fascinated by Bruce Lee's movies as a child to being recognized as what he is today, his life has been a testament to the power of persistence.

Today, as he dedicates his life to empowering others through the Uniearth Humanity and Peace Foundation, GM. Dr. Singh's message is clear: show up for life, no matter the challenges. That's when the extraordinary happens.

GM. Dr. Jasbir Singh

GM. Dr. Jasbir Singh, born in Kapurthala, Punjab, is a globally recognized martial arts master, peace ambassador, and humanitarian leader. Inspired by Bruce Lee at a young age, he began his martial arts journey in his hometown, where he trained rigorously and achieved high ranks, including 5th Dan in Taekwondo from Kukkiwon, South Korea, and 7th Dan from the World Karate Federation. He has represented India in numerous international championships, winning accolades worldwide.

Driven by his belief in the transformative power of martial arts, Dr. Singh founded the International Police Forum (IPF), where he integrates martial arts with modern policing techniques to train armed forces globally. His contributions to public safety and peacekeeping have earned him recognition from international leaders, including Joe Biden and Donald

Trump.

In addition to his work with the IPF, Dr. Singh established the Uniearth Humanity and Peace Foundation, which focuses on humanitarian efforts, youth empowerment, and global peace initiatives. His leadership continues to inspire change, combining martial arts' values with a vision for a more peaceful and empowered world.

Official UN Representative
President – UNIGO
President – IPF (USA)
Founder/President – World Sports Martial Arts Council
Global Director – Uniearth Humanity and Peace Foundation
Phone: +1 (408) 612-5881
Email: wsmac.president@yahoo.com / info@ipfpolice.org
Address: 424 Paula court, #18, Santa Clara, California 95050

Gen. Sir Prof Dr. Jasbir Singh

OFFICIAL UN REPRESENTATIVE - PRESIDENT UNIGO / IPF-IGO (USA)

📞 +1 408 612-5881 (USA)
📞 +91 77174 27944 (INDIA)

Certified By:

✉ info@unigousa.org / wsmac.president@yahoo.com
www.unigousa.org | www.ipfpolice.org | www.globeeagle.university | www.iouhhspedu.com

SHOW UP .... DESTINY AWAITS

Have you felt that too much of life has passed by so too late to do anything of significance or to *SHOW UP* any longer? You could be sorely mistaken.

Life is not just your DOB – DOD but is in the dash between where treasures of value are located. You may not see it yet, but when you find the "purpose in the pain", as I call it, you begin to heal and the nuggets there can help shape other lives and ignite the remainder of time you have remaining on the planet we call home.

Where has your life progressed to this point? Is it all you hoped it to be or are you hungry for more? If you will *SHOW UP* right where you are now in thought and dive into this message it might provoke enlightening truths and directions to aid you on your quest.

What is life just mere happenstance - a coincidence or a series of random events? Could it be a guided pathway from others who are in one's sphere of influence? Have you considered it a predestined plan designed before a soul is fully born?

A common question children hear is "What do you want to be when you grow up?". There are those "child prodigies" and those who know at a noticeably youthful age exactly what they want to do, and as life goes on, they pursue that dream - that vision - that pathway. They choose to *SHOW UP* at opportunities needed to make it a reality.

For me, I had no idea how to answer that question. I tend to be one who takes life on a creative platform with an inner trust, that somehow everything is going to work out well. As I feel internally guided, utilizing my faith, I will SHOW UP at random opportunities. I will admit that, had I been one that knew at a youthful age the path I wanted, it would have been a less complex life, but perhaps not as interesting...who knows for certain? The opportunities to *SHOW UP* for those on a deliberately designed pathway may have afforded experiences that I had not the pleasure...however ... visa-versa could also occur.

No one person is exactly like another. Not even "identical twins" SHOW UP with an identity the same. They have similarities, but very individual aspects to their own being. To think that "THEE CREATOR" even designed us each to have unique fingerprints from any other, leaves me awe struck. I have a hard time understanding how there could be that many possibilities, yet that's one of the mysteries of GOD.

It would be wrong to say that there is only one right way in which to *SHOW UP* in life just as it would be wrong to say that there is only one right way in which to think, be, act or believe. We can tend to box in people, places, things and even GOD into attractive wrapped packages, but if we never open the package, then the treasure inside we will never experience. One beauty of human nature is that we are all individualistic. What a boring world we would live in if we were all the same. I find birthdays to be one of the most important holidays in life to SHOW UP to and celebrate the persona of a GOD given gift to the world and how they chose to SHOW UP and share their life with "little ole me."

Opinions & perceptions are as " beauty is in the eye of the beholder," my expanded version of Plato's and Shakespeare's rendition. We all see then believe in our own unique way. Ones' truth may not be fact nor fact always true. To bring clarity in decisions of when, where and how to *SHOW UP*. Wisdom may say to withhold judgement and preconceived opinions of others, do research for discovery, clear your heart by forgiving those who caused you harm, and ask for forgiveness to those you may have done the same, communicate to GOD through prayer & exercise faith that the revelational insight you uncover is" light unto your path".

One way to expand our life experiences is to SHOW UP, as frequently is possible. Each day mark opportunities. We may not always recognize them as such. In modern technology the cellular phone and ear buds have incredible benefits. However, distractions often occur and if not, mindful we may miss out by not SHOWING UP in conversations. Being double minded as multi-tasking takes priority. By making a choice to set the (possible) addictive instruments aside it can allow the parties to converse to all SHOW UP and be present and engaged in activities at hand. Who knows what nuggets they might uncover in those moments! Intimacy broken down as Into-me-see is a critical component in our nature. "No man is an island". We need one another to *SHOW UP*.

"To thine own self be true". The problem may exist when a soul is trying to fit into something they are not thus the "square peg in a round hole" syndrome. With valuable time spent in that uncomfortable even awkward position it can cause regret and dissatisfaction to clutter the heart. Dangers may arise from that place... one being to seclude and stop SHOWING UP as shutting down sets in. Oh, what may we miss with these missed opportunities? That is when "community", of those closest in heart and spirit, are most needed to SHOW UP and lend loving aid with a hand to lift one out of a pit of despair. See, your time to SHOW UP, in this manner, might be to help another in need. It may not be for your gain but theirs to receive.

We just never know what lies ahead and how our lives could take a twist in our path as we *SHOW UP*. It just may be the next steppingstone to something great because we chose to SHOW UP. What if that was the opportunity to meet your soulmate, and you chose not to go? What if that opportunity were to meet a person that could launch your business, or your invention, and you decided not to attend? What is your WHAT IF's; your heart's desire, your vision, your passion, your dreams which could come true just because you chose to SHOW UP?

At the beginning I posed a question *"WHAT IS LIFE... "* in your opinion. Have you reached a conclusion yet? I pose that Life is a combination of all three. Just our journeys take us on different pathways to reach the goal line of that predestined plan, the most pertinent being to our creation, by GOD ALMIGHTY. We can receive empowerment when we are willing to fulfill that calling because we chose the gift and to *SHOW UP* to be GOD's hands, feet and mouthpiece extended.

The takeaway from my message to you is this...

Think about what you may be missing by choosing NOT the opportunities to SHOW UP. Then weigh that to what you may gain; for example, what might be the answer you've been seeking, who might be the person you've hoped for, what healing might you have received, what might be a joy your heart has need of what might be a key to unlock your DIVINE DESTINY! These may motivate you to *SHOW UP!*

My prayer is that my readers find a nugget of value within these words that will light a spark of excitement to open the wrapped box revealing new horizons of opportunities. GOD does not make junk! YOU are of amazing value to this world, and we all need to experience the beauty and wonder

of the masterpiece designed in YOU as <u>YOU SHOW UP walking in your</u> <u>DIVINE DESTINY!</u>

GOD *SHOWED UP* & *SHOWED OFF* when HE created YOU.

So, how about it? Is it your time to ...

SHOW UP...because...*DESTINY AWAITS!*

penned by Jayne Jorden-Gavin
5 October, 2024

BIO & CONTACT INFO

MISSION STATEMENT

To promote inspiration and help others overcome obstacles. Utilizing love for the theater arts & ministry hearted Inspirational writings developed from pursuing life experiences and lessoned gained.

BACKGROUND * INTERESTS * QUALIFICATIONS

Jayne's lifetime array of occupations encompasses service for those in need. With a background of stage performance (beginning at age 3), a creative flare and heart for the "black sheep, disabled, rejected, and under-dogs" in life... it paved the road through varying occupations weaving in ministry opportunities through customer service, management, merchandising, vocational education, training & caring for special needs and disabled population. Her love for cooking and creating recipes as well as decorating and organizing leads to talents effective for event planning and orchestration, floral/interior design, marketing & development. Entrepreneurial minded she developed a Senior Living Community Program which led into the Real Estate & Mortgage lending industry where she could help other achieve the American Dream through alternate pathway than the conventional methods. As the real estate market changed drastically in 2009 so did her life's direction resulting in a season of overcoming tremendous loss. Jayne is acquainted with grief through multiple experiences: the loss of two children, a terminally ill husband, the loss of her father...her "rock", followed by another marriage to a bi-polar alcoholic husband that led to abuse & loss of business and real estate investments finally released through divorce. She currently has the privilege of caring for her aging mother ... a ministry of heart. All enabling and qualifying her as an OVERCOMER producing PASSION in COMPASSION to nurture and counsel those walking through similar journeys.

Since the super-natural side of life holds great interest to Jayne, she developed her personal relationship with Jesus Christ and the love of GOD grew exponentially as she became His follower. This love relationship resulted in ordination into ministry in which she holds a "Care Pastor" position and published writer engaging inspirational messages as her focus.

PROFESSIONAL ASSOCIATIONS

Co-Founder and facilitator of "For You" Professional Women's Network, Founder and facilitator of Biz 2 Biz Network-Marketing, facilitator of PWR (Professional Women's Roundtable), facilitator the Senior Network-Marketing. President of a BNI

(Business Network International) chapter, Board member of The

Alzheimer's Association and currently a member of GSFE (Global Society of Female Entrepreneurs)

Founder

CREATIONAL CONCEPTS, LLC

A multifaceted organization embracing opportunities with aim in serving others with betterment for humanity.

Author

ON MY ♥ Inspirational nuggets found on life's journey

Jayne shares from her heart and life experiences through public speaking and writings. With a heart to minister to women as being a product of overcoming abuse and obstacles which her writings of On My ♥ Inspirational Nuggets found on life's journey came into being...

how to make "Better out of Bitter".

Author

SHOWING UP FOR THE MASTERS PLAN

It' All About Showing UP   Vol II   *International Best Seller*

(a collaborative project)

Author

P.E.A.C.E ... FINDING YOURS

Voices of Peace   *International Best Seller*

(A collaborative project)

Author

BEncouraged NOW... everything is subject to change

A personal inventory & devotional workbook based on a collection of ON MY ♥ nuggets

(in process)

Founder

Be-A-Claus ... for a Cause

ministry.

Partnered with spouse and likeminded volunteers to develop a ministry known as Be-A-Claus for a Cause. Providing opportunities to GIVE like the famous gift giver (S Claus) and LOVE like the Greatest Gift (Jesus).

Costumed to bring smiles to hearts who know S Claus, in one way or another yet may not know Jesus. A vehicle to introduce and be His hands extended, a children's book (in the making), aimed at the children in all of us, describes the "Famous gift giver" meeting the "Greatest Gift". The vision is global in inviting others to "Be-A-Claus" as you become the storyteller and catalyst in gaining volunteers to meet needs.

CONTACT INFO :

Book Purchases
Event Coordinating
Floral & Décor Design / furnishing placement
Lay Counsel & Consultations
Ordained Minister Services
Public Speaking
Q & A
Volunteer Opportunities

CreationalConcepts@gmail.com
OnMyHeart@gmail.com
Location:
Myrtle Beach, South Carolina USA

Website
CreationalConcepts.com

Facebook
https://www.facebook.com/jayne.triplettjorden?mibextid=ZbWKwL

LINKEDIN
www.linkedin.com/in/jayne-jorden-gavin-88238575

It's truly all about SHOWING UP and ASKING

By Ambassador Jean Olexa

My name is Ambassador Jean Olexa, but many call me MS.O. I have seen firsthand the power of SHOWING UP and ASKING, and how the right combination can lead to incredible opportunities. Originally from the East Coast, I now reside in California. My life is a tapestry woven with experiences that have taught me the importance of being present and the magic that can follow an inquiry.

The Essence of SHOWING UP

As an Organizer, I understand that being effective in this role starts with one fundamental principle – SHOWING UP. Whether it's at an event, a meeting, or simply helping someone who needs organization, arriving on time and being fully present is crucial, the act of being there physically translates into emotional and mental availability for the task at hand.

When I assist others in organizing their lives or their spaces, I often remind them that the process involves making decisions. So, while I SHOW UP ready to help, I must ASK questions like, "Do you want to keep this," or "What are your priorities?" This dialogue not only aids in the organization but also empowers individuals to think critically about their possessions and their lives.

Unexpected Opportunities

I've also learned about the power of SHOWUNG UP through my travels. One memorable experience happened while I was visiting my son Tom on the East Coast on the Fourth of July. Admittedly, I was hesitant to join his family to go to his friend's house for the fireworks that night. However, I pushed myself outside of my comfort zone and decided to go, and I am so glad that I did.

That evening turned into an extraordinary spectacle featuring $40,000 worth of fireworks-on an incredible display that was nothing short of breathtaking. More importantly, however, was the social aspect of that night; By SHOWING UP, I made new friends and deepened my relationships with my family. The event has now become a cherished annual tradition, and I no longer hesitate to participate.

I always express to my grandchildren Jada, Ted, Austin, Neil, Nate Xavier, Alana and Allison, the Power of SHOWING UP and ASKING and I remember one summer one of my grandchildren Austin flew to my sons in Virginia and because he showed up he learned about hunting and fishing and got his first deer and was so thrilled that he SHOWED UP and could learn from his Uncle Tom who is an avid fisherman and sportsman.

Another grandson Nate recently went to Colorado to visit friends and went to a baseball game, and he was standing in line and recognized this very famous celebrity and said are you so and so, the person replied yes, I am and he was able to have a discussion with him that thrilled him had he not made the trip and SHOWED UP that opportunity would have never happened.

Encouraging My Daughters

As a mother of two daughters, Kimie and Kerrie. I have always encouraged Kerrie to exemplify this principle during her senior year of college. I urged her to approach the President of Misericordia University and ASK about the possibility of applying for an Internship for an Intern program at Walt Disney World in Florida. She was nervous at first wondering if she should even take the leap. When she summoned the courage to ASK, she was granted a historic opportunity: she became the first intern from her college at that program. This incident reinforced my belief that magic often happens when we ASK, despite our fears of rejection.

There are innumerable reasons we hesitate to request opportunities; often, it's the fear of hearing "no" that holds us back, yet, many times, the response we receive is a positive affirmation. It's crucial not to let fear silence our desires or ambitions.

A Lesson in Persistence

Another story that underscores the importance of SHOWING UP and ASKING involves my daughter, Kerrie who is a physical therapist. She was on the hunt for a job but was apprehensive about reaching out to her neighbor who worked at the location she really wanted to work. After hearing her hesitation, I encouraged her to take the chance. It turned out that they indeed were hiring-and soon, she found herself in a position she loved. This experience taught her that sometimes, simply putting yourself out there can lead to the fulfillment of your dreams.

Embracing Changes

In my myriads of roles throughout life, one particularly surprising career switch involved being a Nanny, so after moving from New Jersey to California I needed a job. So, I ASKED around- and soon found a position that aligned perfectly with my skills and lifestyle. However, as life would have it, an unexpected opportunity arose when my cousin invited me to Slovakia to teach about our heritage. Wanting to embrace this rare chance. I had to make the difficult decision to step away from my current job as a Nanny. In that moment, by SHOWING UP and saying "yes" to the opportunity I was able to embark on a once-in-a-lifetime journey.

Creativity and Community

I have a passion for designing opportunity baskets and creating floral arrangements, which I developed while living on the East Coast. My love for floral art translates beautifully into my current involvement with the Global Society for Female Entrepreneurs (GSFE), a nonprofit organization I am proud to be part of. Whenever GSFE hosts events, I make it a priority to SHOW UP and contribute in any way I can, whether it's through arranging flowers, decorating tables, or helping to coordinate logistics.

Within this community, I have learned that collaboration can lead to astonishing outcomes. Not only does our shared work exemplify the power of SHOWING UP, but the relationships we build help support each other's individual goals.

The Ripple Effect of SHOWING UP and ASKING

My journey has taught me that SHOWING UP and ASKING creates a ripple effect that spreads beyond our immediate circumstances. Every time I've

taken the step to SHOW UP for myself or for others, magical opportunities have unfolded. By encouraging those around me to do the same, I aim to empower them through my life's lessons.

To anyone reading this, remember that every moment holds a potential, it may be a simple call to a friend, visiting a local event, or even reaching out to someone in a position of power. You never know what beautiful opportunities await you on the other side of ASKING.

Conclusion

As I continue to navigate life as Ms. O, I will always advocate for the importance of SHOWING UP and ASKING. There will always be risk involved, but the rewards often far outweigh the fear. Let us cultivate a culture of boldness and inquiry, one that doesn't shy away from opportunities but instead wholeheartedly embraces them. The stories we create and the connections we forge will be endless if we choose to SHOW UP and ASK.

This chapter isn't just a collection of my experiences; it's a call to action. Let's not wait for chances to come to us. Instead let's be proactive, SHOW UP, and ASK for what we desire -with faith in the possibilities that lie ahead.

Ambassador Jean Olexa

Ambassador Jean Olexa is a Business and Home Organizer, and experienced as a Nanny, also an Award-winning author, a mother and grandmother, she is a member of the Menifee GSFE.

She can be reached at: 858-357-7295. Email: geigi8247@gmail.com, website Otobeorganized.com

It's all
About
Showing
Up

The Power of Showing Up to Serve Up and Glow Up

By Ambassador Jennifer Jrock Blake

The Seed of Understanding

The story of my life begins with a little seed planted within me that has profound understanding of the power of Showing up. I am blessed to have spent my life Showing Up for all the seasons and storms of life. When you Show up and serve you grow and glow with new strength and purpose. Each time you Show up, the lil seed is sprinkled with blessings to help you grow and bloom into your garden of life.

This power of Showing up first appeared when I opened my eyes in a new world and Showed up into a new family. Two amazing people Ken and Linda Blake, did the most selfless thing and opened up their hearts and home to bring me into their family, made up of Linda, Ken, and their adopted son Christopher, who welcomed me and adopted me into the Blake family. This was a blessing that helped the lil seed in me begin to bloom and take the first steps to walking into the woman I am today.

The Storm that Changed Everything

One of the most pivotal moments in my life was when I was a small child our family was moving to a new city. We loaded the car the day after a hurricane and hit the road. Little did we know that storm left its mark. While driving east on Interstate 80 traveling through the small town of Silvis, Illinois the car slid through a puddle, hydro-planed and careened down an embankment flipping multiple times.

In those terrifying moments as the car bounced and hit the ground I was thrown from the front seat and flew face first through the windshield landing into the unknown. My family couldn't find where I landed but that lil seed inside me instinctively knew to Show up and it was a miracle that my brother found me.

An Angel, driving an 18-wheeler, saw the accident and stopped to help our family. He lifted us all out of the car and transported us to a local hospital.

I Showed up to Silvis Hospital in Critical Condition, every bone was broken, lungs punctured and collapsed, cuts and bruises from head to toe.

I was immediately sent to ICU and put on life support. The doctors gave me 2 weeks to live, I was there for over 200 days. That lil seed survived that 2-week diagnosis and is living against all odds for over 14,600 days and counting.

Even in my darkest moments the lil seed in me refused to give up and learned the power and importance of Showing up. With the support of doctors, family and friends I left the hospital and came out stronger than when I arrived.

The Journey After Recovery

Then continued watering, that lil seed gave me the courage to take my first steps and head to kindergarten. From the moment I stepped foot in

the classroom a joy for learning and love of school and making friends was born. Reinforcing the belief that Showing up could be full of great fun and opportunities.

Through my education journey I kept nurturing that lil seed, giving me the courage to apply to college, graduate with honors and take the next step to apply to Graduate School. I was blessed to get into a University in Miami Florida but was soon hit by another storm. The week I was to start my first year of graduate school - a hurricane roared through Miami and wiped-out parts of the city and school. I had to adapt, pivot and select new a school.

Within in a few days I Showed up on the campus of Towson University in Baltimore, Maryland to start my master's program and was able to graduate with honors and a Master of Science. This taught me that sometimes

Showing Up can change directions but when it does it can lead down a path to amazing new things!

Embracing the Seed of New Adventures

Upon graduating I was offered a wonderful job in Baltimore, Maryland as District Operations Manager with Entertainment Publications. I Showed Up, served up and embraced my new career with open arms. Within a few short months I grew into a new position of Northeast Regional Manager, and then quickly advanced to take over the West Coast as Division Operations Manager. I packed up my life and relocated 2200 miles to San Diego, California the land of Surfing, Sunshine and Endless Adventures.

I loved my job but after a few years the lil seed whispered a new dream and needed to spread its wings and take flight on a new adventure that landed me in Orlando, Florida. I Showed Up, served up and opened a new women's fitness center, the first one in the state, Curves Fitness Center, then with a little love, sweat and tears, that seed bloomed and expanded into 4 fitness center locations. We cultivated more than just a business but created a community where we celebrated successes, counted calories and blessings, and members became friends that turned into family.

After a decade of owning and managing the fitness centers, adventure beckoned, and the lil seed of a dream took flight, landing me back in San Diego, California for my second tour.

Though I left a huge piece of my heart in Florida, I knew it was time to soar and create new memories and start over on the West Coast.

This new adventure gave me the chance to show up and launch a career in marketing and digital media—an exciting journey I still cherish every day.

Though I left a huge piece of my heart in Florida, I knew it was time to soar and create new memories and start over on the West Coast.

The Seed of Love

Then one sunny Sunday summer afternoon I Showed up with friends to see a good friend and musician play live at a local bar in Pacific Beach. While I was there a young man Showed up. As I was about to leave, the bar tender told me our tab was taken care of by a young man. With that one act of kindness, that young man became my boyfriend and later became my husband. This proved that you never know what will happen when you Show Up. Even Love can bloom.

The Seed of Zen

The Stars aligned, and I was able to Show Up to pursue another passion and get certified in Yoga.

The lil seed grew to learn the power to Show up and serve up. We were given two hands, one to help ourselves and one to help others. I use my heart and hands to help serve others – one way is through my gift and love of Yoga, to teach others to stretch the mind, body and spirit to find peace and joy.

I invite others to Show up on their mats and join a yoga class with me.

I Show up for friends and family on good days and bad in sickness and health – I am there for family and friends – I believe in Showing Up to be there when people have needs.

I Show up as a member in many Organizations to build community to help and serve others. One of my favorites is Global Society of Female Entrepreneurs we don't compete we complete! We Rise by Showing Up and helping others.

The Seed of HOPE

This lil seed continued to grow with love and compassion I was inspired to Show up and create "Pearls of HOPE" With the Mission to "HELP OTHER PEOPLE EVERYDAY."

Through acts of love and kindness we raise funds and awareness for local and global organizations. Discover the joy of giving by purchasing Pearls of Hope, where every donation supports a variety of charitable organizations.

I realized that we rise by helping others and each pearl is a symbol of Hope. Each strand represents people connected through passion and purpose.

Pearls serve as a reminder that something small and basic can create extraordinary beauty. Just like people, Pearls, are not created in a day, they are formed from enduring pressure and overcoming challenges. I learned that the lil seed growing within me through the years grew and developed into a Pearl that Stands out, Shows Up and Shines within.

Reach out and share if you know someone or an organization that can benefit from our support. We would love to help and Show Up for your charity/organization.

Embracing Every Season

As I reflect on my journey, I realize that the power of Showing Up has been a constant theme throughout my life. From my early days with my adoptive family to the challenges of recovery and the joys of new beginnings. I have learned to approach each season with an open heart. The world is a beautiful place and every time we Show up, we can unwrap treasures and blessings that enrich our lives.

My motto "Show Up and Smile" serves as a daily reminder to "See Miracles In Life Every Day." Through all my scars and bruises God gives me the strength and courage to Show Up.

The Seed of Action

As I turn the page and leap into the start of a new chapter, I am reminded that Showing Up is an ongoing process. It's about being present for

ourselves and others, even when it's challenging. When life knocks you down, I urge you to stand up, rise up, and Show Up. Together, we can create a community built on support and love, where we uplift each other to reach our hopes and dreams.

Embrace the power within you, and remember that every time you Show Up, you are nurturing the little seed of strength and purpose that lies within. The world awaits your presence—unwrap the treasures and blessings that life has to offer, and let your journey inspire others to do the same.

Come and join me lets Show Up, Serve Up and Glow Up and continue to grow, connect and help others together.

Thank You, Peace Love & Blessings,

Jennifer Jrock Blake

Ambassador Jennifer "Jrock" Blake

The Co-Director of the GSFE Oceanside, California, she leads with a heart full of compassion and a spirit dedicated to making a difference. Jennifer is an Ambassador of Kindness & Happiness, believing in the power of two hands—one to help yourself and one to serve others.

Her mission is to spread love and light through her passions: fitness, fashion, and fun. Every day is a fashion show, and the world is her runway! Join Jrock on her journey as she continues to inspire and uplift those around her, proving that with a little kindness and a lot of heart, we can all make the world a better place.

Follow on Instagram @JrockJenn

Follow on Facebook @JenniferJrockBlake Email Jrockjenn@gmail.com

50ShadesFab.com

JrockJen.com

It's all
About
Showing
Up

Cloistered Cinderella

By Ambassador Dr. (h.c.) Joan Wakeland

"We cannot become what we want by remaining what we are."

Max Depree

Have you ever thought about why you were born? What was your purpose? Why am I going through what I'm going through right now? If you have at any point thought of any of these questions, I would like to say that you're not alone. Read that quote again and realize that change has to happen! It is inevitable! If you ever feel stuck, show up and ask for help!

Let me share a little about my background. I grew up in Jamaica and migrated to United States in the late seventies. I was a Registered Pharmacist, educated at the University of Technology. I was an Owner/Operator of a Pharmacy but in my 37th year I had to make an impulsive decision to migrate leaving everything behind! I was threatened and feared that my six-year-old son would not have a mother. I wanted to take care of him since I was privileged to give birth to him.

I did not want grandparents or a stepmother to raise him! Call me selfish, and I am okay with that!

I had great parents. My husband had great parents. However, I had seen, not heard, seen how a stepchild was treated unfairly, and I did not want that to happen to him. This was the turning point of my life. I had to make an important decision. In those days holding up a businessperson involved violence and possibly death. Should I stay and face a gunshot, or should I stay and have acid thrown in my face? Should I run for freedom with my six-year-old baby boy? What would you do? I chose to "Run For Freedom" which is the title of my book available on Amazon. Lady Dr Robbie encouraged me to write that book. I did not think that I had the ability to write a book. I started to write it as information for my grandchildren. I wanted them to know how their father and I struggled. I wanted them to know that we were not quitters. When I was finished with the manuscript, I shared it with one of my neighbors who encouraged me that I should have it published. I was very surprised and excited when it became a number one bestseller and international bestseller. I am forever grateful for the support from my GSFE Sister Friends and well-wishers.

My father was a property owner, a Philanthropist and a Justice of the Peace. My mother was a teacher before marrying my father. It was customary for a husband to provide for his wife and children, so my mother did not work. She also had helpers. I had a younger brother. As children, we had the opportunity of going to good schools. We were taught many life lessons by our mother. She gave us many examples through story telling.

I would like to share a story that is indelible in my mind. I was about ten years old. This is not fictitious. We were sitting on the veranda when a man barely made it up the hill to ask for some water and money. He had a lame foot; he was in tattered clothing, and he had a very bad odor. Mother got up, told us to come with her. She told him she would be right back. He sat on the steps and rested a while. She returned with a glass of water and some money. After drinking the water, he asked if he could stay the night.

She told him she could give him some food, but he would have to move on because she did not have a place for him. Even if there was an available room, his malodor would be a deterrent to have him around for a night. She fixed a plate of food and offered it to him. He voraciously ate it! When he was finished eating, he gave her his "God bless you" and hobbled down the hill. As he was departing, mother told my brother and I that this man was a school mate of my father. He was from a family that had money and when his father died, he got a big inheritance. However, he squandered it away on trucks, alcohol, parties, and friends. When he lost his fortune, he also lost his friends. She told us to be kind to the people in need. She also said that we need to recognize who is a friend. However, we should know the difference between being kind and being used. We should value ourselves and know that not everyone that is partying with us in good times will be there for us when hard times come. Remember life has no guarantees! So bad times will happen. When the bad times come, use them as lessons. Start again, pray for guidance and don't do anything hastily!

Before going to bed mother would read or tell us a story! Most of the time it was a Bible story!

We did not have TV when I was a child. We read books, played board games and dominoes. We listened to the radio! We were not lacking the basic necessities.

We were happy because that was all we knew.

My parents were very strict. I was not allowed to date until I was twenty years old. My brother said that I lived in a Convent. He was partially right because my first suitor was a man of the cloth! He was able to go out with his friends. My parents reminded me that I had to make good choices in life as they were not going to be with me all the time. I would be the one responsible for the outcomes if or when I made bad choices. With that said, I would be very careful about the decisions I would make. I knew who would face the consequences! Certainly not Momma or Daddy!

Fast forward, in 2001, I was invited to attend a karaoke event at a restaurant in Menifee. I showed up! I had the pleasure of meeting a woman who sang in English and French. Her voice was beautiful, she introduced herself as Nicole Farrell. I told her I was new in the area. I cannot sing but I love listening to music. Abe, the owner of the restaurant, introduced me to Lady Dr. Robbie Motter that evening. These two ladies, Lady Dr Robbie and Nicole impressed me, they were introducing me to so many people! My life would never be the same again!

I was invited to join them at a NAFE networking event. I showed up and met more people. I realized that Lady Robbie was a great connector because I met so many people through her. Many were influencers in the community who I would have never met if I never left my comfortable rocking chair to initially meet her!

Life was never meant to be simply go to school, get a job, work hard, chase money, buy a car, buy a house, go to church, and then die! My life when I came to the United States was routinely going to work and taking care of my child. I worked Monday through Friday. Saturday was self-care and shopping day everything got done for self-care first. Sunday was church day and preparation day for the next week! Absolutely a mundane life! I was a workaholic!

I got involved in Serving in 1996. I was a member and officer of an American Businesswomen's Association and Kiwanis International before moving to Menifee. I was ready to serve in this community. I am often asked "When do you find the time to do all the activities that you are involved in?" My answer to that is "If you are operating a purposeful way of life and you are passionate about your mission then you learn to prioritize! My mission

was "paying it forward by feeding the hungry" I had to give back to the country that gave myself and my son the opportunity to be successful!" Lady Dr. Robbie Motter was looking for a Director to expand the National Association of Female Executives I asked her if I would be a good fit for that position.

I retired from Corporate America and became the Director for NAFE Rancho Cucamonga Chapter. I volunteered in the Lions Club and served as the President for the General Federation of Women in Menifee from 2018 -2020. I was serving with those organizations because Lady Dr. Robbie Motter was the conduit, she introduced me to them!

She became my coach and my mentor!

She was seeing my ability to lead, my ability to make things happen, my ability to connect and help others to achieve their goals.!

You have seen in the previous paragraphs my life in the area of service. Now I will share how I benefited personally.

I would accompany Lady Dr. Robbie to several functions, many of which were connected to GSFE Chapter meetings. On each occasion I would meet new people and reconnect with others. I started to build relationships with many. Currently I am one of the GSFE Riverside network Directors. I have had great exposures because of Showing Up

I have experienced what "Showing Up" and Serving can do for your community and for you personally.

It has been twenty-three years since I met Lady Dr. Robbie Motter, we both have grown over these years. I am thankful for her support, mentoring and encouragement. Lady Dr. Robbie helped me to move from my rocking chair where I stayed comfortably. I was busy rocking but going nowhere.

Today, you may be in that comfort zone, your time may be consumed with busyness. You may be tired of not getting the results you need, and you are ready to throw in the towels. I am encouraging you not to quit. Instead, take the focus off yourself and help someone. It is in helping others that you will find joy, peace, and achieve what you desire. It's amazing how we need each other, it's amazing how doors open for you when you serve! I learned how to build relationships first. I learned how to listen patiently when people talk about themselves!

I learned how to share resources!

I have learned how to write; encouraging people to live without focusing on stuff that really does not matter!

I learned how to be a connector! I learned how to choose my words and communicate positively!

While serving for the organizations I met mayors for different cities, council men, senators and distinguished people from other countries. I received many awards that are too numerous to mention!

When I showed up at the Long Beach GSFE Chapter in 2020, I met Marlena Martin the Founder and CEO of The Women of Achievement. She invited me to participate in a Pageant. I told her my age, and that I was not interested!

Later in the week she called me back, I changed my mind when she thoroughly explained what her company stood for.

I was sponsored by some friends and enjoyed being there. It was a lot of fun and I met some great people. There were different categories for the participants. My category was Ms. Elegance International. I left there

as a Winner! It boosted my confidence, and I enjoyed every minute of it. My platform was feeding the hungry and I took home the trophy for my presentation! I was a happy person!

In 2022, Lady Dr. Robbie called me. She invited me to join her at the Cherry Hills golf club. She was there to support Nicole and wanted me to do likewise. I showed up. She introduced me to a man that was sitting one chair away from her. She said, "Joan, meet Charlie". Then she added that Charlie was there for the first time. He was looking to meet friends since he lost his wife. He just wanted to meet females. She laughingly said, "I told him I am not looking, but I know a lot of females." I was not looking either and sat between them. Nicole played some songs that I liked so I was shaking my foot and enjoying an Elvis's song when Charlie asked me if I wanted to dance. I said "Sure" When it ended, we went back to our seats. He asked me if I would be interested in seeing Elvis's movie that would be in the theater the following week. I said sure.

Charlie asked for my number, I gave it to him but apparently it was not saved. It is now time to go to the movies and he could not contact me. His only hope was to return to the club and see if I was there. I was not there! He saw Charmaine, who managed the club, and asked her if she knew me. Charmaine called me for permission to give him my number. He called and we had our first movie date night!

The meetings with Charlie became more frequent and after eighteen months we finally committed ourselves to each other!

I would like to encourage single women not to say you will never meet the love of your life. You don't know what God has planned for you. Choose to speak positive words!

I have been without a companion for 40 years. That is a long time. That is the amount of time that Moses had the Israelites in the desert! Some people find their lover when they are young! Others when they are older. I am 83 years old, and Charlie is younger.

We are loving our life and enjoying our blessings!

We are happy, we have fun together. Each day we thank God for another day!

I wish that you will speak positive words to yourself. Show up with an open mind and embrace new opportunities in your journey!

Ambassador Dr. (h.c.) Joan Wakeland

Ambassador Dr. h.c. Joan E Wakeland is an International Bestselling Author, International Speaker, and an Empowerment Facilitator.

Presently, she is the Director of the Riverside affiliate of the Global Society of Female Entrepreneurs in California.

Over the years, she has received many Awards including the "The Lifetime Achievement Award" from the last three Presidents of the United States. She also received the "Call to Service" and numerous awards from Senators, Congress & dignitaries.

She won the title for Ms. Elegance International in the Woman of Achievement Pageant in September 2021. In December 2021, she was honored as Citizen of the Month by The Mayor and City Delegates for her service to the city of Menifee.

Joan received the "She Inspires Me Award" (SIMA) International Global Award from London, England.

In 2022 she was awarded an honorary humanitarian doctorate degree for her service to others.

The title of Ambassador was awarded to her in May 2024.

Contact Information

Email: joanewakeland@gmail.com

Cell: (951) 400-5341

A Treatise About Showing Up and Asking
By Ambassador John Connor

The common thread of this collection of personal stories is based on the need for all of us to "Show Up and Ask." With all the means for remote communication readily available to all of us today, the ease of video conferencing from home, hearing all about it later from someone who was there, reading about it in the next email, and saving all that travel time and money... well it doesn't seem practical or necessary to leave the house.

So, it doesn't seem necessary to Show Up, and we can Ask online during our remote meeting or Ask somebody later who went. What it was all about, who did you see there, what did they say, did anything exciting happen? I mean, if you didn't go you know most of the people who probably did, and everybody knows you anyway, so you can ask them later, right?

You may already be ahead of me. Let's go back it time... When I was a kid, my Dad told me that the Circus was coming to town, so the whole family was going!! Being young and all knowing I informed my Dad that I had already watched a circus show on TV last month. My Dad said "No you didn't, you must be there to get the "roar of the grease paint. the smell of the crowd." So, what was I going to miss? Answer: Totally Everything!

You experience the vibe of a circus on TV or online. You didn't Show Up.

So okay, a meeting up with friends over dinner, or the family holiday reunion, or the 10 th High School Reunion was not as full of things for us to see/hear/smell/taste/touch as a Circus. So then, why did we go anyway??

We are getting closer now to answering the question about, why Show Up!!

When we went to a meeting, an event, a reunion, or a New Years Eve Parade, we went there for more than that. You'll hear about it later. Otherwise, you missed it.

Showing Up at any gathering is important for many reasons, the deeper reason for having the gathering is to collectively share with each other not only your gift of knowledge, but your smiles and sympathy, private concerns, stories of family and life, the reason you came, to meet a new friend for life, ideas about expanding your business, those things and many more.

So now, where does the Asking part of all of this come in? Ask what??

Well, now that you have arrived, this is the simplest part of the Showing Up.

President Kennedy said it in his 1961 inaugural speech, "So, my fellow Americans: Ask not what your country and do for you – ask what you can do for your country." So why did he say that? Because we all need to ask for anything to follow!

Not just questions about what we can do for the group, but also specific questions and ideas about our own individual and business concerns. Asking questions or for help with ideas and problems does help us all collectively move in the right direction, and we all get to the right answers, or make the helpful moves that were asked for, every Ask has a purpose.

At a GSFE gathering are you there to ask for help for your business and for yourself, or what has been going on at the GSFE meetings that you missed, or what can I do now that I am here to help…, yes, yes, and yes.

You are asking questions to help both GSFE, and importantly, yourself!

The more you ask, the more you know, the more you have something to tell.

- Asking for help will improve personal interactions and build trust.
- Asking questions stimulates creativity and individual motivation.
- Asking leads the way to understanding the concerns of others.
- Asking helps us identify and fill gaps in our own understandings.
- Asking questions encourages group participation of final decisions.

So, how do I know all of this to be true?? Well, it all happened to me on my first invitation to join the GSFE organization 3 years ago. I asked Robbie Motter how I could help in a Global Society organization. "I'm on this mountain top in Lake Arrowhead Ca, not exactly a global reach out place!

Well, she says, first you come (Show Up) to our society meetings that are all around SoCal. Then we get (ask) someone to start a chapter here in Lake Arrowhead (Charmaine Summers asked), and then we will use the Tudor House as our meeting location and expand GSFE to the Mountain. All of that was done.

As the GSFE expands around the world, and you get the urge to travel, you should plan on making that trip… not just to Show Up, but to meet all of the new people, so that you can Ask them "How can I help you… now"??

Ambassador John Connor

Born in 1944 Snohomish WA and lived in Perryman MD until 1962
Went to Drexel Univ. PA (Physics) 62-67
Captain in the US Air Force during Vietnam Chem/Bioweapons 67-72
Went to Duke Univ. NC (MBA) 72-74
Work in the EPA NC and TVA TN both Federal Gov Agencies 74-78
Work for Atlantic Richfield Oil (ARCO) CO Tax Mgr and Lobbyist 78-82
Work for Booz Allen as the Western Regional Corp Tax Mgr 82-90
Started my Tax Consulting Co. CA The Western Treasury Group 90-03
Retired and bought a ranch in the Bitterroot Valley MT 03-05
Work for Villa Ford Motor Co. CA as their CFO 05 - 07
Created the Tudor House/BFM Hotel Lake Arrowhead CA 07-24
 Married (Ex) with 3 children Jennifer 72 Tracy 74 Sean 78
Mr. Connor is a proud sponsor of many GSFE events.
Contact: John Connor Cell:949.922.3435 or
Email: JohnTudorHouse@gmail.com

It's all
About
Showing
Up

To SHOW UP or Not to Show Up
By Dr. (h.c.) Kaye Sheffield, M.S., CCC-SLP

Have you ever NOT wanted to show up when everything was planned, prepared, scheduled, and even paid for? I was recently in that position. The trip was planned and even paid for, and I was excited about going, but then I wasn't excited about going. It was out of the country, on the other side of the world. It was a BIG climate change. Did they speak English? Did they have clean water? Where would we stay at different points of the trip? I had so many questions. I felt safe at home, in my cozy surroundings, with all the things and people I was familiar with. But then...I got to thinking!!!

What if I went to Iceland and Norway. I would learn about people in other countries, including the Faroe Islands, another new country for me to visit and learn about. I would meet new people on the cruise and see some old friends in my group of 12. I would get to see new geography, animals, waterfalls, rain, maybe even snow and ice!! It is 100 degrees, sunny, hot, dry, the mountains are brown here in Southern California in the summer. It is cold, green, rainy, green, cloudy and did I say it would be green, and in the 40- and 50-degree range with lots of wind and rain. Then I got excited. I was eager to go. I was very thankful for something new to learn and see. Sometimes it is so hard to leave the familiar, safe, known place where we are and to reach out and learn something new and exciting.

Next challenge:

How do I pack and Show Up for this trip, when it is a totally different climate and a 50-to-60-degree temperate adjustment. Dressed in shorts and a tank top (it was 99 degrees at home), I began to pull out long underwear, leggings, layers of tops that could go together, socks, gloves, a beanie, scarves, earmuffs, and a rain jacket. Oh yes, a change of shoes, in case the first pair got wet. I also picked up my safari brimmed hat with a strap to keep it on in the wind, but I could wear it over my beanie for warmth and to keep my head dry. Flexibility!! I picked up some water repellent at the hardware store and sprayed my jacket and hood, pants, shoes, and hat. All of that would work well for the trip in the new climate we were going to be in.

The Cruise:

When you are on a cruise, they usually like you to dress up some, so I was thankful for the new challenge of how to dress up. Using the tops I picked to keep me warm when outside during the day, how could I make them a little dressier for dinner, and/or a concert or play on board the ship? I was grateful the cruise line we were on did not require you to dress for dinner or evening programs, but some jewelry and scarves helped to make the outfit a little different for the evenings.

We were going south and east once we got off the cruise ship in Bergen, Norway, and taking a train to Oslo. It could be a lot warmer there, so I packed a couple of short sleeve tops and a pair of capris or shorts. Also, a light sweater or jacket for cooler evenings.

I was getting eager to go, once I began to make a list of the items I needed to take. I went to AAA and looked online for maps, information, highlights

of the various cities and towns we would be in. That got me even more excited. We would be able to see some gorgeous waterfalls, steep cliffs, fjords, and mountains. We could walk, hike, bike, swim on the ship, and even zip line at the ski jump area in Oslo. What fun we could and would have. I was beginning to get really excited! This was a once-in-a-lifetime experience.

My backpack looked good to take for the flight. I would also take a medium-sized suitcase, nothing too big and heavy to haul around, that could be checked in on the plane, for all my clothes and shoes, etc. I like my backpack as it has pockets! I could put my flight and travel information in one pocket with some reading material for the plane. Other pockets are good for extra clothing (in case your suitcase does not arrive with you), a jacket or sweater if the plane is cold, umbrella or things that you may need to wear when you disembark. Another pocket I usually put in some snacks, nuts, dried fruit, beef jerky, and an extra baggie if I only eat ½ of my sandwich at the long layover stop on the way. In another pocket on my backpack, I put medical needs, supplements, a mask (if someone near me on the plane is coughing, I can put it on), my medicines, contact lens case, extra glasses, sunglasses, Band-Aids, Kleenex, cough drops, etc. In the last pocket, I put electronic equipment, chargers, earbuds, writing materials, a small book to write daily events (otherwise I can forget easily what we did on what day and in what city), and a small bible or devotional materials. I also bring along a small bag or backpack that I can take on day trips. In this smaller bag I will bring a jacket, umbrella, disposable poncho, water, snacks, hat, sunglasses, sunscreen, whatever I might need when I am out during the day or on excursions.

Before my trip (now I am getting really excited), I checked with my doctor and/or travel nurse for where I am planning to go, to make sure that I had all the correct medicines, shots, and some medicines that I might need while I am there (such as sea sickness medicine, for the cruise). I made sure that I am medically covered and that I have emergency insurance to cover any accidents. I like to also get insurance for the trip in case there are cancellations or changes of plans. I refilled my prescriptions and over-the-counter medications. I always pack my sunscreen with SPF of at least 30 in my suitcase. I also bring a long-sleeved sunblock shirt to wear, long pants, a brimmed hat and sunglasses.

When I am on my trip, I try to remember some healthy habits, such as eating healthy while I am out. I love to try new foods from the countries I am in, however I try just one or two at a time with other foods that I know my body is used to. I also bring along charcoal capsules and/or ginger chews or drops from a drug store to settle my stomach if it gets upset with what I am eating.

One of the biggest problems that I find on trips is that people, myself included, don't drink enough water. I get excited about what I am seeing and doing and forget to drink water. I always take an empty bottle with me as I check in at the airport, and once I am finished with security, I fill it with some good drinking water in the airport. It is important to remember to continue drinking water throughout the day.

If you are in a different time zone, you may need to remember to rest if you need to catch up with the time difference. When in a new area, I like to get out in the sun and walk a little as soon as I can after arriving. I like to get my body acclimated to the new area as soon as possible. It is wise to stay awake during daylight times as much as possible but take a nap when you are tired. It is wise not to push yourself too much so as to get exhausted. Exhaustion can lead to illness and injury. It is also helpful to get exercise while you are there, and planning ahead of your trip for hikes, trails, bike

riding areas, etc., may be helpful. In planning my trip, I try to do all these suggestions, then RELAX.

Okay, now I am ready to travel and take that beautiful trip to Iceland and Norway. Now I can SHOW UP and enjoy my time, without questions or worry. Let's GO!

Dr. Kaye Sheffield, (h.c), M.S., CCC-SLP

I am Kaye Sheffield from Calimesa, California. I grew up as an Air Force brat, living in 18 different locations and attending 15 different schools including 3 different colleges and universities. Having attended and graduated from high school in Germany, we were able to enjoy many different experiences, languages, and learned about different cultures. I attended San Jose State University in California and took all the course work and exams to obtain a Master of Arts degree, only to find out that they required a thesis besides taking the exams to graduate. As a newlywed living in Southern California, I found it difficult, if not impossible, to finish the thesis. I went back to college after 20 years, to Loma Linda University, as a single parent, after my 3 children were established in school. I could then work a part-time job and attend and finish my Master of Science degree in Speech and Language Pathology and attend activities with my children and church.

Work sites after my degree included hospitals, convalescent homes, private therapy, universities, and mainly working in the schools. I retired after 22 years working in the school districts but have not stopped working as a Speech Therapist/Speech-Language Pathologist.

Currently I am an affiliate with Juice Plus, a worldwide Health and Wellness company, and I am a Dr. Sears, Certified Health Coach.

I have 3 wonderful successful children, 4 fantastic grandchildren and 2 super bonus grandchildren.

I love to dance, travel, learn, and help others through church, GSFE, Speech and Language Pathology, my dance clubs, etc. I am more than delighted and humbled to have recently received an Honorary Doctorate in Humanitarianism. I have written four book compilations which is an answer to prayer and one of my self-goals. All four books have become Best Sellers, nationally and internationally. I just finished writing my fifth compilation book, which will soon go into print, and working on my own book. I am delighted to share my knowledge, thoughts, and experiences, and would love to be of help and/or assistance in any way the Lord has provided me with the ability and gifts.

Dr. Kaye R. Sheffield, (h.c), M.S., CCC-SLP

(909) 556-8221

Kaye_slp@msn.com

It's all
About
Showing
Up

The Unexpected Call to Show Up:
A Story of Growth
By Kelly Brown

The moment I first had to "Show Up" wasn't really my choice—I was blissfully unaware that I was doing just that. As summer transitioned into my junior year of high school, my parents made a significant decision to move from Chicago to California.

This experience was a true lesson in learning how to Show Up, embracing the dual challenge of Stepping up and Growing up. Initially, I found myself thinking about my role as the eldest of six siblings. Compared to the upheaval my younger siblings faced, my own situation seemed minor. I hardly had grounds for complaint, aside from the bewilderment of having my parents pull me from high school with just two years left (seriously?).

Growing up in the Midwest, attending private schools, and keeping faith central to our daily lives undoubtedly instilled in me a strong desire to Show Up—not just for myself, but for my siblings as well.

Being born overseas and becoming a first-generation American has given me a unique perspective on what it truly means to Show Up.

Passion Made Me Do It:

At 16, I felt a calling: journalism was my passion. I was drawn to speaking, the art of creative writing, and everything artsy. Fashion was my playground; I always had an eye for style and made a point to express myself through what I wore.

I vividly recall sitting by my mom's bedside one early morning, sharing my dreams of pursuing a career in TV and radio. As I perched on the edge of her bed, I confessed my passion. She looked at me and urged, "Pick up the phone and make the call, Kelly. What's the worst that could happen? They'll say no. If they do, just hang up. But if they don't, you'll have to show up."

My mom has always believed that God guides our decisions, but we need to take that first step and ask. Learning to ask for what I wanted was harder than I anticipated, but over the years, I've realized that the uncertainty of not asking is far worse.

That phone call—I can hardly believe it—I think I even called information to get the number. I reached out to the local TV station, hoping for an internship to explore if this was the path for me. I was connected to a kind woman named Christine, and I'll never forget our conversation. From that moment on, everything changed. Doors began to open, leading me down a path I had only dreamed of.

Time has softened my initial resentment towards the move. Looking back, I realize it was a pivotal moment that led me to the people and experiences that have shaped my life. I wouldn't trade it for anything.

At 19, the idea of finding a soulmate seemed like a distant dream. Yet, as I navigated college and life, I discovered that opportunities often arise when we simply embrace the journey.

My upbringing equipped me with the tools I needed to pursue my passions. Life's challenges, from failures to disappointments, have been instrumental in shaping my character and understanding my true potential.

Embracing My Journey

My journey has been a long one, marked by perseverance and ongoing challenges. Recognizing the struggles I've faced has shaped me into the person I am today. My bond with my mother remains incredibly strong; she has been an unwavering source of wisdom and unconditional love.

I truly believe that my deep faith has guided me through many uncertain times. As a first-generation American, I often felt the weight of cultural expectations. In my strict Catholic Middle Eastern upbringing, dating—especially outside my culture—was frowned upon. Yet, my husband, Pat, became my steadfast supporter. His friendship helped me navigate my struggles and encouraged my personal and professional growth, profoundly influencing who I am now.

When Pat and I first met, we were both grappling with our own challenges. I yearned to embrace the life of a typical American girl, while he sought stability and a deeper connection to faith. This year, we celebrated 26 years of a happy marriage and over 30 years as each other's soulmates and best friends.

As I sat down to write this chapter, I initially feared I would struggle to find the right words. However, I realized that the title of this book truly reflects my essence today.

Together, we are proud parents of two remarkable children—one navigating college and the other embarking on a career and adulthood. I hope they see that hard work and the pursuit of their dreams are not just aspirations, but achievable realities. I'd like to share a little story that illustrates how children absorb lessons at any age, even if it's just a fraction. During a successful period in my interior design career, I decorated between 40 to 60 Christmas trees for clients in just 45 days each holiday season. I began this venture when a client requested my help with her elderly mother's tree, as she was unable to decorate it herself. This act of kindness sparked a word-of-mouth phenomenon, and soon it became a beloved holiday tradition. I found myself taking on businesses that wanted festive decorations, and my enterprise thrived. The local newspaper even dubbed me the "Tree Diva."

This journey, filled with love, faith, and hard work, continues to inspire me and those around me.

The Ripple Effect of Showing Up

I'll never forget a moment from when my daughter was still in her booster seat, full of giggles and creativity after art class. As we drove home, my phone rang. It was a friend reaching out, asking if my husband and I would like to donate to the Children's Hospital and attend their fundraiser. My immediate response? "Absolutely! Just tell us what you need!"

Once I hung up, my daughter turned to me with big, bright eyes and said, "I want to do something for the Children's Hospital too!" I was taken aback and asked, "What do you have in mind, sweetheart?" I half-expected her to suggest a toy from her room, but I was eager to hear her thoughts.

Then she said, "Mom, I can paint something for the hospital, and they can sell it to raise money for the kids. What do you think?" My heart swelled with pride, and I told her it was a fantastic idea. I promised to share it with the committee.

That evening, I called my friend and said, "You won't believe this! My daughter wants to paint something for the auction." I made it clear that, regardless of whether they accepted her idea, I would ensure she felt proud of her contribution.

A few days later, I got the most exciting call: they loved her idea and wanted to feature her artwork as a live auction item! No pressure, right? With a burst of creativity, my daughter spent weeks crafting a beautiful piece that captured the spirit of the hospital.

When the event day arrived, my husband and I sat at a table, keeping our connection to the artwork a secret from our friends. We were ready to bid up to $2,000 to create a buzz and support our girl.

As the auctioneer began, he shared the heartwarming story of the young girl who had overheard her mom discussing donations. The bidding kicked off at $500, and up went our paddle! Before we knew it, our magic number was eclipsed, and my daughter ended up raising a staggering $7,000 for the hospital that night!

What began as a simple act of kindness turned into a cherished tradition. Each year since, children's artwork has been showcased and hung proudly in the hospital hallways. Generous bidders receive copies of the pieces, while the originals remain as a testament to the creativity of young hearts. It's hard to believe it's been 15 years since it all started, but it's a beautiful reminder of the impact of showing up and the power of asking.

Throughout my adult life, I've stayed deeply involved with nonprofits, serving as president of women's networks and organizing successful charity events. From my husband dressing up as Santa to delivering gifts to children in the hospital, our family has embraced every opportunity to give back.

It's moments like these that remind us of the ripple effect our actions can have— showing up for others can inspire them to do the same, creating a cycle of kindness that resonates far beyond what we might ever expect.

The Power of Showing Up and Asking

My husband and I have navigated our careers both independently and collaboratively, each of us growing and evolving along our paths while still working together. There are times when exhaustion sets in, and our efforts fall short of our expectations. During those moments, having someone who shows up for me has been invaluable—it empowers me to dress up and show up for myself.

Over the last 15+ years, we've joined forces to create a business that opens up bigger and better opportunities for growth. As a minority businesswoman, I've learned so much, especially by witnessing my parents embrace the American dream upon their arrival in this country.

As my husband and I continue to build our business and watch our children follow similar paths, I've come to realize that showing up doesn't always mean being physically present. First and foremost, you must mentally engage before you can truly be there for anyone or anything.

At the core of our successful private label manufacturing company is a deep commitment to hard work and a shared vision. While the rewards of our business are gratifying, they don't come without their challenges. Each day demands a relentless dedication to quality, efficiency, and innovation. The ability to consistently show up—whether by managing production schedules or nurturing client relationships—is what truly drives our company forward.

This journey goes beyond financial success; it's about building a legacy grounded in resilience and unwavering belief in our vision. The importance of showing up, both mentally and physically, and the courage to ask for help or support, are central to our growth and success.

WHO I AM TODAY:

As I reflect on my journey, I embrace the multifaceted identity I've cultivated: a successful minority businesswoman continues to grow, a global ambassador, a devoted wife, a loving mother, a loyal friend, and a passionate philanthropist. I believe in celebrating life's moments, always ready to dress up for any occasion —because you can never be too overdressed!

Through every challenge and triumph, I've learned that showing up is not just about physical presence; it's about mental engagement and emotional investment. My experiences have taught me that life is a treasure map, where each moment spent showing up for myself and others leads to richer connections and deeper understanding.

I'm grateful for the lessons I've learned and the people who have supported me along the way. Whether it's my husband, who has stood by my side for over 30 years, or my children, who inspire me daily, I recognize that our journeys are intertwined. Together, we forge a path that embodies resilience, compassion, and unwavering belief in one another.

Ultimately, my story is a testament to THE POWER OF SHOWING UP and asking for what you need. It's about embracing opportunities and being present for those around you. As I continue to navigate life's adventures, I carry with me the hope of inspiring others to do the same—because every moment we choose to show up is a step toward uncovering the treasures life has to offer.

Advice on Empowerment and Taking Action

If you think about it, the concept that "if you believe you can, you can" is a powerful reminder of the potential that lies within each of us. Here are some key pieces of advice to help you harness that power and turn your thoughts into action:

1. Believe in Yourself: Confidence is the first step toward achievement. Trust in your abilities and recognize that you have the resources to succeed. Surround yourself with positive influences that reinforce your self-belief.

2. Set Clear Goals: Identify what you want to achieve. Break your goals down into manageable steps. Each small success will build your confidence and propel you forward.

3. Take Action: It's not enough to just believe; YOU MUST ACT. Start with small, achievable tasks, BUILD Momentum as you make progress, no matter how incremental.

4. Embrace Failure: (SO IMPORTANT) Understand that setbacks are part of the journey. Instead of viewing failure as a defeat, see it as a learning opportunity.

5. Ask for Help: Don't hesitate to reach out for support. Whether it's advice, mentorship, or simple encouragement, asking for help can provide valuable insights and boost your confidence.

6. Stay Committed: Consistency is key. Stay focused on your goals, and keep pushing forward, even when motivation wanes.

7. Celebrate Wins: Take time to acknowledge and celebrate your achievements, no matter how small. This builds a positive feedback loop that encourages further progress.

8. Visualize Success: MANIFESTATION, spend time imagining your success. Visualization can be a powerful motivator, helping you to mentally prepare for challenges and see yourself achieving your goals.

9. SHOW UP: Share your journey and the lessons you've learned. Encouraging others to pursue their own goals not only creates a supportive community but also reinforces your own commitment to your path.

Remember, the belief that you can accomplish something is the first step toward making it a reality. It's all within your power—embrace it, take action, and watch how your life transforms!

Grateful Reflections

I want to extend my heartfelt gratitude to Robbie Motter for the incredible opportunity to share my story. It's a privilege to offer insights to the younger generation, as well as to my peers—both women and men alike.

Each moment we invest in ourselves or in supporting others adds another layer to that map, leading us to greater fulfillment and purpose.

Thank you for accompanying me on this path. May we all continue to SHOW UP and uncover the treasures that life has in store for us.

Kelly Brown C.E.O.
Global Ambassador
 Founder & CO-Owner
PB System & BrownStone Branding White Label/Manufacturing

1133 Camelback Street
#11595
Newport Beach CA 92658
661-331-7967 Cell

IG: https://www.instagram.com/4mrsoc/
kelly@patbrownsystem.com

It's all
About
Showing
Up

It's Never Too Late To Elevate - Just Show Up and Ask

By Dr. (h.c.) "Doula" Lakeysha Mattis

Have you ever found yourself moving through life like the little engine that could—pushing forward, refusing to quit, even when every part of you felt exhausted? I've been there so many times, choo-chooing down the tracks of life with tenacity and hope, yet wondering, does it really have to be this hard? Why do so many things seem stacked against me? These questions repeated in my mind and followed me through different phases of my life. Whenever I felt like I had hit a brick wall or reached the edge of burnout, I asked myself: What am I missing? There has to be another way! Who has the answer to my questions? But I always knew deep down that the answer lay in my willingness to keep showing up and asking questions until I completely understood what I needed to say or do so that I could apply it to my life to bounce back from life's storms.

Growing up in South Central Los Angeles, I learned early that if I wanted to succeed, I had to work harder, push farther, and be stronger than most because the inner and external forces within that reality of my younger years were not so kind. Moreover, the odds weren't in my favor, but I had made up my mind, with the help of my grandmother, to bet on myself to make it out of that environment. My environment didn't offer much guidance or support on excelling or rising above the circumstances surrounding me daily. Many of us in the neighborhood believed that this was just how life was for us, that we had little control over our destinies, and that there wasn't anything we could do about it because the odds were disproportionately stacked against us. But my grandmother's words were always there, like a beacon of light in the darkness, painting a different picture of possibilities for me. She used to say to me, "The sky is the limit; you can do anything you set your mind to do." For many years, I didn't quite understand the depth of what she was saying, but her words stuck with me. Over time, I realized that she had instilled in me a spirit of curiosity and resilience to believe I could do anything I set my mind to.

The Overwhelming Weight of Doing It Alone

For years, I carried the burden of figuring it out independently. Either the people around me thought my dreams were too big, or they simply didn't have the experience to help me navigate the path I was on to do better for myself and not repeat the same cycle that led to nowhere extraordinary. Others were too tied up in their own struggles to support me or help me navigate the treacherous waters that we faced growing up where we did. And so, I did what a courageous few of us do—I became resourceful and decided to take my grandmother's word and live out what she told me was possible. I learned to seek out information, ask questions, and knock on every door of opportunity I could find in search of answers I needed to have hope of living a better life. This act of seeking help, of not being afraid to ask, is a powerful form of courage that we all possess.

But here's the thing about seeking knowledge: it can sometimes feel like you're swimming in an ocean of overwhelm and confusion. Sometimes, the more questions I asked, the more overwhelmed I became by the flood of information, or the specific vernacular used to describe or explain a

process. Some people were kind enough to help me, while others brushed me off, unable or unwilling to see the potential in me to do more with my life. There were days when it felt like the world was determined to keep me small, no matter how much effort I put into stretching beyond the horizon.

Yet, I kept going, I kept showing up, and I kept asking questions. And, just like the little engine that could, I kept chugging along, fueled by the hope that I would someday get the hang of things to take my life to the next level. My grandmother's words echoed in my mind, reminding me that the sky was the limit and that I could do anything. Over time, I learned how to filter out the noise, to focus on what mattered most, and to let go of the rest. That's when I began to see the fruits of my labor—the seeds of perseverance, resilience, and hope planted in me so many years ago began to bloom. This transformation from feeling overwhelmed to feeling empowered is a journey we all can take, and it's a journey that leads to hope and possibility.

The Blessing of Disguised Opportunities

A quote by Steve Jobs resonates deeply with me: "You can't connect the dots looking forward; you can only connect them looking backward." It's only in hindsight that I can see how some disappointments and failures in my life were blessings in disguise. One of those disguised blessings came when I found myself bamboozled out of money—twice—while trying to gain the knowledge I needed to elevate my voice and gain expertise as a Speaker and Author to walk in my vision and purpose. At the time, it was devastating, and I lost big. But in hindsight, those experiences taught me valuable lessons about perseverance, resourcefulness, and trusting my gut feelings. They taught me to look beyond the despair for the sparkles of hope and light that were ignited within my spirit and soul. As the legendary Les

Brown says, 'You've got to be hungry.' Yes, I remember being in a room with Mr. Les Brown and he looked at me and said, 'I can see you coming, but you won't catch me because I'm moving too!' And he was smiling then laughed. That meeting did me well; he affirmed me in a way he would never know. He confirmed that I needed to be on the right track and that he saw in me what I felt. Brilliance!

Remembering the painful moments of being deceived, I know that those moments led me to one of the greatest blessings of my life—my connection with the Global Society for Female Entrepreneurs (G.S.F.E.). Within this organization, I found a group of women who, like me, navigate the entrepreneurship lifestyle. Lady Ambassador Dr. Robbie Motter often reminds us, "We don't compete; we complete each other." As I choose to bounce back from the storms of lifetime after time, I've learned that we are stronger together, and it's a truth I carry with me every day. In G.S.F.E., I found a community that uplifts and inspires me, showing me the power of unity, collaboration, and showing up!

The Courage to Ask for Help

As much as I valued my independence, joining G.S.F.E. taught me that I couldn't reach all my goals alone and we are better together. We have what it takes to make an impact in the world. For the first time, I acknowledged that I needed help in spreading my vision of hope. There's a common misconception that asking for help is a sign of weakness, but I've come to understand that it's a sign of strength. It takes courage to admit that we can't do it alone. And once I allowed myself to embrace that truth, I discovered how much more I could accomplish with the support of others.

Brené Brown said it best: "Vulnerability is not winning or losing; it's having the courage to show up and be seen when we have no control over the outcome." Saying yes has been my way of showing up, being vulnerable, and trusting that I am worthy of being a part of a tremendous T.R.I.B.E. of women who are Together, resilient, inspired, and one to another! And you know what? It worked. People began to show up for me in ways I hadn't imagined. Now that the door has been opened, I have made up my mind to continue reaching out to friends, mentors, and professionals who can partner with me in supporting one another as we move to the next level of our lives, walking in excellence.

Saying Yes to Opportunities

One of my biggest lessons is the power of saying yes. Out of nervousness and fear, when offered an opportunity to show up, I would clam up, freeze up, or revert to a default mental operating system of saying no or not answering back at all. At the time, I thought it got me off the hook and that I didn't have to worry about the logistics, the expectations, and all the work that sometimes comes with saying yes. The planning, the practicing, the being around strangers... Yes, I used to feel this way because I live in a world of chaos and overwhelm. But now, I'm changed as I understand the power of saying yes to what resonates within my spirit and soul to do better for humanity. To be part of the solution to help others heal is not a part of the problem. Now, I must say that I do not always say yes if I don't get a clear and definite feeling of peace. I will not commit to saying yes because I have learned to listen to my inner gut. But more often than not, I attract positive opportunities, always watching for opportunists looking to exploit others for the love of money or some other gain. As of today, whenever a dream or genuine opportunity comes my way, I do my best to show up and say yes. Yes, it costs something—time, energy, or money—but I understand that the benefits far outweigh the cost. As Shonda Rhimes said in her book Year of Yes, "Saying yes... is the key to unlocking the door to the rest of my life." As such, I can see that each time I say yes to an opportunity, I find myself stepping into a new chapter of growth and possibly awakening to more.

Now, I have a new pep in my step. I'm intentional about asking for support and showing up for the opportunities that align with my vision. And in doing so, I've discovered that asking for help isn't a sign of weakness—it's an act of courage. It's daring to believe that I can accomplish everything I've set out to do, that everything on my vision board can come to pass, and that it has the faith that the right people and opportunities will support me along the way.

The Excitement of What's to Come

As I look ahead, I'm excited for what's to come. Saying yes to life and opportunities and showing up has allowed me to rise to greater heights. There's a quote by Paulo Coelho that sums it up perfectly: "When you want something, all the universe conspires in helping you to achieve it." I feel that truth in every part of my being as I continue to say yes and ask for what I desire. By saying yes to showing up, I've opened doors that I never knew existed, and it's so exciting to know that each door leads to new opportunities. I've stepped into rooms where my presence is welcomed, valued, and appreciated, and I remain forever grateful.

The more I say yes, the more I see the desires of my heart manifesting in ways I couldn't have imagined. It's exhilarating to know that this is only the beginning. By tapping back into life and saying yes to showing up, I've positioned myself to receive the abundance and success I've always dreamed of. I want to thank my grandmother, who planted the seeds of

faith, hope, and love within me. And now, I can see what she was trying to show me because today, I can see that the sky is the limit, and I'm ready to soar on high to birth out a bright brilliance to inspire others to do the same.

So, if there's one thing I've learned, it's this: keep showing up. Even when it feels hard, even when you're not sure what the outcome will be, keep saying yes to those opportunities that feel right to you. As Oprah Winfrey says, "The biggest adventure you can take is to live the life of your dreams." And living the life of your dreams starts with showing up. I'm on a journey to manifest in this life all that is destined for me to fulfill my highest level of myself and to do so graciously to manifest a greater world for myself and others.

Dr. (h.c.) "Doula" Lakeysha Mattis

Dr. H.C. "Doula" Lakeysha Mattis, a Rebound and Reset Doula uses her voice and expertise to inspire individuals to tap back in, bounce back big, and bet on themselves to rise from the ashes of adversity to reclaim and rediscover their passion for life to win!

Based in the U.S., Lakeysha Mattis Enterprises is driven by its vision to bring hope, renewal, and transformation through speaking engagements, books, a podcast, rebound & reset retreats, empowerment workshops, and release events to uplift individuals in building positive identities and self-worth through education and guidance, elevating their personal, spiritual, and professional paradigms to birth out their brilliance!

Author, Speaker, Rebound and Reset Doula: Authored books that can be found on Amazon, "Awaken to More: 8 Strategies to Rebound & Reset

Your Life," "Poetic Expressions from the Soul," "How I'm Learning to Reset My Life," and "5 Action Steps To Live Your Best Life Now."

Let's connect

https://drdoulalakeyshamattis.com/reboundandreset

It's all
About
Showing
Up

Showing Up & Asking Allows Me to Continue to Shine!

By Ambassador Dr. (h.c.) Latasha Fennell

I found out early on in life, there are two forces that, when combined, can profoundly impact your journey: the power of showing up and the power of asking. These two forces are often underestimated, yet they have the potential to unlock doors, create opportunities, and have led me to personal and professional success. Showing up and asking actually changed my life, from a lot of missed opportunities to life-changing moments.

One of the most important things I've learned while serving in the United States military was to always be on time and if you're on time your late! I used to think why do I have to be 15 minutes early when it wasn't even the time that was requested. I later found out things happen in life and when you're late you miss out on many opportunities or don't get the seat you deserve because you're late or just plain didn't show up. One of the things I struggled with was the power of asking. As a child, I was taught to never ask an adult why and just do as you were told and as I got older and joined the military it was pretty much the same thing.

However, things were a little different when it came to running my business. Showing up every day and staying late and asking questions was almost the required thing to do. When I started my small business in 2018, I had lots of questions and sometimes I felt too embarrassed to ask them. Some of the many questions I thought to myself were: Can I really do this every day? Do I really have what it takes? Was I even good enough? and Will my business even be successful?

One of the reasons many people struggle to show up is fear. Fear of rejection, failure, or looking foolish can prevent us from engaging fully with opportunities. However, it's important to remember that fear is a natural response to the unknown, and the act of showing up is the antidote to that fear.

Rejections and self-doubt always played a part with me when I first started my business and I often didn't even want to show up to tables and rooms I rightfully belonged in, but I knew that showing up was the first step towards achieving anything meaningful. Whether it's a job interview, a networking event, a difficult conversation, supporting family members and friends or even a personal commitment to oneself, I know that showing up is the act of being present, ready, and open to possibilities.

Many people shy away from situations that make them uncomfortable or anxious. However, those who consistently show up—even when it's difficult—are the ones who are likely to succeed. So, I was determined to be successful, all it took for me to do it, was to just show up.

Take, for instance with my small business, Boss Lady Bling Blingy, every day, without fail, I would arrive early to my shop and watch how many people would come during the hours I was closed versus the set hours I displayed on my boutique door. I even attended every town hall community meeting and participated in every local event to put my business name and my face out in the local community. I made it a point to be present at every opportunity that came my way. Over time, my persistence paid off. I was starting to be recognized by other business owners and locals in the

surrounding areas, got invites to some of the most top private clubs, dinner parties, red carpet events and even was on major VVIP lists, not because I was the best, but because I was there—day in and day out—demonstrating commitment and consistency, but mostly because I showed up.

When you show up, you open the door to possibilities and meet people you never thought was possible that you wouldn't have encountered otherwise. Opportunities often present themselves in unexpected ways, but they can only be seized if you are there to recognize them.

In personal development, consistency is equally important. Whether it's working toward a fitness goal, learning a new skill, or developing a daily practice like meditation, consistency is what turns aspirations into reality. Small, consistent actions compound over time to produce significant results.

I even kept in mind you can be a master and the very best at what you do in life and even be a good person but if you're not consistent with your customers you will lose them. They will find a backup solution due to you not being consistent.

The lesson is clear: showing up, especially when paired with consistency, creates momentum. The more you show up, the more opportunities arise, and the more likely you are to achieve your goals and most importantly, being successful.

While showing up is essential, it's often not enough on its own. The next critical step is asking like-minded people and other business owners. Asking for help, asking for opportunities, and asking for what we deserve are all powerful ways to move forward in life. But you must be willing to also do the hard work. Unfortunately, many people are hesitant to ask because they fear rejection or judgment. But asking is a skill that, when cultivated, can open many doors and create many opportunities that would have otherwise remained closed.

Asking for help is a sign of strength, not weakness. Many people hesitate to ask for help because they fear it will make them appear weak, soft, dumb or incapable. However, asking for help is one of the most powerful things you can do. It shows humility, self-awareness, and a willingness to learn. Moreover, when you ask for help, you allow others to contribute their knowledge and experience to your journey, which can accelerate your growth and success.

Asking for help can also build connections and foster collaboration. When you ask for help, you invite others into your journey, creating opportunities for mentorship, partnership, and support. No one achieves success alone, and asking for help is often the first step in building a network of people who can support your goals.

Asking for what you want upfront goes a long way and people will definitely respect you for just being honest. Beyond asking for help, it's important to ask for what you want. This could be a promotion at work, a raise, or an opportunity to take on a new project and or help finish something that may be too much for you. Many people don't receive what they want simply because they never ask for it. They assume that if they work hard and do their best, someone will notice and reward them. While hard work is important, it's not always enough. You have to advocate for yourself and ask for the things you want.

By failing to ask, many people leave opportunities and money on the table. This has happened to me so many times. Asking for what you want can feel uncomfortable, but it's a skill that can be developed. The more you practice asking, the easier it becomes. And the more you ask, the more likely you are to receive.

The true power of showing up and asking lies in their intersection. When you show up and ask, you are actively participating in your own success. You are not waiting for opportunities to come to you; you are creating them. By showing up, you put yourself in the right place at the right time. By asking, you make your intentions known and take control of your destiny.

Showing up and asking has open many doors for Boss Lady Bling Blingy Boutique. Here are a few things and ways of having a mindset of showing up and asking has benefited my business:

New Collaborations:

By simply reaching out and presenting my vision, I've secured partnerships, like being in private red-carpet events, VVIPS events and organizations, Top female entrepreneur groups, major networking groups and meeting some very important entrepreneur and business leaders.

Event spotlight Opportunities:

Winning Ms. Elite Southern California International 2025 Woman Of Achievement. Presenting my fashion brand in a fashion show during San Diego Design Week, where I closed the event at the San Diego Made Factory, is a great example of showing up and making the most of the spotlight.

Custom Orders:

I've built relationships with clients near and far who request custom pieces, like your Blingy Blazer Jackets for military retirements, custom one-of-a-kind jewelry, and other fashion accessories for fashion events, by being approachable and making it easy for people to contact you.

Awards & Recognition:

Asking for the opportunity to be seen has earned me accolades like the Global ICONIC CHANGEMAKER of the 21st Century: DESIGNER OF THE YEAR 2024 awards. Countless Awards from California State Governor, Assembly, Senate, Mayor and the president of the United States.

Building a Loyal Customer Base:

Engaging directly with clients—via DM, text, and in-person appointments—helps foster deeper relationships that lead to repeat business and word-of-mouth referrals.

By consistently showing up, asking, and being proactive, you too can do many powerful things as well. I've cultivated a strong, dynamic brand presence that leads to more opportunities for growth.

Ambassador Dr. (h.c.) Latasha Fennell
Ms. Elite Southern California International Woman of Achievement 2025
Founder & CEO, Boss Lady Bling Blingy Boutique
2031 Commercial St, San Diego, CA 92113
Phone: 619-617-4586 | Website: BossLadyBlingBlingy.com
Instagram: @LadieBlingy4 | Facebook: @LadieBlingy
Email: BossLadyBlingBlingy@gmail.com | LatashaFennell@gmail.com

Latasha Fennell is a multi-talented entrepreneur, Founder, CEO and powerhouse of Boss Lady Bling Blingy Boutique. She is also a proud active-duty member of the United States Navy, currently serving as a Senior Chief Petty Officer (E-8) of 25 years. Beyond her military career, Latasha is a proud mother of one, co-author, model, celebrity stylist, jewelry designer, and event promoter.

Latasha's deep commitment to charity and community service has earned her numerous accolades, including an Honorary Doctorate in Humanitarianism, an Associate in General Studies, A Bachelor of Arts Degree, 2024 President Volunteer Service Award (Gold) Ms. Elite Southern California International Woman of Achievement for 2025, 2024 Ms. Elite Southern California and the 2023 West Coast Rising Stars Woman of Achievement Award, along with many other community awards and certificates.

As a passionate member of multiple professional organizations, she actively participates in groups such as the Global Society of Female Entrepreneurs (GSFE), EWOMEN Network Orange County, LAKIDZFASHION, All Women Rock, CIM Exclusive Models, San Diego Business Entrepreneur Networking, and Chula Vista American Legion Post 434. Latasha is also involved with San Diego Made, The Red Blazers, and SEEMSS AFRICA, to name a few.

Born in Memphis, Tennessee, and raised in Anthonyville, Arkansas, Latasha's love for "things that bling" has been with her since childhood. After high school, she joined the United States Navy and discovered a passion for fashion and jewelry design, leading her to create Boss Lady Bling Blingy in 2018. Her brand is known for handcrafted, one-of-a-kind jewelry and accessories using luxury fabrics, precious gems, rhinestones and crystals. Her work is featured in magazines, on runways, and at galas, offering custom designs for every occasion.

Latasha believes in creating art from the heart and takes pride in delivering unique and elegant designs that embody sophistication and flair. Her passion for detail and her love for the craft is evident in every piece she creates.

Whether you're looking for a stunning custom-made jewelry piece or have a design challenge in mind, Latasha is ready to make your vision come to life.

It's all
About
Showing
Up

A SHOWUP Journey Through Life
By Lee Horton

Hello, I am Lee Horton, I was born In Boston, MA., I grew up and SHOWED UP in a family of 3 sisters and 2 brothers. Because of the nature of my dad's work, we moved a lot, so I kept SHOWING UP. We moved to Maine, then to Florida, then to Arizona, then later to the Orange County area, and then finally to Riverside County.

Setting Roots in Riverside County

Riverside County is where I was able to lay down roots in a place that would become central to my identity. Joining the workforce at the Sun City Family Restaurant in Sun City, CA which is part of Riverside County, I dedicated over 40 years to this establishment, I made it a point to show up every day. It wasn't just a job for me; it was an opportunity to connect with my community. I took pride in learning about my customers, remembering their names and favorite orders, and building lasting relationships. My commitment to being a listener and a source of support for them became a hallmark of my character. Even today when I SHOWUP there to eat people still come up to me and thank me for my kindness to them over those years.

The Heart of a Mother

As a mother of four children, three daughters and a son, who tragically passed away—I faced the complexities of motherhood and grief. Each child played an integral role in my life, shaping me into the compassionate and nurturing woman I am today. My experience as a mother has fortified my resilience and capacity for love, urging me to create meaningful connections with those around me.

A Love Story

My marriage to Bud, who was the love of my life, brought me immense joy and companionship. Our bond was one of profound love and understanding, a partnership that defined much of my later years. Following Bud's passing in 2017, I experienced deep grief, mourning not just a partner but a best friend. At about the same time I lost my mother and several other relatives, it was really hard but yet, in true fashion, I picked up my life with grace, embracing new opportunities to connect with people who would enrich my life.

Embracing New Friendships

Recently, I joined the Menifee GSFE (Global Society for Female Entrepreneurs) Network, an organization focused on community engagement and support. The Director, Dr. Christine Park, exemplifies true leadership and the individuals who show up are truly A sisterhood. I look forward to their monthly meetings in Sun City. This new chapter in my life exemplifies my willingness to meet new people and make meaningful connections, embodying my belief that life continues to offer

rich experiences, no matter what the circumstances. My inherent love for dressing up and showing up at events highlights vibrant spirit, reminding everyone around ne to embrace life fully.

A Beacon of Kindness

I totally care about my friends and try to be there for them, I have supported many causes that help to change the world over the years and inch to take each day to touch a life, shake a hand or give something to cheer them up and put smiles on their faces.

I want to be recognized not just for my kindness but for my unwavering commitment to being a friend. Many have told me that my smile and my presence light up any room, and I want to be renowned for being a loyal companion. I want to always be a "forever friend," someone who is there through thick and thin. I am direct, supportive, and I deeply care about the people in my life, making me not just confident, but a pillar of strength for many.

Proactive in Creating Change

My impact goes beyond personal relationships; I am also dedicated to supporting causes that make the world a better place. I try and take each day as an opportunity to contribute positively to my community and beyond, embodying a proactive approach to life. Whether it's volunteering, advocating for community initiatives, or simply extending a helping hand to someone in need, I believe that every small act can create ripples of kindness.

Conclusion

I believe my life's journey is one marked by resilience, love, and a ceaseless dedication to my community. From my decades at the Sun City Family Restaurant to my role as a devoted mother and friend, I hope my story exemplifies the power of showing up for others. I know that together spreading kindness can truly make the world a better place. Through my actions, I hope I can remind others of all of the profound impacts of listening, caring, and simply being present for one another. My legacy is not just in the memories I can create, but in the countless lives I have touched and get to continue to touch each day.

Lee Horton is retired but is there for her community and friends, with her caring heart. She can be reached at 951-928-3401

It's all
About
Showing
Up

Why is Self-Discovery Important in the Current Time?

By Lady Ambassador Dr. Lenora Peterson-Maclin

Self-love forms the foundation of personal growth, resilience, and happiness. Throughout history, celebrated poets have beautifully captured the essence of self-love in their verses, offering inspiration and encouragement to readers worldwide. Their words serve as reminders of the importance of accepting oneself, embracing imperfections, and cultivating inner strength. Through poetry, we learn that self-love is not selfish but essential for building healthy relationships, achieving balance, and finding inner peace.

Poets such as Walt Whitman, Maya Angelou, and Rupi Kaur have penned timeless works that explore the journey of self-acceptance and love. Their poetry resonates because it acknowledges the struggles and joys of being human, encouraging readers to find beauty within themselves. The themes of resilience, self-worth, and inner joy are universal, reminding us that self-love is a trans formative force.

Do you have a favorite poet or poem that inspires your thoughts on self-love?

Self-love is essential in life because it serves as the foundation for mental, emotional, and even physical well-being. Here are a few reasons why self-love is so important:

1. **Confidence and Self-Worth:** When you love yourself, you recognize your inherent value. This confidence allows you to pursue your goals and dreams without constantly seeking external validation.

2. **Resilience:** Life inevitably comes with challenges and setbacks. Self-love helps you bounce back from difficulties because it gives you the inner strength to persevere. You know you are worthy of growth and healing, regardless of the circumstances.

3. **Healthy Relationships:** Loving yourself first enables you to maintain healthier, more balanced relationships with others. You can set boundaries, communicate effectively, and avoid seeking fulfillment solely from external sources. It ensures that your relationships are rooted in mutual respect, not neediness or dependence.

4. **Personal Growth:** Self-love encourages you to be kind to yourself while you grow and change. Instead of being overly critical, you understand that mistakes are part of the journey, and you allow yourself the grace to evolve.

5. **Mental Health:** Practicing self-love helps combat negative self-talk and low self-esteem. It fosters a more positive mindset, which is vital for overall mental health, reducing stress, anxiety, and depression.

6. **Happiness and Fulfillment:** True happiness stems from self-contentment. By loving yourself, you can experience joy from within, not just through external achievements or relationships. In short, self-love is not just a luxury—it's a necessity for living a fulfilling, balanced, and resilient life. What are your personal thoughts on the role of self-love in your own life?

7. **Boosts Hope and Positivity:** Self-love can help you cultivate small moments of joy or gratitude, even during depression. By focusing on

things that bring you comfort or peace—whether it's a hobby, time in nature, or connecting with friends—you can shift your focus from the overwhelming sadness to more positive experiences, which can improve your overall mood over time.

Ultimately, self-love during depression is about giving yourself grace, patience, and care in a time when you need it most. It reminds you that your worth isn't diminished by what you're going through, and it provides a lifeline to healing.

Many spiritual beliefs emphasize the importance of self-love as a vital aspect of personal and spiritual growth. Across different traditions and philosophies, self-love is often viewed as an expression of divine love or a necessary step toward inner peace and enlightenment. Here are some key spiritual perspectives that recognize the value of self-love:

These can also heal trauma: self-love.

1. Christianity:
    In Christian teachings, self-love is often linked to the concept of loving others. The Bible encourages believers to "love your neighbor as yourself" (Mark 12:31), implying that self-love is a prerequisite for loving others fully. Christians who practice self-love understand it as part of recognizing their worth as children of God. This love includes self-care, forgiveness, and gratitude for life, all of which honor God's creation in them.

2. Buddhism:
    In Buddhism, self-love is viewed through the lens of compassion. Practicing Metta (loving-kindness) begins with cultivating kindness and compassion toward oneself before extending it to others. The

Buddha taught that one must love themselves before they can love the world: "You, yourself, as much as anybody in the entire universe, deserve your love and affection." Self-compassion is seen as key to inner peace and breaking free from suffering.

3. Hinduism:
    Hinduism teaches that the self, or Atman, is divine and connected to the larger universal spirit, or Brahman. Recognizing this divine spark within yourself through self-love can lead to enlightenment and the realization that all beings are interconnected. The practice of yoga and meditation in Hinduism often encourages self-reflection, inner peace, and self-care as part of spiritual progress.

4. Sufism (Islamic Mysticism):
    In Sufism, self-love is connected to the idea of divine love. To love oneself is to honor the divine essence that resides within each person. Through deep inner work, like meditation and prayer, Sufis aim to purify the heart, find unity with God, and learn to see oneself and others through the lens of divine love. Self-love, in this context, is about recognizing one's inherent worth as part of the divine creation.

5. New Age Spirituality:
    In many New Age spiritual practices, self-love is a central theme. It is seen as essential for manifesting positive energy and living in alignment with one's highest self or purpose. Practices like positive affirmations, self-care rituals, and energy healing (such as Reiki) are often used to cultivate self-love and raise one's vibration to a higher spiritual level.

6. Native and Indigenous Beliefs:
    Many Indigenous and Earth-centered spiritual practices emphasize the balance between self and the world around us. Loving and

respecting oneself is part of maintaining harmony with nature and the community. In these traditions, self-love is often intertwined with self-respect and the recognition of one's role within the larger circle of life.

7. Kabbalah (Jewish Mysticism):
    In Kabbalah, self-love can be seen as part of the spiritual journey toward understanding one's soul and its divine origins. The tradition teaches that every soul is a unique reflection of God's light. By embracing self-love, individuals are able to connect more deeply with their spiritual purpose and bring divine light into the world through their actions.

8. Taoism:
    Taoism teaches about living in harmony with the Tao, or the natural way of the universe. Self-love in Taoism is about embracing your true nature and living authentically. It involves self-acceptance and aligning your actions and life with the flow of the universe. Taoists believe that loving oneself is key to finding inner peace and balance.

9. Spiritual Humanism:
    Some humanistic spiritual beliefs focus on self-love as a means of honoring one's full potential. These views hold that self-love allows you to recognize your worth, talents, and unique purpose, which are seen as expressions of your spiritual identity. In this framework, loving yourself is also about honoring your connection to the greater good and the collective well-being.
    In many spiritual traditions, self-love is not seen as selfish or egotistical but as a recognition of the divine spark within each individual. It's about cultivating inner peace, compassion, and balance, which then radiates outward, helping to foster love, kindness, and connection with others and the universe.

Lady Goodwill Ambassador Dr. Lenora Peterson

Ambassador Dr. Lenora Peterson-Maclin is a popular and well-respected motivational speaker who has given digital, and in-person talks in countries including the United States, the United Kingdom, and many more. Since 2012, she has represented the National Community Service

Organizations/The United States President's Volunteer Service as an Ambassador. At the United Nations Women USA, Dr. Lenora Peterson-Maclin serves as the certified Global Goodwill Ambassador for Companies for National Voluntary Community Service of Uniting Humanitarians. The People's Choice Awards is a nonprofit organization, and she serves as its chief executive officer. She represents the Commonwealth Entrepreneurs Club as its Global Ambassador. Dr. Lenora Peterson-Maclin, the Woman Ambassador, has accomplished a great deal. This remarkable woman, who is also very modest, is deserving of universal acclaim. She does everything with her whole heart, not for recognition but to make people's lives better.

Lady Ambassador Dr. Lenora Peterson-Maciln has a Ph.D. in theology, specializing in the fundamental laws and principles of the kingdom of God. She is a Ph.D. graduate with a Doctor of Philosophy in Theology from Luther Rice College & Seminary and The Sure Foundation Theological School received on April 19, 2013. In January 2021, she finished her Humanitarian Response to War and Disaster courses via the Harvard X Online program.

She is certified in business consulting and has a human rights consultant certification from the United States Institute of Diplomacy and Human Rights (USIDHR). She became Lady Ambassador Dr. Lenora Peterson -Maclin, Ph.D. in December 2022 after being admitted into the Platinum Jubilee of (the late) Queen Elizabeth II of the United Kingdom.

Throughout her illustrious career, Ambassador Dr. Lenora Peterson-

Maclin has received numerous awards and accolades. To name a few, she was awarded the 2022 Humanitarian Award, the 2022 Superhero Award from the UK, and the position of International Human

Rights Chairperson by the United Businesswomen Association of Nigeria and the Diaspora. A certificate of appreciation for her global humanitarian services and work was presented to her in London, UK, in December 2022 by the Global Association for Female Entrepreneurs. Also, she was honored as an esteemed adjudicator for International Women's Day and received the HERA Award in 2022. The Nelson Mandela Award and Humanitarian Medal were given to her in 2021. She is the recipient of the Princess of Peace Award from LOANI (U.K.) and Future Leaders Entity (Egypt). She has been honored with the 2020 We Are the Change Award, has contributed to the nonprofit publication LOANI's "Expert Global Leaders Book," and has been profiled in many issues of LOANI's magazine. She has received a Leader of World Peace Award given by

H.E. Prof. Amb. Abdullghani Yahya Al-ebarh, Nobel Peace Prize Nominee, was an Asian World Peace Prize Nominee, and was the Presenter of the 2021 World of Peace Award from Pioneers in the World of Peace. The late Georgia Congressman John Lewis presented her with a certificate of Special Congressional Recognition for Outstanding and Invaluable Service to the Community in 2017, and Secretary of State Brian P. Kemp (currently serving as the state's governor interim) presented her with the 2016 Secretary of State Outstanding Georgia Citizen Award.

She also organizes celebrations meant to recognize the contributions of exceptional individuals. Around twenty-five women were recognized in her 2022 All White Dinner Gala & Trailblazer Women of Excellence Award Ceremony, which she hosted. She presided over a 2021 dinner/dance and fundraiser in which three Georgia state officials were recognized with the GIA Men of Excellence Awards. She has presented awards at special ceremonies in New York City in 2014, 2021, and 2022 and in Chicago in 2016 and 2019. Moreover, Lady Peterson-Maclin has other Counties to celebrate a total of a thousand winners of important Prizes.

Stephanie Cirami, President of IAOTP, stated, "There was no question that we needed to have Ambassador Dr. Lenora Peterson-Maclin on our panel. She has a wealth of experience and skill. She has our highest regards as IAOTP's Top Global Ambassador and Humanitarian of the Year for 2023. In 2023, she will be attending the Annual Awards Gala, which we are looking forward to. "She was honored with inclusion and presented with a copy of THE 100 MOST SUCCESSFUL WOMEN AROUND THE WORLD BOOK 2021. In 2020, Lady Ambassador

Dr. Peterson-Maclin released her book, "The Lady the Level the Loyalist." She started the publication "Humanitarian" and also manages it.

In December 2023
A new book called: You're Already Rich 'was released in publication on December 2023

Ambassador Dr. Lenora Peterson has received from the Federal Republic of Nigeria special team in Nigeria has reported to us about your quality leadership and great achievements in the areas of Education, youth welfare, youth employment and development. As a result of your sterling performance over the years, The Committee on special commendation has awarded Ambassador Dr. Lenora Peterson with the World Youth Summit Outstanding Leadership Award (golden plaque) and the Global Humanitarian Award (golden medallion) by Global International Alliance Advocate University USA.

In addition to her work as a Licensed International Chaplain Minster, she founded the nonprofit organization Vision in You Outreach Foundation, Inc. 501c3. She established the highly regarded GIA (Global International Alliance) honorary certification in Humanitarianism and   sponsored Dinner/Award Galas and Celebrations in several places around the United States and

International Chaplaincy program. She has served as its president since the year 2016. The International Association for Continuing Education and Training (IACET) approved Global International Alliance Online University as a nonprofit distance education institution.

(IAOTP) Presented her the Lifetime Achievement Award Honoree of 2024 "

02-2024
United States House of Representatives
Jay Phillip Obernolte California's 33rd State Assembly district
Certificate of Recognition to Lady Amb. Dr. Lenora Peterson-Maclin
California State Senate Rosilicie Ochoa Bogh
California's 23rd State Senate district)
Presented certificate of Honor to GIA Program
        04-20-2024
Tom Lackey California State Assembly representing the 34th district,
Corticated of Honor to GIA Program
        04-20-2024
Global Society for Female Entrepreneurs (GSFE) USA, Canada & UK
Present Prestigious Honors and award to GIA C/O
Lady Amb. Dr. Lenora Peterson-Maclin 04-20-2024

From Shy Girl to Confident Woman: My Journey of Showing Up
By Liliana Venegas Rogers

It has been a long journey—from the quiet little girl to the painfully shy teenager, to the 'invisible' worker, to the confident, strong, and visible woman I am today.

This story is for all the beautiful souls out there who think they can't... My hope is that my story inspires you to believe that you can, to push yourself, and to show up, time after time, until you reach your dreams.

I remember it like it was yesterday—a cold, typical afternoon in Bogotá, Colombia, where I grew up. I was a normal 15-year-old, walking around the neighborhood with my girlfriends when we bumped into a group of guys that my friend Cristina knew. As they approached, I felt it—a wave of shyness washing over me, locking me in place. I couldn't talk, I couldn't smile; I was paralyzed. It was so obvious that one of the guys joked, "Where did you guys get her? The military?" They all laughed. I wanted to disappear. I felt so small, so awkward, so invisible.

That day, I told myself: "Liliana, you have to overcome this shyness. You can't live like this."

It would take years before I truly showed up to face that challenge.

I graduated as a software engineer, worked for big companies, and on paper, I was doing well. But inside, I knew I was missing opportunities—opportunities to grow, to lead, to connect—because I was still hiding behind my shyness and lack of confidence. I just wanted to do my job and stay invisible.

My love for life and adventure kept pushing me forward. I moved to the United States by myself as a software consultant, traveling across the country. If I struggled to socialize in Spanish, my native language, you could imagine how hard it was in English! But this challenge was a blessing. It 'forced' me to finally start working on myself. I took self-development classes and seminars, determined to break free.

I'll never forget the first time I tried to break a wood board in a workshop. On one side, I wrote what I wanted: confidence, ease in making friends, social comfort. On the other side, I wrote what was holding me back: shyness, self-doubt, low self-esteem. I was terrified of change. I cried and couldn't break the board with my hand. After several attempts—and the entire class cheering me on—I finally broke it with my foot. That moment, in the year 2000, marked the beginning of my transformation.

Over the next decade, during my marriage and while raising two kids, I made small improvements, but nothing radical.

The second BIG leap came after my divorce. I found myself without family nearby or male friends to help me set up my new home. But instead of feeling helpless, I showed up and rose to the occasion. I went to the store, bought the tools I needed, and taught myself how to do it all—painting, assembling furniture, hanging blinds, installing dimmers, even putting together a huge trampoline for my kids.

It felt amazing. It felt freeing to do everything by myself, knowing that my

kids had a beautiful, comfortable place to call home thanks to my effort.

It felt amazing. It felt freeing. I didn't need anyone to do it for me. Sure, help would have been nice, but I realized I didn't need it.

As a newly single woman, most of my friends were married, and I faced a choice: stay home or start going out and enjoying life on my own. This was the third BIG leap. I began going to restaurants, concerts, museums, and seminars by myself. At first, it was nerve-wracking. With each outing, each conversation, it became easier to connect with others. I found myself meeting amazing people, and my confidence grew with every step.

In 2018, after being laid off from my corporate job, I decided to take the biggest leap of all: I left my engineering career behind and followed my passion—to learn about the power of the mind and help other women. I became a life coach.

This chapter of my life has been incredibly rewarding. I've grown, learned, and continued showing up. My confidence is stronger than ever, and my shyness is a distant memory. I am now living my purpose, and every woman I help brings me joy, confirming that it was all worth it.

Today, I choose to be visible—no more hiding. I love my blue hair, and I love being different. Every time a woman tells me she likes it but wishes she had the confidence to do the same, I hope I'm inspiring her to show up, own her beauty, and embrace her uniqueness.

I want to be a beacon of love and light to everyone around me, and now it feels natural.

Looking back at that cold afternoon in Bogotá, I never could have imagined I'd become a social butterfly, but I did. And it all started with showing up.

If I did it, you can too. Who knows what's waiting for you if you show up?

Liliana Venegas Rogers – Hypno-coach

Certified practitioner of LOA, NLP and Hypnotherapy

Email: Liliana@Femelocity.com

Phone: 888-333-8106

Website: Femelocity.com

YT: http://www.youtube.com/@femelocity

FB: https://www.facebook.com/liliana.v.rogers

It's all
About
Showing
Up

My Story
By Minh H Dannerstedt, PhD

How you show up is how people see you, understand you, discover you, feel you, and have an opinion about you. It's the way people interact, are responsible, respectful, engage, express, to make decisions.... It's the way the connection starts, how communication unfolds between people. We all learn through our own experiences, our learning, our effort, courage, our mistakes, our losses, how we get back, how we restart, how we continue, and achieve.

From my memories, I started to show up at a younger age, maybe at 8 years old. Being a child in a family with 7 children, I could understand that it was a lot in everyday life for my mother to handle. She had many responsibilities that cannot wait daily busy with her children for school, meals, homework, clothes, nurturing us, educating us ...

In a natural way, I started to take care of my younger siblings with what I could. I felt happy to give my mother a hand. I felt nurtured by my mother, and I nurtured my younger sisters and brothers to help her.

My father focused on his work and life had its difficulties. When I was 6 years old, although my father had graduated and was working, he received a scholarship for internship at Cornell University in the United States, for observation and study further.

Although it was a great opportunity for my father, professionally, for my mother it's quite challenging- not only financially but in daily life too. We were 5 children then. My mother moved to Dalat, 300 km from Saigon, where my grandmother resided, to get some help. I was too young to understand the real challenges, but all seemed to flow quietly and peacefully. My maternal grandmother showed up as most mothers would do, helping my mother with the young children.

Life was certainly not easy, but my grandmother and mother made it comfortable and joyful for us.

I grew up in Vietnam, in a time of war. There was fear, insecurity, and risks in daily life. My childhood was around my grandmother, mother, and 5 of us, school and daily life.... Everybody made an effort for a harmonious life. We were safe and happy as children.

After my father came back, our family moved back to Saigon. We continued to grow, learn and adapt with my parents and life was challenging sometimes, - as for many other families.

When I finished high school, I had an opportunity to travel to Europe to continue my studies as my elder sister was studying and living there. We stayed together in a small student place. My sister was married and had a little baby girl. When I arrived, as I had to wait until the next school year before I could start, I showed up to offer to babysit their baby while her parents were busy studying during the day, as I had some experience when I helped my mother to take care of my younger siblings at home.

Showing up is a choice. Showing up is courage, an effort to discover new opportunities and new opening doors...

During my student years in Belgium, I met my husband. He was studying Medicine, but after 2 years, he realized he wanted to study Engineering and decided to go back to Sweden for Engineering school. I stayed in Brussels with my sister to finish my studies.

In the meantime, the war in my country ended and many major changes followed. That period of time was hard for almost a year, I could not get any news from my family. I did not know what happened to my family.

Life went on. After I finished my studies, I went to Sweden to meet my boyfriend. I could stay at his parent's house, and I had some short-term jobs.

One day, I heard that the department of Oriental Languages at the University of Stockholm was looking for a teacher to teach Vietnamese, as there was a big aid project from Sweden to build a paper mill in Bai Bang, in North Vietnam.

I went to the University to ask about this position, thinking that I could teach Vietnamese language. A Swedish Professor of Japanese received me, and after talking with me, he asked me to prepare a learning booklet to teach Vietnamese to the staff who will travel to Vietnam for the paper mill project, - which I did- adapting to the needs to learn to speak Vietnamese to communicate at work.

Before that, I had finished an intensive 90-day Swedish language studies at the University and could manage to speak Swedish quite well. This did help me a lot to teach the Vietnamese Language class in Swedish.

I prepared learning material with many lessons, from easy texts and grammar to texts with more vocabulary for the students to acquire more words and master general conversations.

At that time, I had to type the whole learning booklet, draw the pictures and photocopy all pages in small numbers of booklets. I was accepted to teach Vietnamese language class at the University, and I was very happy. The students who came to study were engineers, staff who would travel to Vietnam for the paper mill project.

I worked at the University for a couple of years, got married and had one baby boy. I was young and happy to have a job I liked while my husband pursued his studies.

Again, showing up did help me to have this opportunity.

If I did not have the courage to go to the University and ask for details for the Vietnamese course they planned for the paper mill project, I would have missed an opportunity to go beyond myself and teach at the University of Stockholm. I have learnt so much from this experience.

During that time, when we were living in Stockholm, I tried to get news from my family but could not get any. I was praying that my family was doing fine, as we did not receive any news.

One of the students learning Vietnamese had an opportunity to travel to Vietnam. He offered to visit my parents for me. I was very happy, and he came back with news that my family is doing well, with some pictures. A short time after, when letters and courier were regular again, I could correspond with my family regularly and we were very happy.

As we planned to get married, his parents wanted to invite my parents to come to the wedding so both families could meet. We did the paperwork for my parents to attend the wedding, but the process was long and difficult with all the administrative process. We understood the situation and hoped that there would be another opportunity in the future. We had another opportunity to ask for help to get visas for my family, and even if

that could take a long time, we trusted that things would work out.

When my husband had finished his studies, our first baby was one year old. We moved back to Belgium, to be closer to my sister. My husband found a job soon after and we were busy with the baby and his work.

One day we got the news that my family would be arriving in Sweden soon. My sister and I, with our son of 2 years old, traveled to Sweden to meet and welcome my family. How happy we were, as we had not seen my family for 9 years. I am thankful for all the help I got, for showing up, asking for help, for trusting and making an effort in daily life.

Meeting my family again after 9 years was a big gift of happiness for us. I could not describe our feelings to have my family so close.... My husband and I did the best we could to help my family adjust with the new life in Sweden. I traveled there very often with my little son to visit.

Showing up inspired me to inspire others and it does make a difference. This has motivated me for the next steps in my life.

Life continued while I took care of my two small children and built a family.

A friend who was professor in literature shared with me that he had learnt energy healing techniques, and he applied them daily with results within the family. I found this quite interesting, as I believed that Nature, the Universe and the Cosmos have powerful solutions for the needs of humans on Earth that we still have to discover. If we can be aware, tune in, connect, learn and make research to understand deeper, we would benefit much more from the magic and great power of Nature.

Sometime after, I was invited to a presentation on energy healing. I showed up and was very interested to learn more about this energetic and spiritual approach. If the cosmic energy can create the vast universe, re-establish our balance, we certainly have much to learn and discover. And I did, for many years, while taking care of my three children.

After a few years of practice and teaching, I gained more experience and was invited to teach in many countries. The most beautiful thing is that through daily practice for many years, I could expand my understanding and feelings of energy healing to a broader dimension. I had greater balance, more energy, and felt joy in contributing to the community and society, with simple healing techniques and breathing exercises to recharge and renew, both on a physical and spiritual level.

Showing up is magic each time. It opens the mind, ignites curiosity, expands confidence, making us more professional, authentic, positive and visionary. It opens many opportunities. I was grateful for the opportunities coming my way.

Life went on and our family was blessed to welcome another child, and we were now a big family of 4 children. I was really busy with four children, and the spiritual energy healing classes. Being a mom is my first responsibility for our family. I took the time to fulfill my duties for my children, keep them safe and nurtured, happy and balanced. At that time, my husband had his office at home, and we could always have one of the parents present at home when the other had to travel. Things worked out well, and we were grateful.

Years later, my husband's work offered him a position in the company in California, USA. We had an opportunity to move to California.

My son, who was studying at a university, stayed in Belgium to finish his studies. The 3 younger daughters came with us to the US. A new life started for us. Much to adapt, much to learn, much to show up, and much to discover. I was busy with our daily life and adjusting to the new life. My

main focus was the children, school, activities, and daily life. There was so much for us to learn and adapt, but we were all happy with this opportunity. In California, I could see my father often, as he has lived here for many years.

It took a few years before I could get back to my teaching activities. My main focus in a new country was taking care of my children and adapting to their new life.

Time went by faster than we noticed. My children are now grown up and they have their work and family.

More than a decade ago, I discovered the Beauty and Wellness industry and became a Wellness consultant. From my understanding, being balanced on a spiritual energy level goes in parallel with wellbeing and vitality. I learned more in Health and Beauty and have gained many experiences since.

Five years ago, I showed up at a presentation and decided to be certified as a Coach and Trainer in Communication and Relationships. BANKCODE is a scientifically validated methodology in Personality Code to predict in less than 90 seconds the buying behavior of people. I was fascinated by this Art and Science and the depth of the impact in applying this system both in business and personal life.

Communication between two or more people is the foundation of all human interaction, message and conversation. The verb, the word, the speech, all have frequencies. Choosing another word to adapt is matching the frequency to adapt. I have understood that life on Earth is about helping people, through our activities, work or any creativity, in community and society. People helping People. Whatever we do, the ultimate impact is about helping another person.

The BANKCODE methodology has a connective mission to Make people matter. Understanding the codes of another person allows us to adapt our words and approach to the code language of the other person, creating a more connective communication- in all relationships.

If we can speak the language of their personality code, they would feel heard, felt and more related to us. I think this approach is very human, more from heart and emotional intelligence.

If we can tap more into our emotional intelligence and spiritual intelligence, with a simple system, human communication can reach a higher level, with more consciousness, more understanding and respect, and one by one, humans will be creating more connective frequencies through communication and connection, for a society with more love and authenticity.

I am grateful for what I have learnt and the experiences I have gained throughout my life, from a young age until today. I am thankful for my mother and father, my teachers at school and all the people who showed up at different stages of my life. I am thankful for my husband walking the path with me through ups and downs, loving and caring for our children. I am thankful for our four children, for being present in my life, making me a happy and proud mother.

Thank you for reading my story, why I showed up at different situations to discover and learn.

Minh H. Dannerstedt, Ph. D.

Dr. Minh H. Dannerstedt, PhD

Dr. Minh H. Dannerstedt started Energy Self-healing Workshops in Europe and was invited to teach in several countries on different continents.

She received a Certification of Doctor of Philosophy from the Open International University for Complementary Medicine in 1998.

She is also a Certified Hado Instructor guided by Dr. Masaru Emoto.

Dr. Minh H. Dannerstedt is a Certified Coach & Licensed Trainer in Communication & Relationships for Business & Personal life.

https://codebreakerglobal.com/crackyourcode/communicating

#oneworldonelanguage #makepeoplematter #makekidsmatter

minhdann@gmail.com

Your LEGACY Matters
By Dr. Nephetina L. Serrano

The great use of life is to spend it on something that will outlast it.
William James

Living in a world where a pandemic has seemingly changed life forever as we know it, many of us have suffered losses and the longevity of life feels uncertain. The contemplation of life and its true worth and meaning challenges us to re-examine our definitions of success. Why do we do what we do? Is success a thriving career, a happy family, fulfilling health and wellness and the ability to move financially in this world at leisure? That probably sounds like a pretty good life to most. When life is all said and done, and we face the inevitability of our mortality, we have to examine if our possessions and our experiences on earth will even be remembered when we are gone. How will we live in a way so that after we take our last breaths those who succeed us can carry our torch of purpose and vision, extending our life's meaning into the years to come? We must ask ourselves: "What lasting impact do we want to make in the world?" By answering this question, we began a quest of creating a legacy of success and excellence that far exceeds death. It extends past our finite existence and reaches into the future with hope. Creating legacy is indeed true success.

As a woman of God and wife of 35 plus years, I have overcome many difficulties, challenges, and tragedies, including the more recent loss and sudden deaths of loved ones indirectly due to Covid-19. Building legacy has become more important to me now, than ever before. It is absolutely essential for us to determine our purpose, and establish success in that purpose, while committing to building our legacy. We must be intentional in this quest because tomorrow is not promised.

A great man once said: "The power of a person's life is in the stories they leave behind." Our legacies are not just about what we've created, but about the story that we are a part of and share. In truth, we are always part of a bigger narrative. Our story is never just about ourselves. There have always been events, actions and people who intersect with our stories. Our challenge is to see the larger narrative, recognizing how others have shaped us and how we impact others.

We should not limit the pondering of legacy to old age or when our loved ones die. Every day we should reflect about the meaning of our lives, being intentional to live each minute towards that greater purpose. My life journey forced me to consider legacy at a very young age. Although I grew up in a loving home, the dysfunction of my parents' relationship weighed heavily on my teenage mind. My parents' relationship would later dissolve, but not before I left first. I ran away from home, leaving my last year of high school.

Walking away from being an A student to being a high school dropout was devastating. My goal was to finish high school and go away to college, never to deal with that life again. Things didn't quite happen the way I planned. I needed to secure a healthy space for me to live and be, with wisdom even as a youth, to preserve and prioritize my own sanity and well-being. I solemnly promised myself in those low moments of confusion and

transition that I would not be a statistic. My life would mean something, ensuring that the next generation that I would impact would not have to endure the hardships I had to survive. After securing my living situation, I wound up going back to school the very next year and finishing. I kept that promise to myself.

It was at this moment I had to make very adult decisions at a time when most youth my age were celebrating their impending independence, only starting to scratch the surface of their ultimate vision of life. I had to decide in those moments what legacy I wanted to establish on the earth. Who was I? Who was I to become? What did I have to do to survive and ensure that I was not labeled just another at-risk teen with a bleak and pre-determined fate? Renowned speaker Steve Saint says, "Your story is the greatest legacy that you will leave to your friends. It's the longest lasting legacy you will leave to your heirs." At a tender age, I had to direct my choices towards who I wanted to be on the earth and how I wanted to be remembered.

Being a teen who worked to support herself while going to school wasn't easy either. However, I persevered and was rewarded with opportunities for doing so. I had already started working at the early age of 14 with the Philadelphia Mayoral Summer Youth Program. After that, there weren't many jobs that I didn't get on a first interview. My gift of articulation that I was once teased for by my peers, would actually take me far. From there, my first job was an assistant secretary position in the Counseling and Psychology Department of the elite University of Pennsylvania's Wharton School of Business. I built a life, step by step, brick by brick, of serving others, developing my skills and gifts and delivering those gifts in excellence. Years later, full circle, I am now Ambassador, Dr. Nephetina Serrano, Marriage Counselor, Empowerment Speaker, Award winning International Best-Selling Author, Certified Life Coach, Relationship Expert, and Mentor.

I have been able to break generational curses of a dysfunctional marriage with my husband of over thirty years, Dr. Richard Serrano. We both are co-founders of Covenant Marriages, Covenant Rescue 911 and Covenant Marriages Institute. We support couples in crisis and transitional phases within their marriage to achieve balance and stability in life and in business through Biblical principles. We also co-host "Your Marriage Matters" on Dominion TV which has aired in over 35 countries around the globe. In addition, we hosted the RISE Up Series airing via Zoom and streaming LIVE on Facebook. We went on to co-author the book, The Marriage Corporation which highlights the organizational needs of a covenant marriage.

I am the Publisher of Marriage CEO Magazine, a publication tailored to meet the relationship needs of couples, especially those leaders in the community, marketplace and ministry. I am also co-author of and contributor to Make It Happen, When Doves Cry: "Stories that Heal," The Price of Greatness, No Matter What You Can Make It and the RISE UP Women Who Lead Building Legacy Anthology.

I have received many awards and certificates including The City Council of Philadelphia Citation, recognizing my contribution to women. I have also received awards from The Echoes of Africa, The Mayor's Commission on African and Caribbean Immigrant Affairs, Women of Wealth, Publishers Golden Eagle Award and ACHI Magazine's Woman of Inspiration. I was named one of Success Magazine's 100 Best Life Coaches in 2021. I also received both the California Senate's Recognition and Legislature Assembly Game Changer Award. In addition, I was awarded The Assembly Member 61st District Jose Medina 2021 County of Riverside Influencer Award. Most recently, I was recognized for Mentorship at The Lady in Blue Sapphire Awards of GSFE by Robbie Motter.

A life rich with accomplishments and honors. A life of pouring into others so that they experience success in their endeavors and relationships. All because I dared to commit to the legacy I envisioned. However, establishing a legacy of success is not just about the accomplishments and honors that one receives. It is not merely about money and assets as much as it is about you, your life, your impact in the world, the lessons you have learned and sharing your personal story. It is about the people that we are able to truly invest in and touch during our journey. I recognize that I am and have always been a part of the bigger narrative. And one day, the challenges I have had to overcome will be a source of inspiration to someone who feels the odds are stacked against them, but still has the audacity to build their vision by any means necessary.

Here are 7 Key Steps in Establishing Success by Building Legacy:

1. **Get clear on the woman in the mirror and what impact you want to make in this world.**

My moment of clarity began when I was a young teen forced to provide for herself, find a place to live and defy the odds stacked against my favor. Until you are clear on what you would like your legacy to be, you cannot start building it. Stop wasting time and start to build! Establishing success in this area is not something you happen upon, rather you must be intentional and understand your why.

2. **Begin building your legacy today. Tomorrow is not promised; our days are numbered.**

We must start now, as we have seen in the most recent decade, time waits for no one and none of us know when we will cease to be no more. Start a family tree. Even begin writing out traditions so your family does not lose sight of the ties that bind you all together. What do you want your family, friends and the world to know about you? What words of wisdom, recipes or experiences do you want to share that may encourage, uplift or inspire the next generation in this lifetime?

3. **Seek opportunities to serve others.**

Part of our purpose on this earth is to serve one another. Serving helps to build up others. Remember, you matter, your life matters, and what you do for others matters.

4. **Discover creative ways to make a difference in this life, making the world a better place.**

None of us are perfect. Oftentimes we experience failures along our journey, however, we don't allow those failures to get in the way of our success. We take the fall, but we get back up. We become the change we desire and the hope we need, first for ourselves, then for others.

5. **Develop your skills. Find 2-3 things you're good at and explore them.**

What are those things that you find yourself doing relentlessly, without thought that brings you joy? It could be making pies for your neighbors, feeding the hungry, fostering children, teaching self-care seminars, coaching, mentoring youth, etc. Do those things.

6. **Be the change that you are looking for, sharing love and kindness and providing hope to others.**

Everyone needs to know they are not alone. We must inspire hope in

knowing that no matter what, we can and will overcome any obstacles.

7. **Never stop believing in the POWER of ONE.**

It takes one person to make a difference. So why not be the ONE? Don't be afraid of those times when you must stand alone to establish your legacy. You can eventually find your tribe that will inspire you in your journey.

I hold my head high knowing that my legacy of excellence is established in the world, to be a beacon of hope for the next generation and inspire them to be successful in their own right, on their own terms. You, yes you can make a difference in this world and in this life, here and now. See where you are making the most impact in life and do that more. This is true success. We influence people every day by what we say, do, write, create, and share. And all of that influence adds up. It took overcoming and enduring many of life's ups and downs, victories and hardships, to be able to find my purpose, define my own version of success and establish my personalized legacy of success on the earth. And I share that with you so that you can do the same. May we use the power of our lives for the lasting good of those we touch to further impact our families, communities, and the world. Remember, Legacy is true success.

Ambassador Dr. Nephetina L. Serrano

United Nations Ambassador for Peace, Relationship Expert, The Marriage CEO ®

Her Excellency Dr. Nephetina L. Serrano is the Chief Publisher of Serrano Legacy Publishing. She is an International Inspirational, transformational speaker, a committed Influencer who is changing the game and making a difference in the lives of, women, girls, and couples around the world. She is a Certified Counselor, Certified Life Coach, 8x Best Selling Author, and Mentor.

Dr. Serrano is Co-Founder of Covenant Marriages, Inc., Covenant Rescue 911, a 24-hour hotline for couples and families in crisis and Covenant Marriages Institute. Co-Author of the Book, "The Marriage Corporation," Publisher of Marriage CEO Magazine "For the Entrepreneur Who Leads, Building Legacy." Married to His Excellency Ambassador Dr. Richard Serrano, daughter Brande Serrano.

Dr. Serrano has received countless awards and certificates, honoring and acknowledging her Humanitarian contributions, nationally and globally including the prestigious President's LIFETIME Achievement Award 2022 and 2021, signed by President Joe Biden. Success Magazine named her one of the 100 Best Life Coaches of 2021, The City Council of the City of Philadelphia honored with a CITATION recognizing her contribution to women. She also received awards from The Echoes of Africa, The Mayor's Commission on African and Caribbean Immigrant Affairs, The SIMA Global Award, Women of Wealth Award, "Publishers Golden Eagle Award", Carl Wilson Humanitarian RED Jacket Award, Women of Achievement Ambassador Queen Award and crown, ACHI Magazine Woman of Inspiration Award 2019, State of California SENATE recognition in honor of GSFE Senator Richard D. Roth 31st District California Legislature Assembly Game Changer Award, Assembly Member 61st District Jose Medina 2021 County of Riverside Influencer Award, Catalyst for Change Girls with Pearls Award and many more.

Covenant Rescue 911

www.marriageCEOs360.com

DrSerranoministries@gmail.com

116 BALA AVE, SUITE 1B, BALA CYNWYD, PA 19004

SHOWING UP: NEVER STOP BELIEVING
By Ambassadors Nicole and John Farrell

Hello, my name is Nicole Farrell. I love showing up at Global Society for Female Entrepreneurs, (GSFE) events and several others. There is always something we'll learn from one another. It's amazing when I think about what I hear, I learn something new all the time.

When I show up, I listen to everyone, the speaker, my sisters, they all have some personal stories to share. We support each other and we share our thoughts and help each other. We learn by listening then reflecting on the story everyone is sharing.

Even on a personnel basis or as in general, we all have different answers or opinions, and we choose the one that fits our needs. It could be medical advice or suggestions, marital situations, children and grandchildren, or your fundraiser ideas.

What I love is at one of our GSFE monthly luncheons, one of our members suggested that we bring some never used items from our home that we might have received as gifts in the past, but it might be a double of something we already have. She suggested that we bring such items to the luncheon, and we would then hopefully have enough nice gifts to make baskets for some of our fundraisers, I thought that was a superb idea! For an event, we exchange ideas as to what to wear, everything on the table there's no limit, what we can talk about. We learn from each other; we can even borrow a dress, a purse or whatever.

When I do a show up, I learn from our customers. I am learning from doing shows as well – it's never ending. For instance, using a flash drive or music track sent to my text; I had no idea how to do that. It's difficult sometimes but I learned!! John and I named ourselves "Dinosaurs" when we talk about computers.

John, my husband, loves to talk to people especially our veterans about their experiences in the service; he'll spend hours talking to our service men. John's eyes get watery as he relays their stories to me. Thank you for your sacrifice, Sir.

John wrote, one day a few years ago, during the lowest time of my life I was on a walk. I wasn't a religious man but that day something touched me. I stopped and I said a prayer, I immediately felt a "warmth" all over me, then I knew that I'd be all right. A few days later, what I didn't realize then, I met my wife to be, "Nicole"! I thank the Lord for my wife of over 30 some years now and still going strong! Since that day we have been blessed with 18 grandchildren between us. We started our lives together "with nothing "but we fought our way through" Since then, our lives have been "just one in time moment after another." Many times, we have come so close to losing everything then finally we have come to a point in our lives when we can finally enjoy our time together. Never stop trying, never stop forgiving, and never stop believing.

Ambassadors John and Nicole Farrell

John and Nicole moved to Menifee in 2006. Nicole struggled with cancer plus, a brain tumor, and by the grace of God, she's back doing very well.

Nicole is a member of Global Society of Female Entrepreneurs, GSFE, and John is an Ambassador of the same organization.

She is also an Ambassador for the Menifee Chamber of Commerce. Nicole entertains at several nursing homes and resorts. She's been in the entertainment business for over 30 years, and has had weekly shows at Menifee Lakes Country Club, French Valley Cafe, Cherry Hills Golf Country Club. Etc. Nicole is also an International Best-Selling Author in 3 different books. She's a minister who has officiated weddings as far as Lake Arrowhead and here in our local community.

John has been married to Nicole for over thirty-two years. He worked as a general manager for a Cadillac dealership in San Diego for 30 years and retired in 2006 and moved to Menifee which Nicole and John both love with a passion.

John enjoys time with their big family of seven kids and eighteen grandchildren, he loves cooking, yard work, listening to music and watching movies with his wife Nicole, and most of all taking road trips in his little red convertible. He is also Nicole's sound engineer, roadie and greeter as they still do several shows in the area.

John has received several Certificates from our Congressman, State Senators, our Mayor of Menifee as well as from the President of the United States for his volunteer work in our community.

YOUR FIRST & SECOND APPEARANCE (ASK & ASK AGAIN)

By Ambassador Dr. (h.c.) Omenesa Oruma-Akomolafe

Spring 2024, I was diagnosed with Cough Variant Asthma. After 40 years of never having asthma and being able to breathe naturally, I started using inhalers, being awakened in my sleep by attacks and sudden loss of breath. One day while I was at work, after crying my eyes out to a friend of mine on the phone, expressing my pain towards this terrible disease and how the steroids are affecting my vocal cords, a dementia patient walked out of her room and told me to my face that I suffer from asthma because I am not asking what I want from God. She went ahead to give me a book and told me to read it during my shift. The few pages I happened to read was about a young girl who developed asthma because her mom did not listen to her countless requests, of telling her mom to stop the car because her younger sister (Mother's Daughter) was having an asthma attack while seated at the back of the car. Her mother ignored her and took it to be, 'One of those things'. Her daughter died that day. Her sister eventually developed asthma along the way. What a powerful relationship this shows between asking and the fear of not asking because of the fear of being rejected. I strongly doubt this woman got asthma just from that single event. I'm sure years and years of not being able to ask for whatever she wanted caused her body to respond in the way it did. And mind you, the patient who gave me this book was a psyche patient. She was the unlikely person God would use that day, but He did. My tears were my ask, and reading the book was me showing up. I later went on to order the book on Amazon to read and own it for myself.

Our world was created with words. Light was brought into the world by a pronouncement, "LET THERE BE LIGHT," and there was light. Could it be that darkness erodes certain aspects of our lives because we haven't spoken light into it? We haven't spoken positivity into it? We haven't paid attention to that gap in our lives. Therefore, there is so much toxicity and sickness in that area. After seeing the Laryngologist in desperation to bring my vocal cords back to normal, she asked me if I had been experiencing some changes in my singing prior to using steroids. I said, "Yes." This means that the steroids only magnified an existing issue. For the past 40 years, I'd been singing without technique and professional skill. I am a Gospel Singer, so for lack of a better word, I sing passionately and forcefully. I am also a Pentecostal preacher, so my passion shows up in my speaking and singing technique, which excites and inspires the audience, but wrecks my voice.

If I had the technique and skill, this wouldn't be an issue. Surely not all gospel singers have this issue. Why? Because they practice and do warmups in the morning or before they sing. They drink hot/warm water. They drink honey. They cover their necks with a shawl in a cold room. When they don't have to talk, they don't. They sleep with a humidifier. They don't yell or scream. They coat their throat with lozenges, and most of all, they go for singing lessons or voice therapy, or at least they watch YouTube videos on warmups and singing skills.

What does this have to do with asking? You cannot expect miracles to happen in your life if you are not part of the miracle. This is where showing

up comes in (which is a form of asking). In my philosophy, we show up twice. Let's talk about the first appearance. We'll talk about the second appearance soon.

FIRST APPEARANCE (THE FIRST ASK)

Before you ask, you ask. You ask by surveying what needs to be done so you don't even have to 'ask' in the first place. Take your medication so you don't need to seek healing. Study so you don't need to fidget and wonder if you're going to pass or not. Take care of the voice God has given you, so you don't ruin it or need therapy, surgery, or even stitches. Protect yourself. Guard your heart. If we can only do what we know to do, we wouldn't sin against ourselves and then need to repent and ask for forgiveness. We ought to stop sinning against ourselves by showing up for ourselves. By making an appearance in every aspect of our lives and taking opportunities seriously.

I didn't give myself asthma, but the havoc the steroids had caused was only made possible because from the beginning, I did not show up. I did not ask what it would take to continue singing so beautifully. Therefore, life offered me the opposite of beautiful (hoarseness, flat notes, etc.). When you don't ask, you still get an answer. I'll explain this below in the barriers of showing up (Number 4).

Now, here is how I eventually showed up in that vocal situation. I observed the symptoms that took place in my body after inhaling several puffs. I wrote them down and after a month of wounds in my mouth, thrush on my tongue, dizzy spells, tiredness, weight gain etc., I picked up the phone and told my doctor that the inhaler was killing me. I was taken off steroids, which didn't make sense because steroids are what manages asthma. I was given a COPD inhaler instead, and I haven't had any problems ever since.

Calling the doctor was my 2nd appearance. We'll go more on my 2nd appearance real soon. Let's talk about how suffocating your needs (not asking) can cause serious damage in your life.

You see, when you don't ask, you suppress. You keep it all in. You don't express how your salary needs to be reviewed. You don't talk about your marital issues that are killing you. You don't explain your dissatisfaction towards how you are being treated. You don't admit that you don't like the house. Sooner or later, rats will infest the property. A strong stench could start smelling in the home. Electricity shortage could occur in the whole neighborhood, and a whole flood to drudge every city except yours. I know it seems farfetched, but it happens. When you bury your emotions, you bury yourself.

Not only is not asking guaranteed to recede your knowledge, handy information, and enhance an alone complex, it frustrates you and increases low self-esteem. Doors fly open when you ask, and there are many ways to ask. You can ask by using affirmative words daily as a mantra until what you say comes to pass. You can design a vision board. You can also constantly pray for it to happen.

BARRIERS TO ASKING

1. Not being aware of what you really want:

In 2023, I really wanted to meet a specific talk show host who I deeply admired and still do. I spoke to Lady Dr. Robbie Motter about it, and she said, "Just put it out there in the universe and see what happens." I did. The VERY SAME DAY, Facebook advertised that this was giving $200 to people who wish to be on a particular show that was to celebrate her upcoming season in the park, but she wouldn't be there. The ad requested

a few minutes' shoot, expressing why we wanted to attend the show. I was on break at work. I was wearing my scrubs, and I looked like a train had run over me. Nevertheless, I sleeked my hair back, made sure my face was moisturized, put on some lip balm, and I recorded it.

A few hours later, I was confirmed to attend the show. I attended the show and signed my book in hopes of giving it to her producers. She surprised us by showing up in person. I hugged her and asked to have an audience with her. She was humble and invited me to her dressing room. I talked about my testimony in the book and how I moved to New York. She was intrigued and thanked me for coming. It wasn't until I left that I realized, "I DIDN'T ASK FOR WHAT I WANTED." What did I want? I wanted to sing on her show. I wanted to share my inspiring story as a guest on her show. I was so star-struck that I didn't think through what I would do should the opportunity arise to ever meet her, and so the opportunity came, but I did not show up accordingly. The moral of what I just shared is that it is not enough for you to ask. You must know WHY you are asking and WHAT you are asking for.

You must know that you deserve whatever it is you are asking for, and you must be ready for the moment when and how it presents itself. I admit, I was not ready, and I felt I lost the opportunity of a lifetime. But in summer 2024, I booked a ticket to go to her actual show, and I made sure I wore my crown and sash so I could be noticed. Her producers moved me from the 3rd row to the 2nd row. She spotted me and came up to hug me. All throughout the show, I told myself that one day, I would be seated on her show as a guest. I booked another ticket to attend her show for the 3rd time. I'm going to keep on doing that until I become a guest.

2. We are taught not to overstep our boundaries: Some cultures tell you to not look in the eye of an adult. If you can't look into the eyes of an adult,

how are you supposed to garner confidence to ask for what you want with your head down, let alone not looking into their eyes? You end up not asking at all. You end up learning to be " content" with the card life plays for you. That's danger. If you don't play the game, the game will be played for you, and when the game is played for you, it's usually not being played in your favor.

3. Fear of being rejected: " JUST DO IT" is what I say. I was granted an audition as singer/and or author of the year in an award organization. I was not considered a nominee for Singer Of The Year, but for the author of the year. So, I emailed the organization and asked if I could be given a 5-minute slot to sing at the award ceremony because I am actually a singer before an author. As of the time I wrote this chapter in this book, I hadn't received a reply, but you can email me at ooooruma@gmail.com to find out if they ever responded to me and how it panned out.

4. Get rid of pride: Remember when I stated, "When you don't ask, you still get an answer." If you don't know it, you won't produce ripe results. You will definitely produce something. You could produce hate, delay, bitterness, and even divorce, but whatever you produce will certainly not be ripe or worthy of anything. Be careful. Get rid of ego (Stop Edging God Out). Get rid of pride.

5. Not believing you deserve it: You do! All those evil things said to you as a child or even as an adult are not true. You are special. You are needed. You are relevant.

6. What are your fears? Why do you believe you can't get this thing? Tell yourself that what you fear will not manifest, and if it does manifest, what is the worst that can happen? Ask again, and again and again, until you get what you want.

7. Make sure you are asking someone who has the power to give it to you while you are cordial and asking in confidence. Not asking someone who CAN help you will unnecessarily expose you. Be concise and be specific in asking for what you want.

THE SECOND APPEARANCE (SHOWING UP/ASKING AGAIN)

Showing up is another form of asking. What you order is what you get. If you are standing outside, you will be rained on. Rain in this context is a good thing. Rain makes things grow. If you are in the right place at the right time, you will be rained on. Your crops will grow. Your seeds will flourish. Famine will be eradicated. Your land will be green. All this because you showed up outside. All this because you subconsciously asked to be rained on.

I work in 2 nursing homes. It is emotionally draining. Angry people everywhere in the building. Depressed patients and disenfranchised staff. How do I keep showing up at work? Right when I get off work at 7 am, I tell myself, "You are not calling out today." You see, the prior shift would have already dealt with me in a way that I'd have already told myself, "I can't come in the next shift. I have to rest. I need a break. I can't stand this supervisor, etc.)." All these narratives would have done a good number on me, and by the time I get to my house, more than likely, I'll call out from work.

One day, I realized I had called out so many times that my supervisors began to call to ask if I was coming to work even though my name was on the schedule. That's when I realized that I had misrepresented myself and given myself a false and negative reputation of me because I didn't have the wisdom to ask for a smooth shift.

I began to ask God to give me a good shift, happy patients, astute staff, bountiful supplies on the floor, strength in my body, no pain in my back, kind Supervisor, peaceful shift. The more I prayed this way, the less I called out until I didn't call out at all. Now they know that if I call out, it must be for an unavoidable reason.

When you don't show up, you lose. You lose your integrity. You lose your opportunity. You lose the fruition of your desires. In some cases, you lose your rights. You lose your plea. Imagine you missing the opportunity to defend yourself in court as not guilty, but your absence automatically bids you " Guilty".

IN CONCLUSION

I am writing my thesis. It is hard. The writing rules are daunting. It is stretching me to write in a style that I am not used to, and I know that if I don't sail through this season. I will not graduate. I am following the rules to get what I want.

In as much as you are in control of your life, there are some hidden codes and some unspoken rules. You already know you should greet before you start a conversation. You should also know how to leave a tip for the waiter even though it's not mandatory. When you follow the rules, your desired results will be granted. In my case, my graduation will be guaranteed. I encourage you to follow the rules, and the ultimate rule you should follow is the rule to show up and ask……. and remember, they are synonymous.

Ambassador Dr. (h.c.) Omenesa Oruma-Akomolafe

Omenesa Oruma-Akomolafe is a Gospel Recording Artist, Renowned Speaker, Evangelistic Preacher, Award Winning Artist, Confidence Coach, Narcissistic Abuse Healing Practitioner, Philanthropist under the umbrella of Yellow Relief Foundation(365 Baby Deliveries In One Year), UN Ambassador, Joe Biden Lifetime Achievement Award, UK Parliament Awardee, Author, Actress, Model, Pastor of The Delivery Ward Church, Affiliate Pastor at Ben Oruma Ministries & Vineyard International Christian Ministries, Founder of Praying For My Husband Ministries, New York Director of Global Society For Female Entrepreneurs, USA Coordinator for Rev Sam Oye's Prophetic Prayer Conference, CEO Of The Conglomerate: Omenesa's Mansion, Proprietress of Pearls & Pauls Emotional Healing Center, Thanatologist at Angels On Duty, Certified Nursing Assistant, President Of The Aaron Sisters. She loves to travel, journal, swim, and eat mint chocolate ice cream.

"It's All About Showing Up:
The Journey of Maew Voecks"

By Pramuan "Maew" Voecks

In a world where many seek recognition and fame, few shine as brightly as Pramuan Voecks, affectionately known to her friends as Maew. Her story begins in the serene village of Sawanlealok, Sukhothai, Thailand, where she was born into a lively family with six brothers and four sisters. In the heart of this vibrant household, Maew's journey as a dynamic chef took form, guided by the hands of her beloved mother.

From the age of nine, Maew found herself deeply entwined in the kitchen, helping her mother prepare meals for their ever-growing family. At first, the task felt like a burden. She found herself fuming as she chopped vegetables and stirred pots, frustrated by what she believed was an endless cycle of cooking for others. What she didn't realize then was that each meal was not just a chore—it was a lesson, a cultural heritage wrapped in fragrant spices and rich flavors. Every culinary endeavor opened her eyes to the incredible range of authentic Thai food, each dish telling a story from a different region of her beautiful country.

The Move Abroad: A Culinary Awakening

Adulthood ushered in significant changes for Maew, especially when she met her husband, a Navy gentleman whose service in the military would significantly shape their lives. In 2000, their journey led them to Hawaii, a paradise filled with shimmering beaches and the aroma of fusion cuisine wafting through the open air.

She also had to increase her learning of English; she knows the basics, but each journey helped her to enhance this skill.

Upon arriving in the Islands, Maew recognized that her culinary skills could bring joy to a new community. She dived right into the local food scene, showcasing her authentic Thai dishes to the delight of both locals and tourists alike. Her passion for cooking quickly turned into a sensation; her customer base expanded rapidly, and her food became the talk of the island.

"What is in your Pad Thai?" folks would inquire, mesmerized by the perfect balance of flavors. Maew always replied with humility, "It's made with love." The genuine appreciation she received made her realize that cooking was more than just a profession; it was her way of "showing up" in the lives of others.

But as the Navy life often dictates, their time in Hawaii was ephemeral. Maew faced yet another transition as her husband received orders to Northern Seattle. Many would have felt daunted by such uprooting, but Maew embraced the change, ready to again share her culinary talents in a new environment.

Navigating New Landscapes: The Art of Adapting

Arriving in Northern Seattle, the climate was different, the culture distinct. Yet, the very essence of cooking drew her in. Determined to make her mark, Maew scoured local neighborhoods for job opportunities and soon found herself cooking. The more she showed up—at work, in markets, in community events—the more connections she built, and friendships flourished.

Her culinary prowess was unmatched. As she navigated the world of food in a new terrain, Maew discovered that her authentic Thai recipes were a breath of fresh air for many locals. Her passion resonated deeply with the community, and it wasn't long before she became a well-recognized name among food enthusiasts.

Yet, cooking was just one facet of her life. Beyond the kitchen, Maew was an unyielding humanitarian. In every community she settled in, she sought ways to reach out, uplift, and make a meaningful difference in people's lives. She volunteered, organized food drives, and offered cooking classes to underprivileged children. Her heart, big and warm, led her to find initiatives that inspired others and brought smiles to countless faces.

Settling into Menifee: A Culinary Dream Realized

After the family's tour in Washington, they relocated to Menifee, California, where Maew once again faced the challenge of adjusting to a new life. Even in this new setting, she quickly landed a role within the Food Department at Pechanga Casino, where her culinary creations continued to elevate customer experiences. Her reputation for cooking delicious Thai food spread, making her a beloved figure within the local dining scene.

But for Maew, this was still just a chapter in her ongoing story. The dream to again open her own restaurant had always lingered in her heart. In Bellflower, California, that dream became a reality when she opened a Thai restaurant that quickly became a cherished establishment. However, the daily commute from Menifee to Bellflower proved exhausting.

In September of 2022, she made a bold decision—she would open a restaurant closer to home. Thus, Melody's Thai Cuisine was born, a beautiful fusion of flavors and creativity nestled in the heart of Menifee.

It was during this time that Charmaine Summers introduced Maew to the community and to GSFE (Global Society of Female Entrepreneurs). Maew enthusiastically supported the events Charmaine sponsored in Menifee, participating in activities like Line Dancing, Karaoke, and other various events. She even hosted the Menifee GSFE Chapter at her restaurant, further solidifying her role as a community anchor.

From the moment Melody's opened its doors, Maew showed up every day, bringing not just her culinary expertise but a radiant smile that could light up any room. Her inviting presence created a warm atmosphere where customers felt welcomed. It didn't take long before her restaurant became a community hub, a place where patrons returned not only for delightful dishes but for the joy of being in Maew's company.

Recognition and Awards: A Testament to Impact

With her dedication and the quality of her food, Maew attracted substantial recognition. Melody's Thai Cuisine was featured in the Menifee Business Spotlight, celebrating its impact on the community. One of the most profound honors came when Maew was named Menifee Citizen of the Month.

Her accolades didn't stop there. She received numerous awards from dignitaries who admired her commitment to culinary excellence and her contributions to the community. Notably, Maew earned the "Call to Service" award from the President of the United States—a recognition not just of her culinary talents but her humanitarian spirit.

Yet perhaps the most heartwarming occasion came last year when many members of LOANI/GSFE from London showed up at her restaurant for a networking event. As a gracious host, Maew embraced each guest, her beautiful smile and infectious energy setting a warm tone for the evening.

Professor Caroline Makaka, the founder of Leaders of All Nations (LOANI), was among the attendees. After witnessing Maew's inspiring presence and powerful impact on everyone around her, the organization presented her with the World Class Superhero award. This accolade recognized Maew's extraordinary ability to inspire others and restore their sense of purpose, even amidst challenging circumstances.

A Legacy of Love and Service

Her family is very important to her, this year she took a trip back to her home in Thailand to see her Mother Yuan who is 88, Her mother had no idea she was coming, and when she opened the door and saw her daughter a big smile came upon her face. Maew while there for ten days took her on many journeys to see the beauty of Thailand and to experience many of the varies tastes of the exquisite food her county has.

Maew's journey has not just been about cooking; it has been about connection, community, and uplifting others through kindness and generosity. Her kitchen serves as a space of warmth, camaraderie, and joy, a testament to the power of showing up and asking how one can make a difference in the lives around them.

Beyond the restaurant walls, Maew has cultivated friendships and alliances, becoming a beacon of hope and motivation. Her life illustrates that the simple act of "showing up" can spark profound change in both familiar and unfamiliar communities. Through her cooking, she has created a bridge between cultures, showcasing the rich heritage of Thailand while embracing the vibrancy of her American surroundings.

As she looks toward the future, Maew plans to expand her culinary influence further. Her vision includes using her platform to empower aspiring chefs and young cooks. She dreams of organizing culinary workshops for children and adults alike, instilling in them the belief that they can, through their passion and dedication, create something beautiful.

With every Pad Thai prepared, every Curry simmered, and every grateful customer served, Maew Voecks continues to embody the spirit of kindness and a commitment to service. She has shown that it is not just the act of cooking that nourishes but the way one engages with one's community and the lives of others.

Conclusion

In a world that often celebrates individual accomplishments, Maew's journey echoes a profound truth: it is about showing up and asking not just how one can succeed, but how they can uplift those around them. Her story serves as a reminder that with love, dedication, and a genuine desire to make a difference, one can transform their life and the lives of countless others. Maew Voecks is more than a chef; she is a champion of hope,

transformation, and humanity, forever changing the culinary landscape wherever she goes.

Pramuan "Maew" Voecks

Chef with many years of expertise in preparing Thai food. She is also a restaurant owner of Melody's Thai Cuisine in Menifee, CA. She can be reached at 951-449-2272.

Healing, Showing Up, and Finding Love

By Ambassador Dr. Randi D. Ward

"Sometimes the universe shows you your direction even if you don't know the way." I heard this insightful quote from a character on the Hallmark movie Love on Safari filmed in South Africa. These words deeply touched my heart because my life has been a perfect example of this quote.

My life journey has been filled with many ups and downs, many twists and turns, detours, and winding roads with bumps and cracks. As a survivor, a fighter, and a huge dreamer, I had to learn to deal with these obstacles and roadblocks. I proudly have faced every challenge head-on and have thankfully emerged stronger each time. I transformed my trials into triumphs and allowed my perseverance to be a beacon of my success. My resilience and determination have turned obstacles into steppingstones, proving that no matter how tough my path, I have been able to overcome anything with the grace and guidance of loved ones and Almighty God.

Losing my beloved husband Bill after 48 years of being together and sharing so many memories was one of my most difficult tragedies though. I put him in the hospital on November 14, 2019, after our family doctor diagnosed double pneumonia. Bill woke up wheezing loudly, feeling dizzy, and barely able to breathe. He never complained and always said he was fine, but I knew he wasn't. He did not sleep well. His gasping to breathe would keep both of us awake often. When I forced him to see a doctor on previous occasions, the diagnosis had always been severe allergies. I tried not to worry, but I knew there had to be a more serious reason for his troubling condition. On this day, I once again forced him to go see his doctor and then had to force him to go the Emergency Room. He could be so stubborn when it came to his health.

After the hospital ER doctor examined him, Bill was put on oxygen immediately and admitted into the hospital as soon as a room was available. He was so unhappy about this. I felt bad for him, but he needed to get help I could not give him.

We hoped the hospital could get rid of his pneumonia easily and quickly. Many tests were run, including daily chest x-rays; various treatments were administered, but sadly, he was not improving. In fact, each day he became weaker. He was being fed intravenously but was losing weight. He became so frail and thin. I barely recognized my handsome husband now.

Higher levels of oxygen were needed as the days and weeks passed. He became completely bedridden. The doctors were totally puzzled. They could not even decide what kind of pneumonia he actually had. Was the cause viral, bacterial, or environmental? No test determined this. Eventually, it was decided the pneumonia must have been caused by something connected with the environment. Bill's hobby was restoring old cars. He was a master at creating beautiful cars. This work did involve much unhealthy work though---body sanding, sandblasting, painting, engine rebuilding, etc. Even though he wore a protective mask, it most likely was not enough to keep him from inhaling toxic substances.

The doctors, my son Mark, and I as well as Bill tried to remain positive that a cure would be found. We knew the doctors were doing their best to help

him. The nurses also were so compassionate and helpful. Even though Bill was suffering, he was always the model patient—so easy to take care of. The hospital staff really admired his strength and pleasant personality.

Frustration from the doctors finally led them to do a lung biopsy on December 6. This was being avoided because it is a very unpleasant, painful procedure, but they finally decided it was the next needed step to help Bill. We were devastated when the results given to us on December 9 revealed Stage 4 Lung Cancer. Until this test the doctors never suspected cancer. They were as shocked as we were. On December 14, Bill had a serious medical episode—a possible mini-stroke and was put on a CPAP machine at the highest oxygen level, which still was not enough. We were told by his doctors his chance of survival was now Zero Percent. How could this be possible? I went into immediate denial. They must be wrong. I prayed for a miracle.

On Sunday, December 15, Bill and I made the agonizing decision to slowly turn off the CPAP machine. It was the hardest thing I have ever had to do. We were told he would die in a matter of a few days of a heart attack, a stroke, or suffocation. He chose to die peacefully. We would not get our miracle. Drugs were administered to put him into a deep sleep. Around 11:35 p.m. that night, Bill passed away. I could not be there. I had watched him suffer so much; I could not watch him die. The two adult children of one of my best friends were there when he took his last breath. They said he died peacefully with a smile on his face. That was somewhat of a comfort to me that night when I received the phone call.

I went into shock later though. I never imagined that the day I put him in the hospital, he would never return home. My life was shattered. I am a very strong woman and have been through many personal traumas in my life: learning to walk so many times over five decades, surviving a near-fatal car accident requiring eight months of physical therapy, etc. Losing Bill was the worst. For months, I blamed myself, the doctors, and even God for his death.

For the next year, I did the grief counseling I needed: first at a nearby church group and then with an online therapist after COVID shut our world down. It helped, but I needed more. I was so lonely with no family close, except my dog Savannah. She was grieving as well.

One year after Bill's death, I wrote this poem to honor him.

My Year of Grief

My heart is being torn into tiny pieces once more.
Memories of the suffering of the man I still adore.
Still plague my mind every second of each lonely day.
Evil lung cancer destroyed my love and took my Bill away.

One year has passed, but I am still haunted by my relentless grief.
Nothing I do truly eases my emotional pain to give me needed relief.
I try to keep my promise to him to stay strong and continue to dream.
But as much as I want to do this, it is not as easy as it might seem.

I try to keep so busy, but I feel I have lost my joy.
There are not many things in life I now truly enjoy.
So many reasons exist why I have these problems moving forward.
I am confused and have no idea what things I want to move toward.

Bill was my life, my love, my partner, my everything.
He was there for me and made my heart sing.

He was my "earthly" savior who taught me how to accept love.
I have no doubt he was sent to me from God and Heaven above.

When I needed a special person to share an incredible fulfilled dream,
I went to him.
When I needed someone to hug me when things were not quite right,
I went to him.
When I needed a friend to explain to me why things were not as they
seemed,
I went to him.
When I needed a man to hold me in his arms and make my life so bright,
I went to him.
When my creative mind was so full of crazy ideas or I wanted to share a
secret,
I went to him.
When my life became overwhelming and just became too much,
I went to him.
When my mind was filled with unpleasant thoughts I needed to forget,
I went to him.
When the cure for all these was simply a gentle, sweet, and loving touch,
I went to him.
When I wanted to travel and explore a faraway land,
I went to him.
When I wanted to celebrate a completely unique and joyous day,
I went to him.

I really believed my life would never be happy again. But then what I consider
one of my unexpected miracles occurred. I turned to Facebook for comfort
and companionship. I started connecting with incredible people around the

world. One day in May 2021, I received a message in Facebook Messenger from a man I did not know. We had one mutual friend on Facebook. I am always careful, but I was intrigued after examining the profile page of this Pakistani man. Masood looked so kind—so sweet. We began writing to each other which led to voice calls and video calls. I was still in deep grief. Masood saw me at my worst---often crying, without makeup---in other words, a total mess. He patiently listened to me and only offered advice when I asked for it. We became close friends quickly as we talked for many hours every day. We often lost track of time during these long chats. The more we shared our thoughts and our feelings about so many things, our friendship grew into a deep love for each other---a romantic love. We were both shocked at first. We had not planned this. I was not looking for love again, but it found me. I was Masood's first true love. He often says he had been searching for me all his life, and now he had found the woman he was supposed to be with.

One of Bill's last words to me before he passed away was to keep my heart open to love. He did not want me to live the rest of my life alone and without love. Bill truly loved me and always put me first. I adored him.

I really believe that Bill and God sent Masood to me to help me heal. I will always love Bill and never forget him, but I have happily started a new life with Masood. Masood and I met in person in London in December 2022 at a LOANI (Ladies of All Nations International) award conference. He came to meet me. In January 2023 we met again in Dubai, UAE. I was there as an online university Chancellor to present Honorary Doctorates to recipients from Nepal and Bangladesh. Manila and Davao City, Philippines, would be our next destination. During this trip in October 2023, both of us were receiving LOANI awards as World Superheroes and attending a United Nations Day event. Every time we were together was magical. We knew without a doubt we were meant to be together. We became engaged and

started working on his USA visa.

On April 3, 2024, Masood arrived at Maynard Jackson International Airport Terminal in Atlanta, Georgia. On April 21 he and I were married in the garden area at the Manor House at Lake Arrowhead, California, in front of some of our closest friends. My Matron of Honor was International Leader Professor Caroline Makaka. My Bridesmaids were Legacy Builder Dr. Angelica Benavides, GSFE Founder Lady Dr. Robbie Motter, Entrepreneur/ Business Owner Dr. Jaya Sajnani, International Fashion Designer Dr. Chebra Dorsey, Celebrity Boss Dr. Dawn Anderson, Her Royal Majesty Queen Eden, Educator/Entrepreneur Dr. Susie Mierzwik, Publisher Dr. Angela Covany, and Domestic Violence Activist Dr. Suku Moyo Mackenzie. The Best Man was Entrepreneur Dr. Darryl K. Horton with Groomsmen Hall of Fame Magician Dr. Kenrick "Ice" McDonald, Singer/Actor Prince Fleet Easton, Educator/Coach Steve Mierzwik, and Media Guru John Farrell. Singer and Reverend Nicole Farrell officiated our lovely international wedding. My wedding party consisted of amazing international celebrities---people like family to me.

I created the entire wedding script. I wanted it to be meaningful. The ceremony included a prayer, personal wedding vows Masood and I wrote, the lighting of candles, a unity sand ceremony, the song "We Only Just Begun" (originally performed by the Carpenters and sung by Nicole plus a French song she sang) and two songs from Opera Singer Chelsea Snow. We danced to a couple of songs before going inside for the reception. The weather was perfect---sunny and mid-70s. (It had snowed there the weekend before. We were blessed to have great weather.)

The bridal party wore fashions representing their countries of Zimbabwe, India, Mexico, Canada, the Philippines, and of course, the USA. Masood and I wore Pakistani attire. He bought me a beautiful pink Pakistani dress.

Later I also wore a gorgeous Indian gown (a wedding gift from Dr. Jaya) for some of our wedding photos. The flowers were white silk rose bouquets and boutonnieres.

Lady Dr. Robbie decorated the outside with silk daffodils and gifted us a delicious and pretty wedding cake. The reception tables were covered in yellow tablecloths. At the reception Kenrick performed a magic card trick, Prince Fleet sang, and Chelsea Snow performed again.

In May we honeymooned in Orlando due to a resort gift from Dr. Angeline Benjamin. Disney World and Epcot entertained us that week. We connected with some close friends, too.

Our wedding was so special---beyond my wildest dreams. My new life with Masood is a true blessing. He is an incredible husband, as my Bill was. I cannot imagine my world without Masood now.

What if I had not "shown up" and not replied to Masood's first greeting that day in May?

I repeat once more, "Sometimes the universe shows you your direction even if you don't know the way."

I dedicate this chapter to Masood and to Bill---the two men who have filled my life with such joy.

Ambassador Dr. (h.c) Randi D Ward

Ambassador/Dr. (h.c) Randi D. Ward is a 50+-year-veteran American Educator/former Egyptian ESOL teacher; Co-Owner-RM Infinite; Former owner/teacher---Rise Up and 6 October Nursery (Egypt); Author of Because I Believed in Me (My Egyptian Fantasy Came True) and Random

Wanderings; Blogger/YouTuber; Writer--all genres; International Co-Author---37 anthologies (15 best-sellers); 18-time best-selling master editor/editor of 3 magazines; Visionary Book Coach certified in 4 categories, including NLP; LOANI Visionary Global Goodwill Ambassador; GIA Chaplain and Georgia Representative; International Speaker--15 countries; World Traveler--62 countries; and African animal advocate. Awards include IAOTP's Female Visionary, Hall of Fame, Educator of the Decade; 2020/2022 "She Inspires Me"; 2020 Woman of the Year-Language Arts and Writing (Top 100 Registry), 2020 Marshall University Star Alumni/2023 Distinguished Alumni; 2020/2023 Beautiful Survivors Awards; 2021 USA Presidential Service Award; 2020/2024 Nelson Mandela Humanitarian Awards; Three Honorary Doctorates; 2024 LOANI/GSFE/GIA 50 Top World Humanitarian Leaders; 2023 Top 50 IAOTP Fearless Leaders; 2024 Global Iconic Changemaker; Georgia Outstanding Citizen; Two LOANI Superhero Awards; Expert World Leader; Featured on 4 American billboards and numerous international newspapers/magazines/podcasts/TV/movies/zoom conferences (live and virtual).

www.randidward.com; randiteach@yahoo.com; rminfinitel@gmail.com

SHOWING UP
Brings Amazing Thingsto One's Life
By Lady Ambassador Dr. (h.c.) Robbie Motter

SHOWING UP is like following a treasure map; you never know what treasures will come your way. Each moment of presence, each decision to engage with life, opens a door to connections that might have otherwise remained hidden.

As I reflect on 2024, I can confidently say it has been an extraordinary year for me and the members of my nonprofit, Global Society for Female Entrepreneurs (GSFE). The series of events I experienced and the stories I became part of, both new and old, have reaffirmed the power of showing up - each instance a testament to how our lives can intertwine in the most unexpected ways.

Rediscovering Connections

One of the highlights of my year occurred in January when I had the honor of serving as both a speaker and a judge for the "Women of Achievement" pageant on the Queen Mary in Long Beach, CA. One of the contestants was one of my valued members, Sue Phillips from New York, City, who brought supportive guests to cheer her on. To my astonishment, I was reunited with Geoff Phillips, Sue's brother, whom I had not seen since the late 1980's. Geoff had previously been one of my clients for many years during my years doing government contracting and helping small business owners. As he approached me and playfully said "Guess who? I 'm part of your past," my heart swelled with joy, it took only a heartbeat for me to recognize his familiar voice and South African accent. We dove into a vibrant conversation, retracing the incredible business moments we had shared across New York, Washington, DC and California. We laughed about the fond memories, reminding ourselves of the profound connections we forged so long ago. Had I chosen not to SHOW UP at that event, that precious moment of reconnection would have been lost forever.

A Touching Surprise

Another unforgettable experience unfolded in Lake Arrowhead, CA. I consider myself someone who is not easily surprised, but 39 plus individuals managed to catch me completely off-guard. At a gathering, they presented me with a heartfelt book titled "A Leader with A Heart of Gold." This book was a compilation of stories that reflected my impact on each of their individual lives. As I flipped through its pages, I was struck by narratives chronicling encounters that spanned over 25 years.

To bring this project to life, they had to reach out to those whose lives touched, gather their stories, and keep the entire endeavor under wraps. I was astonishing to learn that even those I saw regularly kept this secret. As I read their heartfelt worlds and memories-some drawn from experiences in Hawaii, others from the East Coast, California and International Connections-I was overwhelmed with emotion. The love and respect emanating from each narrative confirmed the lasting bonds we had formed.

The book's official launch on April 28th was met with incredible success, achieving both US and International Best Seller Status on Amazon, a fitting testament to my enduring legacy. The book is available to be purchased on Amazon.

At this same meeting I was gifted with a check for me personally and told to use it totally for me, which I did. I planned a trip back to my birthplace Hawaii for ten days. I had not been home for five years and I saw it as a wonderful opportunity to also launch our "Voices of Peace: A Global Perspective" book with 100 coauthors sharing what Peace means to them.

We launched the book on July 7th in Hawaii on International Peace and Love Day, it immediately made #1 US and International Best Seller on that day in several categories. I took the book and took photos holding the book at all the great world renown places in Honolulu like the Royal Hawaiian Hotel, The Hilton Hawaiian Village, The Moana Hotel, Don the Beachcomber, Iolani Palace, Pearl Harbor and numerous other locations.

While in Hawaii I was also invited to be a guest at the Mrs. Hawaii Filipino Beauty Pageant and also reconnected with beautiful friends I had not seen for years. It was great to eat some food items I love from the Islands and to enjoy the beauty and Aloha that Hawaii is about.

Embracing the World

February brought another remarkable opportunity when I and other GSFE members were invited by LOANI (Leaders of all Nations) to attend their Gala and other planned events in the Philippines, and which for me also offered the opportunity to speak at three different events in the Philippine's.

As part of GSFE, we thrive on collaborations like this, which allow us to connect with women around the globe. LOANI's reach spans 195 countries, drawing us to locations we had only dreamed of impacting.

Growing up in Hawaii, I was surrounded by many Filipino friends, but I had never imagined speaking before them one day in the Philippine's.

This adventure significantly broadened my understanding of cultural exchange and global community. I found immense joy in sharing stories and wisdom with entrepreneurs from diverse backgrounds, who were equally passionate about empowering one another.

Providing Opportunities to Others

One of my greatest passions is being able to help others soar to higher heights than they even imagined and through GSFE this past year we were able to do many things. Through a collaboration with GIA (Global Alliance Association) and LOANI we did an Honorary Doctorate Humanitarian Doctors degree graduation in Lake Arrowhead and 28 of our GSFE members were able to receive that distinction, we had international visitors from London and Canada join us at this event.

Also, this year we had members that received Ambassador of Kindness and Love titles. Individuals serve because it's their passion. But it's a great feeling when they get honored and recognized for the work they do.

I was blessed this year of receiving so many International Humanitarian and Peace awards, and a Royal Ambassador of Peace Award, as well as another Ambassador title that of Ambassador of Happiness and Kindness. In May, I was presented the title of Queen of Ohanaeze Kingdom of California USA by His Majesty King Ozor Dennis Okafor, King of Ohanaeze Kingdom.

I remember when I was presented with my Lady title in London 4 years ago by Professor Caroline Makaka the CEO and Founder of LOANI, I was in shock and now to also receive two Ambassador titles and a Queen title is like a dream. The work we do, we don't look for awards, but when we get them, it's so nice to know others appreciate our efforts.

I also never thought I would ever be on the cover of a magazine and this year I was on three different covers, two different LOANI Magazine issues and one Celina Fashion Magazine. All also featured stories about the work I and my nonprofit do. I was also able to get several of my members on Magazine covers as well.

Opportunities presented themselves to me to be a coauthor in seven books this year, they are: "Expert World Leaders," "Leading with Heart and Soul," "Power of Networking"," Voices of Peace: A Global Perspective," "What are you Wearing? The Inspirational side of Fashion," "You are Enough," and now this book. It has been such an honor to be in these books with the other dynamic GSFE coauthors, as all the books achieved #1 US and International Best-Selling status.

What makes me the happiest is that I am able to SHOW UP and nominate my members for a variety of US and International awards. I was able to do over 200 nominations so far this year, offer opportunities for many members to be coauthors in books that achieved bestselling status, found them podcasts to be guests on, and speaking opportunities. We even got to SHOWUP on a cruise which was the first time for many and have another one planned for Dec 2024, we went to Americas Got Talent that was a fundraiser for GSFE, and we nominated 77 to be presented with an award on International Kindness Day November 13. Every year, we offer an online conference with dynamic speakers and trainings to help them grow their business. GSFE is there for its members.

As the leader of Global Society for Female Entrepreneurs, a 501(c)(3)

nonprofit, and my dedicated team, we strive to help our members totally understand the power of SHOWING UP and ASKING. Being there for them and sharing opportunities are something we are proud of, as together we truly can make a difference in the world to bring Kindness, Peace and Love.

One thing we know is we don't compete, we complete each other, and we are ONE.

The Dance of Transformation

These experiences highlight a universal truth: timing and presence matter, in each interaction-from a casual chat with an old friend to heartfelt discussions with new colleagues - I saw how the fabric of our lives interweaves through shared experiences and mutual support. Life often presents us with choices, it invites us to take part in opportunities that may seem daunting at first. Yet, when we choose to embrace those moments fully, we find ourselves enriched in ways we never anticipated. This year, through all these encounters, I came to understand that by simply showing up and being present, I've unlocked doors to immense personal growth and enriched my community.

A Call to Action

As I reflect on my journey, I urge you to remember the power contained in showing up. Whether it's attending a live or zoom event, reaching out to an old friend, or participating in unknown territories-your presence,

your voice, and your willingness to connect can culminate in beautiful transformations.

What treasures will you find when you SHOW UP? It could be an unexpected reunion, an inspiring story, or perhaps a chance to touch someone else's life profoundly. The possibilities are limitless, and I encourage you to seek them out.

Join me as we continue to cultivate connections, advocate for one another, and inspire through our stories, Together, we can transform moments into memories and relationships into powerful collaborations.

So, ask yourself, are you ready to embrace the adventure that lies ahead? Are you willing to show up and welcome the extraordinary into your life? The world is waiting for you.

Lady Ambassador Dr. (h.c.) Robbie Motter

Lady Ambassador Dr. (h.c.) Robbie Motter is the Founder and CEO of GSFE (Global Society for Female Entrepreneurs) a 501 (c)(3) nonprofit whose mission is to Empower, Inspire, Mentor, Educate and Connect individuals to be successful entrepreneurs. We are a global network with live and zoom monthly meetings. Check out our website at gsfeus.com. She is also an award-winning author, speaker and personal and business coach.

She can be reached at rmotter@aol.com, or 951-255-9200, also same number for WhatsApp just add US code. She can be found on Facebook and LinkedIn as Robbie Motter, her personal website is robbiemotter.com

"Be the CHANGE You Want to See in the World"

By Dr. Sara M. Lypps, MBA

What does "showing up" mean to me? I don't believe that life is simply like a dress rehearsal. Even when you're backstage, and especially when you don't have an audience, it's important how you see yourself and not just how others and the world see you. As a single mother of four children the past thirteen and a half years, I have always made it a priority to set a positive example. Whether you're front stage or backstage, it's always "SHOW TIME!"

One example of this is when my boys were young and we used to spend a lot of time at the park, especially when we were killing time waiting for their older brother and sister to get out of school. While my boys played on the playground, I didn't just simply sit down and watch from the sidelines. Instead, I would walk around the play area and look for trash to pick up. This was not only to make sure the area was safe for my children to play, but also to do my part by leaving the park cleaner than when I got there. "But when you do a charitable deed, do not let your left hand know what your right hand is doing." (Mathew 6:3) One time, I was with my boys at a very large park in Oceanside, California where they had several soccer fields. When my boys were a little older, maybe six and eight, and I was walking laps for exercise while they rode their bikes and scooters. After they did three to four laps of a nearly one-mile track, they would go to the center of the park where there was a large playground. One day I was walking by myself and I started picking up trash, as I often did. There were usually several birthday parties and events on the weekends and small items of trash would often get overlooked. That day, I started picking up water bottle caps, streamers, juice box straws, candy wrappers, and lollipop sticks until my hands were completely full. I clearly remember telling God that I would gladly pick up more trash if I only had a bag to put it in. I "ASKED" God for a bag, and within two to three seconds, a plastic grocery bag started blowing across the grass field and across the sidewalk only a few feet in front of me. I looked up to the sky and to the heavens and said, "Okay God, now you're just showing off!"

The importance of what's going on when no one is watching is extremely important to me, but sometimes we just need to "SHOW UP" for others; even when there are many watching. For me, it's not about having spectators but about doing what needs to be done when someone is truly counting on you. There are many times in my life when other people really needed help, and I rolled up my sleeves to lend a hand because they "ASKED."

More often than not, I was the one that my friends and family would call when it was time to move their home and office furnishings, plants, and anything else that required a large vehicle and a little muscle. I guess that was one of the advantages of always owning a large vehicle as well as a flat-bed trailer. The right man for the job, or in my case, the right WO-MAN for the job. My late husband was a granite slab contractor, and I was very comfortable driving a large truck while hauling a heavy trailer loaded full of goods. I guess it's no wonder that for several decades, I was the go-to girl when it came to moving stuff around the county and from city to city. I once helped transport a twenty-foot box trailer full of exotic plants and expensive concrete cast pots and benches from San Diego to Los Angeles.

Now, driving the cargo up over 100 miles was the easy part, backing up in a narrow alley to the drop off point was an entirely different story. There were two vehicles parked parallel to where I needed to unload, and there was no margin of error. Very slowly and carefully, one foot at a time, one inch at a time, I arrived at the perfect spot to successfully unload our precious cargo. City driving definitely requires a complex skill set, and especially when you've got forty feet of vehicles to maneuver.

A funny story about "Showing Up" that recently happened was at a loft house build at my local church. Now if you're not familiar with what a loft house is, let me give you a better description of exactly what I'm talking about. A loft house is a very small structure, usually about fourteen by eighteen feet and twelve feet tall in the center. They're primarily designed to fit a lot of modern conveniences into a small space in a very cost-effective manner. Our church has been doing these loft-house building projects for several years, this was our 89th build. The homes are premade in the church parking lot in sections and then transported to Ensenada, Mexico where the pieces are then constructed together to make a house. We work with local church leaders in Mexico that help decide what family will receive the new home, free of any cost. By our standards, the loft house is the size of a master bedroom. However, for these well deserving families, it is a safe self-contained living space, with all of the modern amenities including carpet, windows, doors, and appliances. Many of these families are used to sharing literally a shack made out of various building materials, not designed to withstand the elements. This is an absolute blessing for these families.

Now let's get to the funny part of this story. I "SHOWED UP" to help with the loft house build one Saturday morning. I'd been wanting to do this for years, but the weekends were always jam-packed with sporting events for my kids and the opportunity never presented itself, until now. I was excited to be able to "SHOW UP" and serve; I even baked chocolate chip muffins to share with the crew. I brought my hammer and a smile and got to work. I immediately started directing other workers and created a system to help our part of the project go more smoothly. I had a sixteen-year-old young woman, her father, and two elderly gentlemen that I was directly supervising. I grew up in the construction world and was married to a contractor for many years, so I felt that I was a natural born leader in this department. My team and I were making progress until something unexpected happened.

We were all hammering panels, and a few guys were cutting out holes for the windows in the top portion of the loft and an opening for the front door. I was helping and supervising, supervising and helping, when all the sudden something very unexpected happened. One of the older gentlemen that was assisting with the cutting, which required the help of a skill saw, got his glove caught in the quickly moving blade of the skill saw. Now, when we said we were prepared to put blood, sweat, and tears into this build, we weren't kidding. Blood began to splatter across the side of the house, literally. I immediately reacted by saying, "Sir, can you please step away from the skill saw?" he replied by saying, "I'm fine" and he attempted to grab the saw and continue cutting. Very quietly as not to embarrass the man, I repeated, "Sir, can you please step away from the skill saw?" This time the man agreed, and we exited stage left into the lower level of the church, in order for me to discretely assess the dire situation. I knew if the man had seriously hurt himself, he would most likely go into shock, and I need to act swiftly. Fortunately, once he removed both of his gloves and I was able to see the extent of his injury, I quickly determined that it was only a minor cut. Unfortunately, when it comes to skill saws and table saws, most accidents require stitching the cut or often at times attempting to reattach finger(s). While I "SHOWED UP" that morning to participate in a loft house build, I ended up trading my contractor hat for a nurse's hat. I

set up a triage station for my patient, immediately grabbed a bag of ice, and located the rather large first aid kit. As soon as we entered the building, the gentleman got lightheaded and wanted to sit down. However, I still needed to assess the situation, which required me to stay calm while he removed his gloves. I hoped for the best but expected I may find something much worse; thankfully, all his digits were accounted for and fully attached. I began gathering all the medical supplies I needed while he iced his hand. Once I got the bleeding to stop, I determined he didn't need stiches, but it was still a big painful cut that needed attention. I cleaned it with rubbing alcohol, applied Iodine, and wrapped it in several bandages. I gave him a pain killer, but beforehand asked if he was on any blood thinners and if he had a preference between Ibuprofen and Acetaminophen. Although the churches' fancy first aid kit only had Ibuprofen, I happened to have extra strength Acetaminophen in my purse. I told him to take two now and another two in four to six hours before the pain set back in. I also asked the man when his last tetanus shot was, he said that it had only been a few years; you want to get a tetanus booster at least every ten years to be safe and protect yourself from tetanus. I brought him an ice water and even left him with a lollipop; I had one coincidently on my person. I "SHOWED UP" when this man needed me and continued to be on God's payroll. I got back to work on the build. Only fifteen minutes later, I got another patient, this one not nearly as serious but still they received the royal triage treatment.

This book is not only about "SHOWING UP" but that also the power is in the "ASK." I often tell my fellow female entrepreneurs to have their "ASK in GEAR." The clearer the "ASK," the easier is it for others to "SHOW UP" and support you in your "ASK." For many of us, it's not easy to "ASK" for help. But the interesting part is, people inherently want to be helpful and support others along the way. If your "ASK" isn't clear, it makes it more difficult to properly be of assistance. So "ASK" away and see what blessings may come your way.

On the other hand, when someone else has an "ASK," make sure you're paying attention so you can properly be of service. Earlier this year, if the head volleyball coach of my youngest son's high school team hadn't had his "ASK in GEAR," the team wouldn't have had snacks and meals provided for all of the players throughout the season. As a mom of two teenage boys, I refuse to let anyone go hungry on my watch. So, when the coach "ASKED" during our parent/player meeting at the very beginning of the season if any parents would volunteer, I couldn't stay quiet. I waited to see what parents would raise their hand to volunteer to be in charge of snacks; no one raised their hand. The coach added, "The varsity boys get all of the attention and the junior varsity boys don't get any love." He added, "Many of these boys have their last meal at noon and then don't get done with games until 8 o'clock at night and are "HUNGRY" since they're literally starving." Still waiting for someone, anyone, to raise their hand, I immediately went into full on "Momma Bear" mode when I looked around and saw no one stepping up. I reluctantly raised my hand, and said, "I'll do it if someone else does it with me." Who else offered to help with this huge "ASK" you're probably wondering? It was another single mom; Single moms are Super Heros!

Little did we know that providing snacks for away games for fifteen hungry teenagers would morph into providing meals for home games, which soon turned into hosting a full blown "Snack Shack" with all of the extras. I used my connections with the local grocery stores as well as a few local restaurants that graciously donated snacks and even meals to feed our starving players, as well as the dozens of hungry opponents, their siblings, and parents. I remember thinking, "What did you sign up for?" Once I asked the coach what our players needed, I quickly shifted into fundraiser mode and became a "WO-MAN on a MISSION." The coach commented that all of the junior varsity players had mis-matched shorts, many were

too short or had holes in them. Miraculously, only after the next two home games at our deluxe "Snack Shack," did we earn enough money to not only buy the entire team new shorts, but even got an extra-large pair for the coach. With a clear "ASK" and a clear "MISSION" and "VISION," we were able to accomplish an incredible goal.

My advice, "SHOW UP" with your heart on your sleeve and watch the magic happen. One person can make a big difference and that is compounded exponentially when we "SHOW UP" as a team and as a community. Go out into your community and be the "CHANGE." One small act of kindness can create a ripple of "CHANGE" that moves across towns into neighboring cities and states, and then across state lines, across the country and around the world. So just "SHOW UP" and be the "CHANGE" you want to see in the world.

Dr. Sara Lypps, MBA

Dr. Sara Lypps is a Licensed Financial Advisor with Lypps Financial and Insurance Services. She is passionate about financial education for women and helping families to get financially fit. Currently, she is working with corporations to implement a Comprehensive Wellness Program that not only helps the businesses to save significantly off their payroll taxes but also provides a variety of additional benefits to the employees and their families, all at zero out-of-pocket expenses to the business or the employee. Families across the country are reaping the benefits of this amazing program. Her passion is changing peoples' lives and she lives up to her role as a liaison for change in turning our current "Sick-Care" system into a true "Healthcare" system.

Please feel free to reach out to her at: (760) 497-5821 or DrSaraLyppsFinancial@gmail.com and don't keep her a secret!!

It's all
About
Showing
Up

Unleashing the Power Within: A Journey of Showing Up, Asking, and Transforming Lives"

By Saskia Christian

Prologue:

Join me on an incredibly transformative journey of personal growth and empowerment. Discover the power of showing up, engaging with others, and fearlessly pursuing opportunities. Through these experiences, I have connected with inspiring community leaders, contributed to impactful projects, and participated in global empowerment initiatives. This chapter is a testament to the incredible potential within all of us when we step out of our comfort zones, advocate for ourselves, and embrace the unknown. Let's dive into my life-changing entrepreneurial experience.

A Life Transformed: Empowerment and Impact through the Global Society of Female Entrepreneurs.

It all started with a fortuitous encounter with Dr. Angeline Benjamin, the Virtual Thursday Networking Forum Director, at a local chamber luncheon. Dr. Angeline was ushered to my table. After we introduced ourselves and listened to each other's platforms, Dr. Angeline said to me "I love your energy, and I believe we should connect." Little did I know that those words would be the spark that would lead me to an organization that would change the trajectory of my career and personal growth. Dr.

h.c. Angeline Benjamin introduced me to the Global Society for Female Entrepreneurs (GSFE), founded by Lady Amb. Dr. h.c. Robbie Motter, Founder/CEO GSFE GSFEUS.COM. My life was forever changed by this encounter, as it set me on a path of personal growth, empowerment, and making a difference in the lives of others.

A Journey of Empowerment: How GSFE Transformed My Professional Life

Dr. Angeline's introduction to GSFE opened up a world of opportunities for me. Joining the Global Society for Female Entrepreneurs (GSFE) made a profound impact on my life. It provided me with a supportive community of like-minded professionals who believe in the power of women supporting and uplifting each other. It gave me a sense of belonging and support, something I had rarely experienced during my corporate era. I was able to host my first BoostThru Annual Resilience summit with 15 speakers, most of which were GSFE members. I asked several speakers to give a 30 mins talk on a preselected topic. I pushed past my skepticism and was prepared to receive a yes or no. To my surprise, I received a "Yes" within two weeks of my request from nearly everyone I approached. Wow!! Others and I were blown away by how quickly professionals committed to the cause of healing and empowering the professional community without compensation and without mostly knowing me for more than three months. That complimentary virtual summit with the theme of "Emotional Intelligence for BreakThru" garnered over 100 registrants who gave heartfelt testimonials about its impact on their personal soft skills development and transformation.

Through my GSFE sister connections, I was able to make significant strides in my professional journey. I had my first TV show interview on HSBN hosted

by the amazing Rena Neal, a fellow GSFE sister. I also made an unforgettable appearance on the show of my fabulous GSFE sister Joy Ruffen, a classy professional who is an outstanding TV producer, professional stylist and TV host. I felt so much at home on her TV platform, and it was a great opportunity to be visible on over 37 social media platforms as a result of one interview. My appearance on the Joy Ruffen show also opened me up to a whole new community of women leaders- Leading Ladies Leaving Legacies where I continue to market my business events and special promotions. Wait there is more! I also had the honor of having My BoostThru business brand featured in Celebrity Boss magazine founded by another fellow GSFE member, the outstanding Dr. Dawn Anderson, former editor in Chief of Atlanta Business Journal. After being in the GSFE organization for only a few months, I was able to be featured on the August cover of Celebrity Boss Magazine right after our amazing founder Dr. h.c. Robbie Motter graced the cover for her nonprofit org. In my magazine feature, I presented my visionary approach to professional assistance which is BoostThru's three component wellness framework.

Our GSFE Founder Dr. Robbie also graciously connected me with an amazing C-suite woman executive leader and coach, Dr. Karen Hills who is the Founder of Sister Leaders community. Because I showed up and inquired about being a part of her conference agenda, I was able to secure the last speaker spot Dr. Karen had on her conference lineup. I had invaluable opportunities to talk at the 2023 Sister Leaders conference and to contribute my article on Women leaders maximizing their influential power in the 2023 Sister Leaders magazine. What a privilege to be featured on such a massive platform for the empowerment of many fellow minority women leaders to help them maximize their influential power and lead at their full potential! Those unmatched opportunities allowed me to encourage and empower women to step into and conquer senior leadership and executive roles in their careers.

My active involvement in GSFE also provided me with unparalleled visibility opportunities, including TV and magazine appearances, press release citations from 400 premium news outlets, and collaboration on an impactful anthology "You are enough" that was created by the fabulous Lady O, our GSFE New York Chapter Director. That anthology gave me a golden opportunity to revisit the period of my childhood to adult years and embrace how my experiences from living in four different countries formed me into the confident Executive Trainer, Trauma and Resilience life transformation coaching consultant and overcomer I am today. What truly sets GSFE apart is its belief in the power of women supporting and completing each other rather than competing. It's all about Community Over Competition. Our Founder Dr. Robbie's motto is "We don't compete, we complete." This inclusive and welcoming atmosphere gave me a true sense of belonging, something I had never truly experienced during my corporate career era.

As an entrepreneur and resilience ambassador, I have witnessed the transformative power of becoming a member of GSFE. Under the guidance of our visionary leader, Dr. Robbie, I learned the importance of showing up and fearlessly asking for what I needed. The opportunities for personal growth, speaking engagements, and career development that GSFE provided me are beyond measure. Dr. Robbie's servant-style and exemplary leadership opened doors I never thought would be possible. Most importantly, I also experienced the power of giving back in kindness to this beautiful GSFE community of women leaders. My receipt of the 2024 GSFE Kindness award for my virtual chapter, Global Author Icon and Global Visionaries Leaders awards from Global Visionary Convention underscores the importance of transformative leadership, paying it forward and showing up with kindness every opportunity you get. I am grateful for

and will cherish each and every one of these awards.

Seizing Opportunities: How Showing Up Transformed My Entrepreneurial Journey

One of the key aspects of my entrepreneurial career has been my involvement in various publications. By showing up at online LinkedIn events, panel discussions, and in-person networking events, I have been able to connect with like-minded individuals and seize opportunities that typically wouldn't be available to me. For example, by simply showing up to an event where one of my business family members, the fabulous Julie Jones was emceeing, I had the opportunity to meet the founder of "The Art of Connection :365 Days of Gratitude Quotes by Business Owners, Influencers and Entrepreneurs "anthology. This chance encounter led to my work being published under a special calendar date of mine (Aug 31st) in an international bestseller book series and even appearing in the Library of Congress in 2024.

Another unforgettable instance where showing up made a significant impact was when I agreed to participate in an online mental health panel discussion. Through this experience, I connected with an amazing integrated health coach Melissa Deally who later introduced me to The Founder of The Global Resilience Project initiative, Blair Kaplan Venables. Blair presented me with the opportunity to contribute as a co-author in her second "Global Resilience Project" book- Resilient A.F.: Stories of Resilience. Even though I was hesitant at first to coauthor another book compilation due to competing time demands and project priorities, I quickly realized that this collaboration would provide unparalleled international exposure for the personal story about my dad 's disappearance to be used in the healing and encouragement of so many around the world. The book made its debut at the pre-Oscar's gift lounge in March 2024 and will be displayed at the Emmy's gift lounge in September 2024 allowing my personal journey to be showcased to celebrities, influencers and media personalities. Wait, there is more on the incredible exposure gift this book collaboration brought me. Fellow co-authors of that Resilient A. F. book and I are being featured on a billboard in NY Times Square. To top it off, I was able to make meaningful connections with my other amazing contributing authors! It was an opportunity I couldn't afford to pass up.

Connecting Globally: From TV Shows to Global Summits, My Journey of Empowerment

My journey has also enabled me to make guest appearances on several other TV shows and podcast platforms, focused on mental health, wellness, and resilience. From appearing on the Mission Accepted podcast, which reached audiences as far as Australia, to my feature on Deborah Drummond's 262 Mission Project summit speaker series "Standup Speakup, Showup," that is being aired in Fall 2024 on Apple and Amazon TV in celebration of 2024 Women's History Month, I have had the priceless opportunity to connect with audiences worldwide.

Another remarkable opportunity presented to me through GSFE was the chance to join a LOANI (Leaders of All Nations International) call one weekend and meet exemplary world leaders. Despite conflicting commitments, I couldn't pass up the opportunity to connect with outstanding global change agents and represent my birth country and the United States of America. That experience allowed me to forge friendships and strategic partnerships with LOANI members dedicated to peace, women's empowerment, cooperation, and sustainability. As a result of showing up and saying yes to being an author contributor to this book,

Volume 3 of Lady Dr. Robbie's amazing book series "It's All About Showing Up: Power is in the Asking," my networking story will be unveiled along with many others in time for the 2024 Global Visionary Convention.

Empower and Elevate: A Transformative Journey of Connection, Growth, and Impact

One of the most transformative and unforgettable moments in my personal and professional journey was attending the 2023 Empower and Elevate conference, an annual event hosted by my remarkable business coach Colleen Biggs, a renowned expert in high-performance leadership coaching. This conference was not just an ordinary gathering; it was a life-altering experience that would forever shape my path and leave an indelible mark on my journey of personal growth and success.

The Empower and Elevate conference platform provided me with a unique opportunity to be a panelist and connect with a diverse group of inspiring and talented women leaders. It was a gathering of like-minded individuals who shared a common goal of empowerment, growth, and excellence. The atmosphere was electric with positive energy, enthusiasm, and a palpable sense of camaraderie. From the moment I stepped into that conference venue, I knew that something special was about to happen.

Embracing the networking opportunities presented at the conference proved to be a game-changer for me. As I engaged in conversations, exchanged ideas, and shared experiences with these incredible women, I felt a powerful sense of connection and belonging. It was a space where we could support and uplift one another, celebrate our achievements, and learn from each other's journeys.

The connections I made at the Empower and Elevate conference were far from superficial networking. They were genuine and authentic relationships that paid significant dividends for my career advancement. Through these connections, I gained invaluable insights, mentorship, and guidance from women who had walked the path before me. Their wisdom and expertise served as beacons of light, illuminating the way forward and inspiring me to reach new heights.

But the impact of attending this conference extended far beyond my own personal and professional growth. It became a source of encouragement and inspiration for countless women entrepreneurs and visionaries in our community. As I shared my experiences and the lessons I learned during a panel discussion at that forum, I witnessed firsthand the transformative power of storytelling and vulnerability. My journey became a testament to what is possible when we dare to dream big, take risks, and support one another along the way.

The Empower and Elevate conference was truly a gift, not just for me but for all those who crossed paths with me. It sparked a ripple effect of empowerment and elevation that continues to reverberate in our community. The connections forged at this conference have blossomed into collaborations, partnerships, and friendships that transcend boundaries and make a positive impact on the lives of many.

Looking back, I am filled with gratitude for the opportunity to attend the Empower and Elevate conference. It was a turning point in my journey, a catalyst for growth, and a reminder of the power that lies within each of us to create meaningful change. The experience taught me the importance of embracing opportunities, stepping out of my comfort zone, and surrounding myself with a community of like-minded individuals who believe in my potential.

Attending this conference was not just an event; it was a transformative experience that continues to shape my path and propel me forward. It serves as a constant reminder of the incredible potential we all possess and the limitless possibilities that await when we come together, empower one another, and elevate ourselves to new heights of success.

The Power of Gratitude, Celebration, and Inclusive Leadership

Showing up for yourself goes beyond networking, building authentic relationships, and pursuing collaboration opportunities. It involves expressing gratitude daily and celebrating the successes of others. When you show gratitude towards those who selflessly contribute to your growth and publicly acknowledge the achievements of others, doors open wide for you. Being intentional about appreciating your own accomplishments and your support network, as well as publicly celebrating others, adds to the momentum and power of your endeavors. By doing so, you may find that you don't have to actively seek out opportunities; people will willingly offer them based on their observations of your generous personality and inclusive leadership style.

Unleashing Potential: A Journey of Recognition, Empowerment, and Resilience

In summary, my career journey has been nothing but extraordinary. It was greatly enhanced by joining organizations such as GSFE and being coachable by the best for my destiny fulfillment, taking full advantage of online and in-person panel discussion opportunities and my participation in collaborations with amazingly talented leaders in the industry for various community causes.

The opportunities, support, and sense of belonging have propelled me to new heights of success and fulfillment. That was notably asserted by two inductions, the Marquis Who's Who in America 2023 honoree listing and the coveted Marquis Who's Who 2024 Top Engineer award for my online activities related to empowering others and for my chemical engineering career contributions. I am grateful for this notable recognition of my hard work and accomplishments over the years in the chemical engineering field. I am also grateful for being handpicked to be The Executive Contributor to Brainz Magazine and its associated global award recognition. That Brainz Magazine coveted title was as a result of me simply inquiring about writing opportunities at Brainz. I had noticed that a professional I was recently introduced to was a Brainz Executive Contributor and I was stoked by that. I immediately applied and had an exceptional interview which reinforced my excellent writing capabilities and unique writing style I bring to the world. I didn't realize that the action of showing up and leveraging power in the asking would present such a golden opportunity to write for a renowned magazine.

As I reflect on the journey, I am truly appreciative for my brand's prestigious recognition since it is a testament to the impact, I am making in the lives of professionals seeking resilience and personal growth. I cherish being a recipient of such prestigious distinctions for empowerment work since I am very passionate about fighting for and encouraging the underdog professionals in the world to greatness. I am forever grateful for the doors that have opened up before me, and I am excited to continue my journey of empowerment and inspiration alongside the incredible women of GSFE and the many outstanding authors and visionaries I have met in my entrepreneurial journey. All that's needed is for you and me to believe in ourselves enough to pursue our dreams and aspirations with intention and impact.

Call to Action:

Are you ready to unleash your networking potential and transform your life? Join me on this empowering journey of showing up, asking, and making a meaningful impact. I invite you to reflect on my experiences of personal growth, resilience, and the incredible connections that have shaped my journey. Embrace the power of community and discover how asking for what you need can lead to profound opportunities.

Together, let's break through barriers, support one another, and elevate each other to new heights. Don't wait for change to come to you—take the first step today! Connect with like-minded individuals and embark on your own journey of transformation. For additional insights on effective and strategic networking, feel free to connect with me at www.boostthru. com/contact.

Believe in yourself, show up, and take action—because the power is in the asking!

Saskia Christian

Saskia Christian, an accomplished Trauma and Global Resilience Expert has a remarkable background. With 17 years of corporate visionary engineering leadership experience, she excelled as a technical leader. However, her path took an unexpected turn, leading her to become a renowned Training Executive, Trauma Healing and Resilience Coaching Consultant, Speaker, and Founder of BoostThru.

Saskia's expertise extends beyond her corporate success. She is a prolific author, with her book "Mindset Mastery" showcasing her ability to unlock mind power. She has authored e-courses on Seasonal Resiliency and co-authored five anthologies, including one Bestseller and an International Bestseller in the Library of Congress. Notably, her story about her father's disappearance in "Resilient A.F: Stories of Resilience" gained recognition at the 2024 Oscars and Emmys gift lounge.

Saskia is a Brainz Magazine Executive Contributor and has received several global accolades. As a Resilience Trailblazer, her work significantly impacts the lives of professionals in distress. Her purpose-driven comebacks inspire hope and resilience, making a profound difference in the lives of those she works with.

Email: saskiac@boostthru.com
Website: www.boostthru.com/contact
LinkedIn: http://linkedin.com/in/saskia-christian
Facebook:https://www.facebook.com/profile.
php?id=100088422974533&mibextid=LQQJ4d
Instagram: https://www.instagram.com/boostthru

It's all
About
Showing
Up

Showing up for Your Self

By Ambassador Dr. (h.c.) Susie Mierzwik

Have you ever seen a child trying out their first two-wheel bike without training wheels? The bike wobbles: Mom or Dad runs along behind. Maybe you learned to ride a bike on your own, with no one cheering you on. You may remember feeling scared or proud. What does riding a bike have to do with Showing Up for Yourself?

Childhood is full of opportunities to try new things almost every day, but what about now? Do we still have the opportunity to venture out in a new area of our life? Or do we feel that Showing Up for ourselves is a thing of the past? We might be excited about trying something new, yet we worry that the "Training Wheels" in the new situation might "Fall Off" and leave us stranded in a place that is unfamiliar, worrisome, or downright terrifying!

Encountering a new chapter in life can be both exciting and daunting! Some new ventures we meet eagerly, such as going on a vacation to a new destination. Others, however, may give us mixed feelings, such as the anticipation of starting a new job. In this case, our eagerness is probably tempered with some apprehension about our new position as well.

How do we prepare for a new chapter in life, when we have been wrenched out of our old life and forced to Show Up for something that we never asked for? There are many situations in life where we may find ourselves dumped on the doorstep of a disastrous situation, we never anticipated whether it is an illness, family betrayal, death, an accident, unemployment, financial mishap, loss of our home or even divorce.

When unwelcome changes are forced upon us, as in the above examples, it can feel terrifying. This fear stems from stepping into the unknown, leaving behind the familiar, even if it was painful or unfulfilling. It's the uncertainty that haunts us. We worry about how life will change, how we'll cope, and whether we will ever find happiness again. This fear is natural, a reflection of the magnitude of our life transition.

However, as gut wrenching as these catastrophic changes can be when they are dumped on us, they can also usher us into a new season of growth that we never expected.

I remember standing at the threshold of divorce in my own life 27 years ago. My husband of 24 years had just handed me divorce papers and told me he was leaving. You could have bowled me over with a feather! I was in such a state of shock. I tried to decipher what these words meant to me. I had believed that were married for better or worse, "till death do us part!" I had plugged along for 24 years, simply accepting the good times and tolerating the bad times, because I assumed that this was the ebb and flow of my life. Yet most of the time I was in such a dissociated state of mind, that I had a difficult time recognizing any feelings at all.

I believed my "Boat" had sailed into rough waters, and if I held on for a time, maybe I would pass into a safe harbor eventually! It was very difficult to identify my reactions during this period in my life since I had grown up in a family where emotions were never talked about or allowed. All of us kids and my dad just catered to my narcissistic mom, so no one else's feelings were ever considered.

For many years while I was married to my first husband, I existed in a dissociated, robotic state where my spirit was not allowed to surface. If I allowed myself to shed a tear, my narcissistic husband would complain that I was having a nervous breakdown. So, all my confused feelings were kept locked up inside. After he left, it felt like my tears would never stop. I came to realize that I was crying not just because I was a jilted wife, but for the quiet, sad little girl who had never been allowed to express her emotions.

At this point, although the landscape of my life felt shattered, it actually turned into an enormous opportunity for growth in my personal development. It was a chance for me to SHOW UP FOR ME; to redefine my sense of self and embrace the possibility of a more authentic, fulfilling future. Although I suffered keenly at the time, when I was forced to "crack open the poisonous shell of my old life," this gave birth to a whole new person inside that was emerging for the first time.

Now I was at a new threshold I had never contemplated. I actually envisioned that "my house was on fire," and I had to save myself. I thought there might be another new life beyond my current one, but to reach it I needed to walk through the fire. This is the definition of SHOWING UP FOR MYSELF.

In my past, I felt like I had to be perfect. If I made a mistake, I berated myself, I had no idea that I was allowed to have needs of my own. I only felt my responsibility as a wife and mother. Once while I was trying to fill out a simple Christmas wish-list at work, I had no idea what to write down. I didn't even KNOW WHAT I WANTED.

Since I was living such a disempowered life until my divorce, facing my future seemed terrifying to me. Yet I knew that God had a plan for my life so after praying for six months for the restoration of my marriage, I realized that He had a Different Path for me. I just had to trust Him and walk through the fiery door of uncertainty even when I had no map or blueprint for the future. It all looked very blurry through my tears.

Any time we are faced with a painful or frightening occurrence in life, we have a choice. We can try to avoid the pain by engaging in addictive or destructive behaviors, such as drinking, using drugs, overeating, or engaging in unhealthy relationships, or we can live in the land of Denial and Pretend that everything is "Just Fine." We might try coping by engaging in the "blame game." We can say that our sad, current circumstances are someone else's fault, and we can choose to be a victim. None of these strategies will solve our current problems. By staying "STUCK" in a situation we can't control, we just prolong the current agony. By refusing to walk through our "fiery door," we just remain in our pain. The problem is Still There. We have just closed our eyes and wished on a magic wand that It "would just all go away"!

The only healthy strategy I learned was to face my situation squarely and JUST SHOW UP FOR ME. In tumultuous circumstances, it is helpful if we can keep a foothold on one thing that is predictable and steady. In my case, I kept going to work each day. I 'Showed up' for my students and my responsibilities, even though I drove to and from my school in tears.

We must 'Show Up" for ourselves in difficult times. Yes, it requires courage, but I know we don't need to face the future without encouragement. There are appropriate ways we can seek help during our current trials by following a three-step formula I call the "IOUs of survival."

The first way I decided to show up for myself was to LOOK INSIDE Me. I realized there were probably things in my past life that I had not known about that caused my marriage to flounder. So, I set about reading many books about personal development to discover in what areas I was deficient. No matter what tragic circumstances we find ourselves in, we can

always seek information about our current dilemma to see what we may have missed along the way. We need to discern if there was information available that could have changed the outcome of our misfortune.

The second way I decided to Show up for myself was to LOOK OUT for appropriate support systems. I engaged in personal therapy, divorce recovery in a group and Bible study. These were three safe venues I could learn about my deficiencies and discover new paths into my future.

Whenever we find ourselves in a crisis, there are always support systems we can access for health, finances, education, career, relationships, or addiction. It is imperative that we access a safety net to guide our new path. No matter WHAT we face, our first step to get out of whatever pain we find ourselves in, is to SHOW UP for ourselves with appropriate people who can guide us, because they have traveled this path before. We need a reliable safety net because our family is often involved in the crisis and is unsuitable to provide the guidance we need. The third way I showed up for myself was to Look UP to God for Guidance and hope. I realized that He had a plan for my life, and although I faced a detour at present, there was a way out if I prayed and relied on Him to guide my path.

One huge challenge I had in SHOWING UP for myself, was to re-discover my new identity. Previously I had self- identified as "Mrs. Flying Pilot (my ex- husband's career), or someone's Mom or Teacher. I could not feel a sense of myself for a very long time.

It took several years of emotional healing and self- empowerment "work" to discover the ME I was, without any attachment to my roles in life.

I chose to DO THE NECESSARY Emotional Growth WORK and SHOW UP to receive all that a new life had to offer. If we DO NOT SHOW UP FOR OURSELVES in every sense, then we are just letting someone else (family, spouse, society) write the script for our own life, and we are only "playing out a part," mindlessly, on someone else's stage!

In one empowerment course I learned that we all have choices in our personal life, and suffering is optional. I learned to make new choices and SHOW UP FOR ME every day, as if it were the last day of my life. I no longer wanted to live on autopilot, where the expectations and definitions of WHO I WAS were determined by family or spouse.

The outcome was not easy. There were some in my family who blamed me for the divorce, even though I was the one who was cast aside. Others couldn't make sense of my newfound self -empowerment and attempted to sabotage my newly discovered confidence and decisions. I realized that it is not always easy to SHOW UP FOR MYSELF, especially since I grew up in a dysfunctional family where personal autonomy and self- confidence were not allowed. I had to discover these values on my own in mid- life.

This ingrained habit of self-sacrifice can make us feel selfish or wrong to focus on our own well-being. Because I had internalized the belief that my value consisted solely in serving others, it led to feelings of guilt if I tried to carve out space for me. However, I had to learn to put myself first to heal my mental and emotional health. It required that I unlearn old patterns of reacting, such as, setting boundaries, and embracing the idea that self-care is not selfish, but necessary. It was a challenging journey, but one that ultimately led to a joyful, fulfilling and abundant life.

So, if You are going through a difficult passage in life, these three keys will lead you along the path until you are thriving again.

I had the chance to talk to a friend recently who is grieving the death of her husband of 55 years. She shared that she is just now learning to "SHOW UP for herself." She confided that during their long happy marriage, her

husband made all the decisions in the family. Now at this later stage in life, she is learning to decide things on her own. So even in the throes of intense grief, she can see herself taking baby steps to Show Up for Herself.

My friend gave me an example of how she took the needed time to just cry, stay home and be still. She had planned an outing with her extended family, but after going through the necessities of the day, she found that she just could not muster the emotional resources to go out with the family. That evening, she listened to the still small voice inside her that begged for a respite. So, she 'Showed Up for herself" at this point by declining the family outing and having an evening to just breathe, cry and deal with her emotions. So, Showing Up for Yourself, can look different at various moments in time,

When life throws us a curveball, it can feel like the ground has shifted beneath us. In those moments, Showing Up for Yourself can feel impossibly hard, but it's also the most important thing you can do. It's about choosing to nurture yourself when you're at your most vulnerable, even when it feels like everything is falling apart. This isn't about being strong in a conventional sense, but about embracing your own softness and pain with compassion.

Showing Up for Yourself means acknowledging that you are hurting. You realize you need care and attention. It's choosing to get out of bed, to nourish your body, to speak kindly to yourself, and to keep moving forward, step by small step.

The emotional reward of this process is profound. It's not instant relief, but over time, you start to rebuild trust in yourself. You learn that, even when things go wrong, you are there for yourself—and that counts for everything. So, showing up doesn't necessarily mean you GO OUT into the world at every moment. Rather it is looking inside yourself to take stock of what YOUR OWN heart longs for at this exact moment.

There's a quiet strength in this self-commitment. You begin to feel more resilient because you've proven that you won't abandon yourself. This emotional reward—of knowing you are enough, of being your own support system—brings a deep sense of peace. It's empowering, because while you can't control life's blows, you can control how you respond. And by showing up, you give yourself the gift of healing, self-respect, and the ability to rise again.

Dr. Susie Mierzwik

Ambassador Dr. Susie Mierzwik

Dr Susie Mierzwik is the bestselling author of Sow in Tears, Reap in Joy, a Transformational Journey. Bit.ly/3icPis6

She is also an entrepreneur and speaker. Her health and wellness business provides a nondrug solution for people struggling with health issues. She embraced this 21st century technology in 2009 and has helped her clients reach a pain free state using this patented phototherapy product. She received the Teacher of the Year award in 2000 and retired from teaching in 2012. She received the Distinguished Woman of the Year in 2014 from her state senator, as well as numerous state and local accolades.

Susie received an honorary doctorate in Humanitarianism in 2022, as well as holding a BA and an MBA.

She is also a coauthor in twelve anthologies, many of which are best sellers. Connect on her website https://susiemierzwik.com to purchase her books. You can also schedule a complementary discovery session, hear her interviews and podcasts, as well as testimonials from clients who have benefitted from her life changing health and wellness business.

https://www.linkedin/in/susiemierzwik

www.facebook.com/susanemierzwik

kinderkat9@gmail.com

Showing Up!!! TODAY and EVERYDAY!!!
A Ceremonial Priestess is Born
By Zulmara Maria

Show up for yourself, your family, your community, your world. How are you showing up today? SMILE!!! It is all good.

Un abrazo,

Your Divine Self

Zulmara Maria

BREATHE!!! BREATHE!!! BREATHE!!!

Here I am standing at the top of Machu Picchu, me the person who never thinks about getting to the top of the mountain, here I am, just breathing and taking in the moment. A true WOW moment and I drop deep into my soul and just say, "show me"? And I close my eyes and my soul, my heart, and my spirit all align to show me...show me why I came to Machu Picchu, why at this time, and what was coming up for me next. It was truly a moment in time, a way of being, a breath of pura vida.

I went to Machu Picchu during my second Saturn Return in December of 2017. It was an extraordinary experience. Machu Picchu had been calling me for years and every year, it was hard for me to go for whatever reason.

Then, in December of 2017, it all came together in such a serendipitous way, that I knew it was my time to be there.

What is so interesting is that I needed to wait...wait for my second Saturn return (more on that later), wait for my guide, Daniel Gutierrez, to be ready through some of his life experiences, and wait for me to be ready. The moment at the top of the mountain was truly epic in so many ways, but mostly because it was DIVINE TIMING. I was supposed to be there at that time.

My Journey

My journey to Machu Picchu began when I was in Mexico in 1994 visiting the ruins there and I had this strong feeling that I needed to visit Machu Picchu. This stayed with me for years and years. I would look at guides, opportunities to go, and the right time, and it was never the right time, until December 2017. I did not know I was at the beginning of my Saturn return, that would come later, I just knew the stars had aligned and I was going.

The trip came together quickly and as I was on the plane, I felt like this was going to be an epic spiritual journey, and it was. I set my intentions, stayed open to the possibilities, and just went to be in the sacred valley to just soak up what was awaiting me.

I arrived on a Sunday morning and had lunch with Daniel and one of the other participants. Daniel shared with us the story of his soul's contract with his mother and her passing earlier that year. This resonated so deeply with me and gave me so much insight into the soul contract I had with my

mother. I began to understand, at a level I had not understood before, what soul contracts were all about. My journal entries revealed so much to me that evening, the clarity gave me peace and understanding. I began to clearly see why my mom and I had chosen to come here together as mother and daughter. I could see all the gifts she had given me and the true symbiotic relationship we had had through the years. I felt she left too soon, I was only 44 when she passed, but something Daniel said stayed with me and I will paraphrase, "My mom said, mijo, our contract is complete, we are complete." And, for the first time, I realized, all in divine timing, in this realm, my mom and I had stayed together for the time we were supposed to stay together. I felt a profound sense of deep inner peace and I knew now why I had to wait for Daniel, who has been a friend, mentor, and guide for over 20 years, needed to go through his experience, before I could benefit from his gained wisdom.

A couple of days into our trip, we did San Pedro, plant medicine. We worked very closely with a skilled and gifted shaman who guided us through our experience. Before taking the medicine, he asked us to choose 3 words for setting our intention and to share them out loud. My words were paz, tranquilidad, y serenidad...peace, tranquility, and serenity. My experience with San Pedro was nothing short of incredible. I felt like I was shown so much about my life that was good. I was laughing, and smiling, and just being with my soul, heart, and spirit as they came out to play, offer me guidance, and give me nudges for my next steps.

Those next steps came that very night when I was processing the experience with the other guests there and I realized I had knowledge and insights into their experiences that resonated with them. I could clearly help them interpret their experience, their life choices, their questions, and their wonderings. One of them even asked me if I was "clairvoyant" and I thought about it and said, "I do have gifts, but I have not worked on honing them." It was a heavy feeling and at times, I did not even know where all of this was coming from, but it was deep.

Machu Picchu

A few days later, we went to Machu Picchu. We were up early; we were the first to get to the mountain to start the climb. I had never planned on getting to the top of the mountain. I was going half-way and spending the rest of the time in quiet contemplation and meditation at the ruins. I had my journal, and I was going to find different places and spaces to write, reflect, rejuvenate, and renew within the sacred valley.

You have to understand, I have never been a "top of the mountain" sort of gal. I have always been a "what goes up must come down" sort of gal, so I never climb higher than what I want to go down. On this day, there were circumstances with our group and Daniel asked me to stay with one of the other members of our party and he was going to go ahead with the rest of the party. She wanted to get to the top, so I went inside and got a "yes, you are supposed to go to the top." So, with an amen, awomyn, aho, and on we go...I started the trek past the halfway mark. It was daunting, crazy, fun, scary, and sacred. To this day, I still cannot tell you how I made it to the top, but I did. I was at the top of the mountain...and after my moment of joy and reflection, I thought...how am I going to get down? I said a little prayer and I let go and let God.

And God came through. A wonderful keeper of the mountain guide...he is the first to get to the top and the last to leave, took me by the hand and guided me all the way down...it was EPIC, and I knew he was the answer

to my prayers.

As I came down the mountain and went to explore the ruins, it started pouring...absolutely pouring rain for about an hour. The ruins were soaked, there was no place to explore, I was tired, beat, and ready to go eat, and I left. On the bus back into town, I was a little disappointed because I did not get to see the ruins and I felt that is what I had come for. Little did I know...that source had other things in mind for me.

My Second Saturn Return

A Saturn return happens when Saturn is in the same place in the sky as it was when you were born. It takes about 29.5 years to happen. Ergo, when you are about 30 and about 60 and about 90 you will experience a Saturn return. In astrological terms, Saturn's Return is seen as a major turning point in a person's life and frequently results in major life changes, perhaps difficulties, and chances for personal development and growth. This is a period of maturing, self-analysis, reflection and rejuvenation. This is a period that sets you up for the next phase of your life. I was in the throes of my 2nd Saturn return, which was officially happening within a month of me being in Machu Picchu on Tuesday, January 16, 2018.

As we completed our time in Peru, I spent so much time reflecting on my experience and I realized I was being called to be a ceremonial priestess, a guide, and a healer. I was a bit surprised, but not really. I had already started a program called Reclaiming your Divinity, which I had been guided to stop, but I knew that I was a guide to many already and this was my call to hone my skills and start learning.

I came back and sat with that for a moment or two and started my learnings. I took classes from various shaman, started learning how to work with crystals and oracle cards, became adept at holding healing space so others could heal themselves, and started practicing ceremonies in my own way with my own touch. I was stepping into being a ceremonial priestess and I was loving it. I dabbled in many different things, and I found what worked for me and was guided to add my own touch to what I was doing. It has been a fantastic journey.

It was in 2023 when I actually learned about Saturn Returns and realized that when I showed up in Machu Picchu in 2017, it was during my Saturn Return...and so much just fell into place. By then, I was already doing oracle card readings, cleansings, and ceremonies for individuals. I was already developing my own style; I was already stepping into my role as a ceremonial priestess. As I reflected on the changes in my life since that time, I could see that I was in the right place at the right time, and I showed up at the divine time for me to move forward. It has been an absolutely great ride.

Fast Forward

So, here I am the year before I will retire from 40+ years in education and I am loving my life more than ever. I am looking forward to retirement and claiming my space as a ceremonial priestess who curates events for groups, individuals, milestones, and energetic happenings. I enjoy teaching, learning, and developing curriculum. I am working with snake energy right now as I gradually shed my old skin letting go of what is no longer working for me. When a snake emerges from its old skin, it has renewed energy, it is rejuvenated, and I am here for it.

In October 2023, I went back to Peru and went to Machu Picchu again. This time, I went with my partner, best friend, husband of 44 years, colleague and soon to be business partner, and again, I had an incredible experience. I did not climb to the peak, but I spent my time in the ruins just soaking in the energy of the sacredness of the space.

I took my favorite stone with me, Labradorite, it is a stone of new beginnings and helps harness your vision and going after your heart's desires. It also brings hope, possibility, and imagination as it kindles your inner fire and passion.

I took several pieces with me to Peru and to Machu Picchu to help heighten and harness my energies as I was focusing on new beginnings, retiring, opening my retreat center. It was a time to focus on endings and beginnings. Last time my three words were paz, tranquilidad, y serenidad. This time my words were dream, clarity, and focus. I went with an open mind of 'show me what I need to know.'

I had an incredible experience. One of the stones was carved as a rose...and on the day we were doing plant medicine, it was the only stone I could find. Well, a rose has a very special meaning for me and my husband because when we were first together, I gave him a rose bud to celebrate our budding love because we were so young. It was the stone I meditated with during the ceremony and the message was clear, you are on the right path with your husband, partner, and colleague. You will make an incredible and successful team as you continue to live your life's purpose and continue your journey.

I had a labradorite mala I took to Machu Picchu, and it broke. It absorbed so much old energy that I was releasing while in the sacred valley, it just broke into its beautiful pieces. I have the pieces, and I am waiting to bury it at the space I will curate for my Roots and Wings Rejuvenation & Renewal Retreat Center, this was my sign that I was breaking with the past and releasing all that no longer serves me.

I have since seen my husband begin to understand what I do and embrace the different things I am doing with all that I do.

In Peru, this time. I was able to envision my future as a ceremonial priestess. I am opening a Rejuvenation and Renewal Center to have a space to do the work I am being called to do. I am coming into my own. I am REJUVENATED and RENEWED!!!

Zulmara Maria Teixeira de Lima, Ph.D.

Holding a Sacred Space for Your Spiritual Growth and Development

Award winning Latina, Dr. Zulmara Maria is a ceremonial priestess who holds sacred space for your financial abundance, physical healing, and healthy relationships. She is available for readings, blessings, cleansings, and ceremonies. Dr. Zulmara hosts wellness events, retreats and private parties for groups and individuals. She will do blessings and cleansings of home and workspaces that are specifically cultivated for you and your needs.

In 2003, Dr. Zulmara Maria founded Roots and Wings and started offering personal, professional, and spiritual growth programs to help individuals find their voice, their strength, their identity, and their purpose in life. Her inspiring workshops focus on achieving dreams, celebrating humankind,

healing the collective, developing as self-actualized individuals, and living a purpose informed life.

Dr. Zulmara Maria is currently the Director of the Long Beach Chapter of the Global Society of Female Entrepreneurs (GSFE), past president of the Long Beach Holistic Chamber of Commerce, certified leader for Infinite Possibilities, co-founder of the RiseUp Leadership Series, founder of Latina Gratitude Month, and a featured author in Chicken Soup for the Latino Soul. She has authored three signature programs: Millionaire DIVAS, ABRAZOS of Gratitude and Appreciation, and Reclaiming Your Divinity.

She has been recognized and honored as a Woman of Distinction from CA Assembly District 70, Woman of Distinction from CA Senatorial District 33, received the Latina of Influence recognition, and honored as a Ms. Long Beach Women of Achievement. She has been featured in VoyageLA as a person to watch.

She specializes in helping others reach peak performance spiritually, professionally, and personally as they cultivate gratitude and appreciation in their lives.

Zulmara Maria is an Educator, Inspirational Speaker, Author, Blogger, and Entrepreneur--Inspiring women to soar while being grounded in their ancestral roots. As the Founder of Roots and Wings, Dr. Zulmara Maria endeavors to inspire others to grow personally, professionally, and spiritually for peak performance.

Zulmara Maria can be contacted at: zulmaramaria@gmail.com or through her website at http://zulmarmaria.com

Zulmara Maria can also be found at:

- Amazon: Zulmara Maria Teixeira de Lima
- Facebook: http://facebook.com/zulmaramaria
- Instagram: https://www.instagram.com/zulmara.maria/
- LinkedIn: http://linkedin.com/zulmaramaria

It's all
About
Showing
Up

www.ingramcontent.com/pod-product-compliance
Lightning Source LLC
Chambersburg PA
CBHW051129120626
46547CB00012B/735